A Vancouver Boyhood

Recollections of Growing
up in Vancouver 1925-1945

Robin Williams

Copyright © 1997 Robin Williams

LOCCN 97-66412

Canadian Cataloguing in Publication Data
Williams, Robin, 1925-
A Vancouver Boyhood: Recollections of
Growing up in Vancouver 1925-1945

ISBN 0-9683107-0-2

1. Williams, Robin, 1925- 2. Vancouver (B.C)--Biography.
I. Douglas, Diana. II. Title.
FC3847.26.W54A3 1997   971.1'3303'092   C97-910525-0
F1089.5.V22W54 1997

Editor : Diana Douglas
Book Design: Patti Smithson
Cover Design: David Marty
Cover Illustration: Kiff Holland

First reprint October 1997

ROBINSWOOD BOOKS
1427 Bellevue Ave. Box 91352
West Vancouver, B.C. V7V 3N9

Printed in Canada by Hignell Book Printing
488 Burnell Street
Winnipeg, Manitoba R3G 2B4

DEDICATION

To Vancouver and Canada,
boyhood home and native land

Acknowledgements

This book is based almost entirely upon the author's own recollections, but also includes a few recollections of former schoolchums. These persons are Buck Barraclough, Edward Carr, Ailsie Falkner Davidson, Walter Firth, James Galozo, Paul Gilmore, Gerry Green, Mary Hamilton Plourde, Robert Handel, Hugh Koonts, Anna Laubach Sumpton, Patricia Lindblom Gray, Ann McDougall Macdonald, and Peter Moffat.

I was fortunate also to interview a few former teachers; Arthur Creelman, Eric Gee, Charles McIntyre, Mollie Nye, and Day Walker Gee. I was most fortunate to gain a better understanding of "Mickey" McDougall, beloved Principal of North Vancouver High School, from interviews with Jessie and Ann, widow and daughter respectively, and from "Mickey"'s son Barry.

The historical material on the North Shore comes largely from the scholarship of my former Latin teacher "Katey" Reynolds. I am indebted to June Thompson of the North Vancouver Museum and Archives for calling this treasure trove of North Shore history to my attention, to the University of British Columbia for allowing me to use it, and to retired U.B.C. professors Paul Gilmore, James Gray, and Arthur Lazenby for helping to edit the entire text of the book.

For photographs to illustrate the book, I am indebted to Jim Galozo, Gerry Green, Hugh Koonts, Ross Johnson, Mae Smith McInnes, Mayor Murray Dykeman and personnel of the District of North Vancouver, David Newman and the North Vancouver School District, the archives of the cities of Vancouver and North Vancouver, and the Vancouver Public Library.

Limitations of time and space did not allow me to use all of the wonderful stories and photographs provided by my Vancouver friends, particularly those from the North Shore. Have patience. I plan on putting together another, shorter book that will bring much of this material together and focus entirely on the North Shore.

I am indebted also to publisher Elliott Wolf and editor Diana Douglas for shepherding me through my first experience with commercial publication, Kiff Holland for the painting on the front cover, and of course my life partner Billie Wallace Williams for her numerous instances of encouragement and assistance.

Olympia, Washington April 5, 1997

Photographs

Cover ~ Painting by Kiff Holland from 1938 photograph by
    Leonard Frank of the Lions Gate Bridge under construction.

Chapter 1 ~ *End of chapter*
- Aerial photo of Vancouver and the North Shore, 1939
- English Bay Beach in summer, 1920's
- Hotel Vancouver, early 1900's
- Mother when single, about age 23
- Father when single, about age 23
- Mother and first child with grandmothers
- Dad's Mother
- Dad's Father
- Mother as a girl of 13 with family in Prince Edward Island

Chapter 3 ~ *End of chapter*
- Lumbermens' Arch in Stanley Park
- My brothers Larkin, Asa, and I with family pets, about 1928
- Mother and her four sons, Balfour Avenue house, late 1920's
- Granville Island and mills along False Creek, 1920's
- Downtown Vancouver, Hastings St., Dominion Bank Bldg., 1920's

Chapter 4 ~ *End of chapter*
- Tom Nye mansion, 230 Carisbrooke Road, North Lonsdale
- North Vancouver ferry dock, 1920's, 30's
- North Star School classroom, early 1930's
- Princess Park swimming hole, boys getting ready in Spring

Chapter 7 ~ *End of chapter*
- Ship launching at North Vancouver shipyard during W.W. II
- North Vancouver High School, sketch by Sydney Baker
- North Vancouver High School, photo of staff, 1938
- North Vancouver High School, graduation classes 1940-50

Chapter 9 ~ *End of chapter*
- Union Steamship Co. dock in Vancouver
- W.W. II, Author in Alaska, 'cat skinning for the Army
- W.W. II, brother Donald in U.S. Army Airforce
- W.W. II, brothers Larkin and Asa on leave, Edmonton
- W.W. II, Author and Asa, North Vancouver, April 1945

Chapter 10 ~ *End of chapter*
- Author when completed writing this book, April 1997

Contents

Dedication
Acknowledgements
Photographs
Introduction

1. A Vancouver Romance   1

2. Roughing it Among the Rich of Old Shaughnessy   18

3. Hard Times and Polio   40

4. North Shore Paradise   72

5. Clouds Over Paradise   128

6. World War II: Waterboy to Fitter's Helper   162

7. North Van High and
   The Remarkable "Mickey" McDougall   185

8. A Queen Charlotte Summer   215

9. Alaska Grubstake   245

10. Epilogue   297

References   303

Introduction

This is my recollection of growing up in Vancouver from 1925 to 1945, years spanning times of prosperity, the great Depression, and World War II.

Vancouver was a different city then, of B.C. Electric streetcars, horse-drawn wagons that delivered bread, milk, and ice door-to-door, Union Steamships that carried people up and down the coast, C.P.R. oceanliners like the *Empress of Australia*, railroads powered by steam locomotives, elevators operated by uniformed attendants, telephones that were always black, lady swimmers at English Bay attired in double-skirted bathing suits, Packard touring cars with wooden spokes and steamer trunks at the back, bootleg liquor, and five cent ice-cream cones.

My family was an ordinary middle class one in most respects, but had its peculiarities. My father was an American forestry engineer who came to Vancouver in 1912 to sell machinery to B.C.'s thriving forest industry. My mother was a Canadian, born in Prince Edward Island and raised in Alberta, making their four sons, all born and raised in Vancouver, Canadian-American hybrids, not at all sure who they were in the mosaic of Canadian identity. Two served in Canadian forces during World War II and remained Canadian. Two crossed the line into the States, an easier place to gain a university education in those days.

Despite the hardships of the 1930s, one can hardly imagine a better city than Vancouver in which to grow up for boys who loved the outdoors. At first my parents were affluent enough so that our first years were spent in Old Shaughnessy, the haven of the rich. The came the Depression, Dad's business went bankrupt, and he moved the family to the North Shore.

Compared to Shaughnessy's manicured boulevards and aloof society, North Vancouver was an outdoor boy's Paradise; a vast stretch of mountain slopes, forest, river valleys, and waterfront, largely uninhabited, a mere 14,000 inhabitants in 1931. Nearby vacant lots were utilized for kitchen gardens, chickens, rabbits, or goats. Firewood for heating and cooking was close at hand from forestland or a local mill. Every boy had his favourite place to fish and swim at a nearby creek, river, or along the waterfront.

My original intention in writing this book was merely to provide stories of my Canadian boyhood for my American-born children and grand-children. But one thing led to another, and what has resulted is something muchbroader and of interest to others, both young and old. I think you will find it entertaining. I hope you will also find it enlightening, about the social customs and attitudes of the times, the very different position of women and minorities, and the wrenching conditions people had to cope with during the Depression, ended only by World War II.

That war changed Vancouver forever. Much is to the better, thanks in part to the kind of people who built Vancouver, predominantly British in origin, but they came from every corner of the world. They built a city so admired only misfortune or bad judgement would cause any of its citizens to leave. I probably suffered from both. But no expatriate forgets where he grew up. I was a Vancouver boy, a Canadian, and for that heritage I shall be forever grateful.

A Vancouver Boyhood

Recollections of Growing
up in Vancouver 1925-1945

1

A VANCOUVER ROMANCE

Vancouver has always attracted the adventurous or eccentric, and my father was no exception. Asa Starkweather Williams was born in the city of New York in 1882 of old Yankee stock and grew up in a three-story brownstone family home not far from Central Park. His father Edward had enlisted in the Union army as a drummer boy at age sixteen, served throughout most of the Civil War, and upon discharge developed a thriving business as a small manufacturer, thus being able to marry and raise a family under comfortable circumstances. His wife, Clara Robinson, was a handsome, sociable, civic-minded woman, so much so that she was the first woman to serve on the school board for the city of New York and was actively involved with Clara Bloomer and other reformers in various social causes of the day.

The household employed a maid, cook and furnaceman, thus freeing the parents from household chores and allowing Asa and his older brother Howard freedom to do pretty much as they pleased. Howard was of a studious nature, but Asa much preferred the outdoors and spent most of his time when not in school roaming Central Park and enjoying other adventures with his neighbourhood pals. The result was that while Howard easily won admission to Cornell University at Ithaca in upstate New York, Asa had to cram for exams with a tutor to gain admission. However, once forced to apply himself, he did so well he was granted a scholarship to attend Cornell also.

This had become necessary, as at about this time his father's health failed, the family income declined, and his mother sold the home in the city and moved the family to Ithaca. There she bought a large, plain family house near the university, took in other students as boarders, and, with her energetic and sociable nature, soon turned the old house into a popular gathering place for the students and their friends.

These were happy times for Asa and Howard in this small college town, and after four years, both graduated in engineering and went their separate ways, Howard to work for the Calumet and Hecla Mining Company in Michigan, and Asa to follow his interest in forestry, first in the East and South, then in the North-west.

The move to Ithaca and enrollment at Cornell set the course for my father's adult life. The university's beautiful location beside Lake Cayuga amidst forest and rolling farmland made it ideal for cross-country running, boating and the study of nature, the very things he loved, so it was not long before he was on the rowing crew and long-distance running team. Moreover, Cornell had the first school of forestry of any American university, and the quality of instruction was so good it challenged the best in Asa. He became the editor of the first professional forestry journal published in North America and developed skill in drawing plant and animal life, an aptitude which later gave him advantage and pleasure during his fieldwork and employment in the forests of Maine, the Carolinas, and in his subsequent forestry career in Oregon and British Columbia.

Once he left the East, he never returned, eventually finding his way to Vancouver in 1912 representing the Empire Locomotive Company and other machinery manufacturers. He had graduated from Cornell at the age of twenty-three, but by the time he reached Vancouver he was a rather confirmed bachelor of thirty, interested in the ladies, but they were decidedly secondary to his outdoor interests; hiking, running, hunting, fishing, and the company of other men like himself.

He took an apartment in the West End, as the area between Burrard Street and Stanley Park was called, drawn to the park's miles of running paths, and exclaimed in letters to his mother back East, "This city is where I belong. It has everything I need or desire; a good living, natural beauty abounds everywhere, and I have plenty of good company. In short, it is Paradise, and I doubt I shall ever leave."

Such was his intent, but within two years disaster struck, and the happy bachelor and forester almost left Vancouver in a coffin. He had prospered so well selling machinery to the booming logging industry that he had acquired his own timber company, logging on Lasqueti Island near the south end of Vancouver Island. As with much of early coastal logging, the trees to be harvested; huge, original growth Douglas fir for the most part, grew on steep, rocky slopes close to tidewater. No roads were necessary. The trees were felled and slithered down the rocky slopes by an A-frame, winch and cable, mounted on a floating log raft, or, if there was a creek nearby, by diverting the water into a hewn log chute.

The logs cascaded down this slippery trough at tremendous speed before crashing into salt water a hundred or more feet below. There, usually in a sheltered bay, they were assembled in booms or rafts and towed to mills located in Nanaimo, Chemainus, New Westminster, or one of the numerous mills along the shores of False Creek in Vancouver.

On the particular day Asa's life almost came to an end, he was making improvements at the bottom of one of these chutes when one of his employees let loose a large log. It sped down the chute and knocked him to smithereens. There he lay, splattered on the rocky shore, unconscious, bleeding and hours away from the nearest doctor or hospital, if he could survive that long.

There were no commercial aircraft, let alone helicopters, in those days, only small, gasoline-powered company boats to bring men and supplies to camp, capable of doing no more than eight knots with a favourable tide. With luck his small launch might connect with a Union Steamship Company boat that made scheduled weekly trips up and down the coast between Vancouver and the main settlements.

For the sake of brevity, all we shall say is that the good Lord was on Asa's side that day. His boom man hauled him into the small boat, and after several hours of rough travel, he was carried into St. Paul's Hospital in Vancouver more dead than alive. There he was operated on by Dr. McKechnie, an excellent surgeon affiliated with the University of British Columbia, and although severely crippled for many months, he survived to eventually pick up the pieces of a promising career.

It took almost two years for his body to recuperate from a fractured skull, collar bone, several ribs and right leg, but fortunately only limited injury to his brain and internal organs.

Because it seemed useless to remain in Vancouver until he had recovered the physical mobility essential for his occupation, he went to California to recuperate, invited to stay with his cousin Olive and her naval officer husband, Albert Cabanis, at Monterrey. There, through gradually increasing the length of his daily walks, he eventually was able to cover a mile or so a day. Being able to do little else, he further cultivated his interest in nature by sketching and drawing whatever he came upon along the seashore and uplands of this superb stretch of California coastline.

By the middle of the following year, 1917, he felt well enough to return to Vancouver to complete his recovery. Again he took an apartment next to Stanley Park, this time as close as he could get, at Englesia Lodge, on the very edge of the park at English Bay. Each day he pushed himself to walk a little further and faster, then to a slow trot, and finally to the point where he could once again cover his favourite forest trails running, now more slowly and with some pain and a slight limp, but well enough to allow him to experience once again the joy of a vigorous outdoor life.

Any man who has suffered severe physical wounds will understand that it was not only his body that needed to recover, but also his spirit, to regain confidence that his mind could still solve problems, that he could competently move among men in business and play, feel the appetite for risk and adventure again, and, equally important, not be found unattractive by the opposite sex.

If Asa Williams's brush with death nearly ended him, his introduction to Eliza Bell Larkin within a few weeks of his recovery and return to business was his miraculous compensation, a prescription for his spirit that not even the best physician could provide. They were brought together on a blind date for a dinner dance at the Hotel Vancouver, and it was a case of love at first sight for both of them.

Bell Larkin was twenty-nine at the time, and not only beautiful but full of fun, a good dancer, story-teller and lover of the outdoors. It was small wonder that she had numerous friends and suitors. Like Asa's mother Clara, Bell was a woman ahead of her times. Before she was twenty, she had taken over and managed her father's business, the only general store and bakery in the small Alberta town of Gleichen, some forty miles east of Calgary. In addition to running the family business, she was the first woman agent in Alberta for the Sun Life Insurance Company and thought nothing of setting off in her model T Ford and travelling for miles around to sell insurance to the surrounding farmers and ranchers. Sometimes, when a storm came up, this meant staying with a farm family overnight, and it was on these long visits in the country, with not even radios in those days, that she acquired her endless repertoire of stories, her skill as a story-teller, and ease among people of every sort.

She was given a head start in her outgoing, confident nature by her father, Frank Larkin, a large, affable man of Scotch-Irish background and a natural leader, who had sold his fishing fleet and cannery on Price Edward Island and moved to Gleichen in 1907. There he built the Larkin Block with living quarters above the street level across from the Bank of Commerce.

Bell, the youngest of his children, had a natural talent for business and dealing with the public, and became his right-hand "man". The general store and bakery served the whole surrounding countryside, including the Blackfoot Indian Reservation nearby, and thus, on Saturdays, when Indian families largely occupied the store, she learned to speak their language, befriended many, and came to know many of their customs and legends.

Bell was eighteen when the family moved to Gleichen, the last of ten offspring born to her Scotch-Canadian mother, Eliza Bell, and not in good health. She had developed tuberculosis in the damp climate of Prince Edward Island, and it was partly on the family doctor's recommendation that 'Captain' Larkin, as he was called, moved the remainder of his family to the drier climate of Alberta. Within a year Bell overcame the disease, and once in good health, became the leader of the pack among the young of this small prairie town. She was into everything, organized a girls' hockey team, parties, dances, and later, weekend trips to the big dances at the Palliser Hotel in Calgary. When her father's health deteriorated, she took over the business entirely.

So, at the time Bell Larkin met Asa Williams at the Hotel Vancouver dance, although six years his junior, she was in no need of a husband to protect and support her. Quite the contrary, she had been accustomed to managing her own affairs for a number of years, was comfortably off, and was on a holiday to visit her sister Flora and numerous friends who had settled in Vancouver.

Through her wide business and social associations, Bell knew just about everybody in southern Alberta, including the rising young Calgary lawyer named R. B. Bennett, a future leader of the Conservative Party and Prime Minister during the disastrous later years of the 1930s. But that's another story. Just now, on holiday in 1917, Bell was having a marvelous time; more invitations than she could accept, to dinner parties, dances, musicals and plays, a merry social whirl for this popular and beautiful young woman from the Prairies.

Young Miss Larkin took it for granted that she would marry and have children someday, but being raised a proper Presbyterian in matters of sex and marriage, she regarded match-making as a matter of faith that the Lord would let her know when the right man came along by the mysterious alchemy of falling in love. In this scheme of things, a decent woman could have many flirtations and beaux, and indulge in vague fantasies and dreams of romance. But anything explicitly sexual in thought or deed outside of holy matrimony with the Lord's designated mate was definitely sin. The Lord had His plan for matching and mating every man and woman in His Kingdom, and when the ordained partners met, He would let them know, more or less simultaneously but in no uncertain terms, that they were made for each other.

So it was with a carefree heart that Bell Larkin accepted the blind date invitation from one of her Prairie friends, Roberta Robinson, married to an American mining engineer. "Bell, I want you to meet one of Ken's best friends. His name is Asa Williams, a young forestry engineer from the States, and Ken and I are both very fond of him. He is a little shy but lots of fun when you get to know him. Won't you come?"

Little did Bell know that when she accepted that invitation, the Lord's will was at work. Nor did Asa. "She is the most beautiful woman I have ever met, and she seems to enjoy my company," he wrote to his mother the following day.

As for Bell, she told her sister Flora, "The moment we met, I knew that he was the man I was going to marry." Both having been smitten by the divine madness of love, they could not rest until they were together again. They dated the next day, and the next, and the next, went for long walks in the park, dinners and meeting each other's friends. They found they had much in common besides physical attraction. Both loved the outdoors, both had grown up in the East but preferred the freedom and informality of the West. Bell soon found that Asa was her match in story-telling, and she was delighted with the sketches he produced during their daily explorations of the beaches and forest trails of Stanley Park.

Before the week was out, she had accepted his proposal of marriage. Asa wrote to his mother enclosing a photo of Bell and a cheque, asking her to purchase the rings at Tiffany's. They made plans for the wedding as soon as Bell could settle her affairs in

Gleichen. Asa's mother answered his letter promptly, saying, "Dear Son, words cannot express my joy and thankfulness that the Lord has provided you with this beautiful young woman. With just one look at her photograph, I know I will love her, too, and am impatient to meet her. You should receive the rings directly from Tiffany's within a few days, and I do hope you will be happy with my choice. With much love and the Lord's blessing on both of you. Clara."

Within a month they were wed at a small gathering of only immediate family and friends in one of Vancouver's Presbyterian churches and took up residence at the Englesia Lodge in an apartment large enough to accomodate the furniture Bell brought from her Gleichen home. A loving wife was just the tonic Asa needed to fully restore his confidence from the near fatal accident. His stamina and ambition returned, and before long his business did very well, in no small part due to Bell's support and skill at entertaining Asa's business friends.

Within a year, even a large apartment at the Englesia would not do, as Bell was expecting their first child, so Asa rented a large family house not far away on Beach Avenue. Here their first child was born, a boy, whom they named Donald Edward after a younger brother of Asa's who had died in infancy.

The house was only a temporary measure, as the West End, Vancouver's first fashionable district, was declining rapidly as a residential district in favour of the newer developments to the south and west, such as Shaughnessy Heights, Kitsilano and Point Grey.

So Asa and Bell made plans to build their own house in Shaughnessy Heights. This area was the city's most prestigious neighbourhood, developed on choice land overlooking the city and given to the C.P.R. as part of its reward for bringing the railroad to Vancouver in 1885.

Asa was not wealthy, but with a promising career ahead and a wife who had investments and income of her own, the trust company had sound reason to finance construction of a relatively modest, five-bedroom Dutch Colonial family home in this neighbourhood of palatial residences. Evidently the C.P.R. had over-estimated the number of millionaires available to build huge homes, had vacant lots here and there, and thought it would be better to let a few middle-income professional people settle among the elite than to leave the lots vacant.

When completed in 1920, 1163 Balfour Avenue was a well-planned two-storey family home, the ground floor consisting of living room with fireplace to the left of the entrance hallway, dining room to the right, kitchen and breakfast nook next to the dining room, bathroom and den at the end of the hall, and up-stairs, a master bedroom, three smaller ones, bathroom and small storage and sewing room. Beneath the first floor, a daylight basement with a separate entrance contained two bedrooms and a bathroom for servants, furnace room, laundry room and fruit cellar.

Approaching the house from the street, one came upon a straight driveway that led along the border of the property to a double garage next to the back porch. In front of the house, a lattice-work fence and hedge enclosed a small lawn and weeping willow shade tree. Behind the house the lot was ample enough for a vegetable and flower garden, a small pond for Asa's two pairs of mallards, and a play yard for the two or three children they anticipated.

Bell and Asa were a happy couple with every reason to feel confident of their future as they settled into their new home. Asa's health was again robust, business was prospering, Bell suffered no ill effects from her first delivery of a strong and handsome son, and now she had her own home in a very respectable neighbourhood. It did not bother them that their new home was unimpressive alongside their neighbours' mansions, for neither Asa nor Bell was socially ambitious or pretentious in relation-ships with people.

To them, home was a place in which to be safe and comfort-able with family and friends, not a showplace to the world. Of course they enjoyed living in the city's most fashionable district, but mainly because the C.P.R. had not spared expense to make

Shaughnessy Heights quiet and beautiful, with curving streets and landscaped boulevards. Besides, it was a practical location for Asa's business, a straight drive down Oak Street in his Studebaker to the Dominion Bank Building on Hastings across from the Cenotaph and Province Building.

The house soon became none too ample for their needs. Within a year, both of their mothers came to live with them, their husbands having passed away. It was the firm belief in those days that one took care of one's parents at whatever sacrifice, just as naturally as one had been cared for by them as a child.

Bell's lovable personality was perhaps to her disadvantage in this circumstance. Both Clara and Elizabeth had other grown children at least as affluent as Asa and Bell with whom they could have lived, and not as far away as Vancouver. But both elderly ladies wanted to be around Bell, and she could hardly take one and not the other. To tell the truth, Bell and her mother-in-law Clara were two of a kind and thoroughly enjoyed each other's company, while her own mother Elizabeth, utterly worn out from bearing thirteen children, then losing three of her sons at sea, had a dour outlook and was taken in more out of duty than love. "The crabbiest woman I ever met" was the way Asa summed up his feelings for his mother-in-law. But again, to tell the truth, he was not much company for his own mother.

From an early age when his family lived in New York City, Asa had felt that his mother was too much of a social and political busybody, spending time on all her causes and church work instead of staying home and taking care of her husband and children. Although he admired and profited from Bell's equally outgoing nature, when it came to marriage he was a firm believer in the Victorian male's view that a woman's place was in the home, an attitude that was eventually to lead to trouble and sorrow in their marriage.

With the arrival of their second son, called "Larkin" after Bell's family name, and with two elderly ladies to attend to, Bell needed some help, so they hired a Chinese cook and a nursemaid-housekeeper, Ling and Frieda. Frieda was a jolly, plump young woman in her early twenties just over from Germany, and was delighted that Bell was interested in her as a person, teaching her the language and customs of Canada, helping her make stylish dresses for herself, in every way treating her more like a younger sister than a servant.

Ling, too, appreciated being treated by Missy, as he called Bell, in a warm and democratic manner, and showed his devotion in his weekly purchases of the household's meat, vegetables and fruit. Every Thursday he took the streetcar to Chinatown, bought directly from the farmers, and returned with the freshest produce at bargain prices, and he always included some special treat found only in Chinatown, leechee nuts, candied ginger, spiced pork or milk-fed squabs.

Bell was an excellent cook too, especially with fancy breads, cakes, cookies and pies, recipes she had learned during her Gleichen days. She always involved Clara, too, in preparing for dinner parties, for Clara loved to entertain as much as Bell and took pride in helping Bell make every dinner a success. Clara was especially helpful with sauces, gravies, and with her knowledge of wines, something Bell had not acquired on the Prairies.

Bell showed the same pleasure and skill at a monthly afternoon party strictly for ladies, not a stiff, formal tea, but an informal gathering where women could talk and share experiences and jokes such as they never could with men present. She had a genius for bringing people together, often inviting women who would otherwise have no opportunity to meet each other and talk in a relaxed atmosphere. Between good food and lively conversation, the women found out how much they had in common once they shook off the stiffness and reserve expected of a Victorian wife and lady.

It was in the 1920s that contract bridge became all the rage among Vancouver's ladies, and every second or third month it was Bell's turn to entertain the bridge club that she belonged to. But these bridge parties never supplanted her ever-popular monthly women's gathering, a forerunner of what women would be doing a generation later in the post World War II women's movement.

Just as Bell had her special relationships with women, Asa had his with men, built mainly around common interests in forestry or outdoor life. With the coming of spring, the perennial boy in Asa became excited as he prepared his fishing gear, light tackle and flies for trout, and a heavier pole, reel, and lures for salmon. Those he always took along on business trips to logging camps or mills on Vancouver Island or up the coast.

In early summer, he turned his attention to his vegetable garden, first putting in a row or two of peas, and later, beans, onions, squash, and potatoes. His pleasure was not merely in the harvest. From the first act of purchasing seed to finding the last squash hiding beneath vine and leaf, tending the garden was a sacred annual ritual, the garden itself a safe and quiet refuge from the cares of the world. There a man could take time to absorb the sun's warmth and let his mind drift with the gentle clouds above, drift safely and slowly above time and space, dwelling upon only that which he found agreeable and reassuring. For Asa, like his father before him, was a dreamer as much as an engineer and outdoorsman.

With the coming of the gray skies and cool nights of October, the fruit cellar shelves shone with quart glass rows of fruits, vegetables, jams and jellies, and Asa spent his evenings preparing for the bird hunt. First came China pheasants among the cornstalks and vegetable fields of Langley, then ducks along the sloughs of Lulu Island or Delta. Numerous paraphernalia had to be inspected for the previous year's damage, repaired, and carefully assembled before the hunt: the canvas-covered duck punt, rubber boots, canvas vest, coat and pants, canvas water bag, light cookware, thermos bottle and rum flask. Wooden decoys had to be re-varnished and put in a gunnysack, duck caller and dog whistle hung by cod line from his coat. There was no end to the special clothing, tools and gear to be made ready, all with a distinctive, musty smell. Of prime importance was a good gun and dog. Asa had both, an Ithaca double barrel 12 gauge shotgun, and Nick, a well-trained, eager black water spaniel, as smart at upland birds as he was at waterfowl.

Bell was unavoidably drawn into these annual hunting expeditions, answering Asa's frequent calls for help in getting ready. "Bell, where did you put...?" or "Bell, would you mend....?" And the night before the hunt, she would rout herself out of bed at three or four in the morning to see that Asa had a good breakfast and carefully provision his mooseleather backpack with a thermos of hot coffee, sandwiches, cookies and ingredients for a hot meal.

But that was only the beginning of the concerns of a hunter's wife. Seeing her husband all packed and out the driveway, Nick perched beside him in the Studebaker touring car, she returned to her cold bed and began to worry. Would Asa and his pals drink too much and fall overboard in their heavy rubber boots?...or get the car stuck in the mud?....or even accidentally shoot one among them while climbing through a barbed wire fence?

She knew she was probably worrying for nothing, and it didn't do any good anyway, but worrying just seemed part of the bargain when you marry and have children. And besides, she never would be able to forget the night three of her brothers were drowned, never seen again, in the cold Atlantic, when she was just a little girl on Prince Edward Island. How could she not worry until she heard Asa's car drive up and he had safely returned? So, trying to get warm again in bed, she prayed quietly, simply, for just one thing, that her husband would be back soon and safely from his hunt.

Even Asa's safe return was not without its price, for then began the nasty business of plucking, gutting, and preparing the pheasants and ducks for cooking. "Bell, nobody prepares wild game like you," Asa would say, her reward for all the drudgery associated with his hunt.

First she had to make sure all the potentially tooth-shattering lead shot was removed, then prepare the dressing, for which she had different ingredients according to the bird, to bring out its flavour and have it juicy rather than too dry. An older, lean bird needed more fat and not too much salt or bread, as that would dry it out. So it was quite an art, but the usual ingredients were chopped celery and onion, dried bread, of course, sometimes chopped nuts, raisins, sausage or bacon for flavour and fat, and a variety of spices. Two or three times she would open the oven door to pour the juices back over the bird, and then, when it was cooked just right, out it came, and the extra juice at the bottom of the pan was made into gravy.

After the bird had been carved, only dry bones were left, but even these were not wasted. They were simmered with vegetables and seasonings and made into soup, which, with fresh baked bread, made excellent fare for lunch or dinner. Such frugality came as naturally from the Scottish part of Bell's rearing as the generosity and affability from her father's Irish heritage, all of which would stand her in good stead for the leaner times ahead.

For ten years after moving into their Shaughnessy home in 1920, life in the Williams family unfolded in the normal and mostly happy sequence of seasons and events. Within two years of Larkin's arrival, Bell gave birth to a third son, whom they named "Asa Starkweather", and yet another son a year later, whom they decided to call "Robin", an abbreviated form of "Robinson", Clara's maiden name.

I arrived in September 1925, which meant that Bell had given birth about every other year since wed, all boys. Each was welcome, healthy, and lovable, but no substitute for at least the one girl they both desired. But it seemed that the genetic cards were stacked against that prospect, so Asa and Bell declared a recess in their procreative activity by one means or another. It was just as well, as four rambunctious boys were about all the house could accommodate, even after both grandmothers had passed away.

Aerial view of Vancouver & the North Shore, 1939

Hotel Vancouver, early 1900's

English Bay beach in summer, 1920's

Mother & Father when single,
both about age 23

Mother & first child, with grandmothers

Dad's mother

Dad's father

Mother as a girl of 13 with family in Prince Edward Island

17

2

Roughing it Among the Rich of Old Shaughnessy

The Balfour Avenue home was suitable from my parents' point of view, but Shaughnessy was not the best neighbourhood for four exuberant outdoor boys. In the first place, the wealthy inhabitants of nearby mansions had few children to play with, and they were usually sent to private schools where they made their own friends.

One might think that my brothers and I felt left out because of this, but quite the contrary, we devised our own fun and made chums outside the district. On the few occasions we mixed with the private school boys, we felt sorry for them. They did not seem to know how to have fun, appeared so stilted and unimaginative, like overdisciplined little adults, always fearful of being late for this or that.

Whenever one of these neighbour boys did break away from his anxious parent or nanny and came over to our house, he made secret plans to come back again to play marbles or Cowboys and Indians, or put together a kite or homemade scooter, or share in whatever else we were up to. One even sneaked out of his house one night and came over to hear mother tell Indian stories.

Mother loved to tell stories, and when adorned with a Blackfoot Indian war bonnet, beaded vest and tomahawk, all gifts of her Blackfoot friends from her Gleichen days, she told Indian tales that curdled our blood. She told these stories only on dark winter nights in the den with the lights turned out, all of us gathered in front of a crackling fire. Mother would enter the room dressed in Indian garb and brandishing a huge buffalo bone tomahawk, her face painted with red lipstick like an Indian warrior, her long black hair trailing down her back.

Doing a slow, curving dance, she stamped her feet in rhythmic cadence, with gutteral whoops and thrusts of her feathered tomahawk. Then, slowing down her excited dance, she placed herself in a squatting position in the shadows of the fire, bowed her head, and commenced a low, mournful moan.

One by one the stories unfolded, whispered in a low, far-off tone, while fire flames and shadows flickered across her ghostly form. Hers were grisly tales that carried us to another time and place. Enthralled, we wished she would go on forever.

The neighbour boy, filled with terrifying tales, quite naturally feared returning home alone, but warmed by hot chocolate and accompanied home by two of us, he begged to come again.

In a few instances these associations with neighbour boys provided reciprocal pleasure. One such boy was Campbell Sweeney, an only child about my age who lived in a huge granite mansion on Selkirk, just a block away. Campbell's father owned a barrel and box factory on Granville Island, so Campbell had all the toys money could buy, whole battalions of lead soldiers and an electric train set complete with tunnels, bridges and switching yard. When all laid out, Campbell's train set occupied an entire room.

Not only did I enjoy playing soldier and train with Campbell, but also I found the formality of the Sweeney household an amusing contrast to my own. Right in the middle of an exciting afternoon of play, a servant would announce, "Tea time," and Campbell and I would recess to the dining room, where we were properly served tea and biscuits by the Sweeney's butler.

Another wealthy neighbour whose children were allowed to play with us was the Mercer family on Osler Avenue. Mr. Mercer was the builder of the new Burrard Street bridge. Although wealthy and socially prominent, the Mercers welcomed Larkin,

Ace and me into their home as chums for their three sons.

It was in the Mercer home that the three of us first savoured a few of wealth's advantages; learning to play tennis on the Mercer's court, then refreshing ourselves with a glass of lemonade and a dash of soda water from a silver decanter. In turn, the Mercer boys were always eager for a game of improvised hockey on roller skates out on the boulevard, an expedition to Little Mountain to watch the Mounties practice cavalry drills or to scamper over the rocks of the mountain's abandoned stone quarry playing Cowboys and Indians.

An outdoor boy's life isn't much without a dog to tag along, and we were fortunate in having a father who understood this. In fact, being more or less a lifetime boy himself, he could not imagine being without his own dog. Since he was a bird hunter, Dad always had a retriever of some sort, in this case Nick, a black, wavy-haired water spaniel with big floppy ears and droopy brown eyes.

Wherever Larkin, Asa and I roamed, we made sure Nick was always along. Big brother Don, of heroic stature to us, was too much older to be part of our little gang. But a dog is special, so special that any of us would have risked his life for Nick, just as he would for us. We knew this because if we ever left the house without him, Nick would bark and scratch at the kitchen door, generally making such a commotion that one of us would have to run back to get him.

As much as we and Nick were inseparable companions, there were times when he made a nuisance of himself, especially when we played Cowboys and Indians or Robbers and Cops up on Little Mountain. The old quarry was a perfect place for such games; rock walls, ledges, crevices and caves for scampering and hiding, as in a Wild West movie. But with Nick along it was difficult to hide without being discovered. Like a dutiful sheepdog, Nick insisted on roaming the quarry to keep track of each of us, and upon discovering one of us in hiding, he would wag his tail and bark, a dead giveaway to a pursuer. The upshot was that we always had to take a piece of rope along and tie him up while we lived out our Wild West fantasies, something he did not like at all. Somehow he had the idea that hide-and-seek was as much his game as ours.

One day Larkin, the most emotional of us, got mad enough to kill to save Nick's life. Nick was a lover by nature and a bird dog by training, not a fighter or trained guard dog. But he, like any male dog, would fight if necessary to defend his territory, our yard.

On this particular day, a neighbour's big, slobbery, bow-legged bulldog wandered up our driveway all the way to the back porch. There was no doubt about it, the bulldog's aim was to pick a fight. Nick was no match for this fighting beast and was soon getting the worst of it. Cornered between the garage and the back porch, poor Nick was on his back, his assailant on top with a firm grip on Nick's throat, throttling him to death. It was a desperate situation. Larkin, hollering, screaming and crying all at the same time, ran into the kitchen, grabbed the butcher knife, and was doing his best to stab the bulldog's back. But the beast would not let go. Blood was foaming out of Nick's mouth, and he was beginning to go limp.

Asa grabbed a bucket, filled it with cold water and dumped it on the bulldog, but that didn't do any good, either. Then big brother Don appeared, and with superior eyes, spotted the bulldog's weak point; two large balls between his hind legs. Don wound up and gave the beast one good, swift kick in the rear. I thought the bulldog's eyes would pop out. His jaws dropped open, releasing his death grip on Nick, and he staggered back down the driveway. That was the last time he bothered Nick, and from that day on, Don's already heroic stature attained Superman proportions.

The kind of dogs people own says a lot about them. Our family always had hunting dogs that were pals, too. Our rich friends had showy collies or Irish setters, beautiful, agreeable family pets, but not much fun, not the sort of dog to wrestle, fetch tennis balls or tag along on expeditions. The very rich seemed always to have large, vicious German shepherds or Great Danes that barked and snarled behind iron gates, or ridiculous, yappy toy dogs like Boston bulls, wirehaired terriers or pompous little black Scotties. But the oddest dogs we ever encountered were the Bucklands' pair of Pekinese.

One Sunday our family was invited to dinner at the Bucklands' home, business friends of father's who lived in one of Shaughnessy's granite mansions. They had no children, human ones that is. Mother dressed all four of us in suits and bow ties and told us to show our best manners because, although the Bucklands were very nice people, they were not used to children.

The Bucklands were really rich, their home like an English castle, with a curving driveway leading to the covered main entrance. A Chinese butler in a starched, black and white uniform admitted us at the front door. We boys had hardly begun to take in the home's rich interior; dark, wood-panelled walls adorned with richly framed paintings, and in every room large mirrors and chandeliers, when two of the funniest-looking, yappy little dogs came running up and sniffed our legs.

They were like fluffy twin mops, with brown hair, pug noses and pop eyes, and around each whirling moppet's neck was a large, showy, silk bow, one in blue, the other in pink. It was the only way we could tell them apart.

Mrs. Buckland, a round, creamy, perfumed lady in flowery silk kimono, called to the excited little creatures, bent forward, swooped them into her ample arms and announced, "This is Ching," and "This is Ping," turning her head first to the one with the blue ribbon, then to the one in pink.

It would be an understatement to say Mrs. Buckland spoiled Ching and Ping. At dinner, Ching popped onto Mr. Buckland's lap at one end of the long dining room table, and Ping onto Mrs. Buckland's at the other. There each of the dogs sat, receiving tidbits of roast beef throughout the main course. Then came dessert. But first, beside both Mr. and Mrs. Buckland the butler placed an additional chair, then a plump cushion and an additional plate, not a china plate, but a large one of silver, in front of both Ching and Ping. Finally, he brought in the dessert on two silver platters; two bricks of Neopolitan ice cream on one, and on the other, a round sponge cake with orange icing. He placed both in front of Mr. Buckland.

Ching and Ping watched the master of the house and the two large silver platters of dessert as expectantly as we did. First, Mr. Buckland served Mother and Dad. He then paused, looked at Ching and Ping, then at each of us boys, none of us sure who was to be served next. We boys glanced at each other, then at our parents, then back to Mr. Buckland. The two dogs, by now sitting up on their silk pillows just as nervously as we, kept their eyes fixed upon Mr. Buckland and the dessert.

Mr. Buckland grinned, we burst out laughing, and to our relief, he served us boys next, perhaps deciding that real children ought to come first, or merely that the Williams boys were, after all, his guests too.

Unsure of whether Mrs. Buckland was just showing off how well trained her pets were, or if the Bucklands lived like this all the time, on the way home in the Studebaker I asked Dad, "Why don't rich people have normal dogs like us?" Dad chuckled and replied, "Well, son, I guess rich people are different."

That was good enough for me. The rest of the way home all I wanted was to see Nick and climb into my own bed. The rich were different, no doubt about that. But I was glad I was who I was, Robin Williams, with my dog, my brothers, my parents, and the Bucklands could be as rich as they wanted with their ridiculous pug-eyed pooches.

Summer was the best season of the year, and Sunday the best of summertime days. That is when the family, Nick and all, would pile into the Studebaker to spend the day at English Bay. Mother saw to packing the steamer trunk at the back with a picnic basket of sandwiches, a cake made especially for the occasion and lemonade, then the beach equipment, swim suits, towels, blankets, pillows and tin play buckets and shovels. On the way down Granville Dad would purchase his particular pleasures, cigars and the Sunday edition of the *New York Times,* albeit a week late coming from the East by train.

Upon arrival at the beach, Dad selected a log within easy distance of the bathhouse and diving float, propped himself up with a pillow and spent the day with the *Times,* while Mother took over as swimming coach. She was a good sport, wading right in with her four boys, the outer skirt of her black swimsuit floating until she ducked in and began our lessons. First she taught us the dog paddle, then the breast stroke, and finally, how to float on our backs.

That was the hardest thing for me to learn; the trick of it being to relax enough to let my head go all the way back until only my nose and mouth were above water. This automatically forces the chest upward and keeps the whole lower body safely afloat. As soon as Mother saw that we each of us had mastered how to float on our backs like this, we were on our own to learn the Australian crawl, sidestroke and backstroke from other boys. By the end of the second summer we were swimming out to the float and learning to dive.

After the picnic lunch on a blanket came special treat time, Dad sending all four of us off to the concession stand at the bathhouse for ice cream cones for everyone and a nickle apiece for each of us to spend as we wished. Choosing among the assortment of candy bars and suckers called for tough decisions, but usually the horseshoe suckers won out. Every fifth one or so had a lucky number beneath the wrapper entitling the purchaser to a second one free, and even one of these fruity delights could last the rest of the afternoon.

Some Sundays we spent part of the day in Stanley Park, feeding peanuts to the bears at the zoo, rolling down the grassy slopes in front of the tea pavilion or sharing fish and chips at Lumberman's Arch. That was a special place, for there, once a year, hundreds of families gathered for the Alberta picnic. Each family brought a casserole to share and chipped into a fund for ice cream, soft drinks and game prizes, everyone joining in like one big family.

While grownups moved among the tables, embracing and swapping stories with old friends from the Prairies, the children ran foot races, played blindman's bluff or engaged in numerous other organized games and contests. Then came the grand finale, a tug-of-war among the adults and a candy throw for the kids. How exciting it was to anticipate the rewards when one of the men stood upon a picnic table, reached into a barrel and flung hundreds of wrapped toffees into the air. Like greedy little sparrows, we scampered after them until all were gone.

Each summer for two weeks we enjoyed a cottage at Crescent Beach, courtesy of the Douglas family, Mother's friends from the Prairies. There each day had its special pleasures quite different from English Bay or the park. The safe, shallow beach allowed Mother to let us out of her sight without worrying, and we spent hours splashing in the warm tidal pools hunting for crabs, digging clams, building huge sand castles or putting together driftwood forts, from which we played our usual war games.

In the afternoon Mother joined us to pick blackberries for pies, but the most exciting event of the day occurred each evening after supper. That is when, upon hearing its distant whistle approach, we ran up the hill at the back of the cottage and stood as close as we dared to the railroad tracks as the Great Northern steam locomotive thundered past on its daily journey from Vancouver to Seattle.

When we were not at the beach we never lacked ways to spend summer days closer to home. Part of the fun was making many of our own toys, contraptions and costumes. A pair of skates served for much more than street hockey. When we nailed a skate to each end of a three-foot length of two-by-four, added an apple box up front, then a discarded broomstick for a handle, we had a sturdy scooter. Off down Balfour Avenue we would go, making an awful racket with our steel-wheeled machines.

We constructed sit-down buggies much the same way, only made faster with discarded rubber-tired wagon wheels, great for careening down the broad boulevards that curved downward toward the city. Homemade kites cost nothing when made of cedar kindling, grocery bag paper, paste made from household flour, and tails from shredded bedsheets. Tethered with string, our kites could fly as high as any store-bought model.

We always made elaborate preparations for expeditions to Little Mountain; homemade wooden rifles, pistols, bows and arrows, raggedy but convincing Cowboy and Indian costumes fashioned from discarded hats and coats adorned with feathers, ribbons, buttons and badges. The abandoned rock quarry at Little Mountain, whose granite building stone was used to construct the Shaughnessy mansions and later the sunken garden of what is now Queen Elizabeth Park, was as close as one could get in Vancouver to a Wild West scene. Huge boulders, rocky shelves, and small caves made the quarry perfect for hideouts and ambushes.

On the way to the quarry we passed the barracks and parade ground of the local detachment of the Royal Canadian Mounted Police, the red-coated keepers of law and order in the Wild West. There the Mounties, brandishing flag-topped lances, practiced cavalry charges, thundering down the field on their magnificent horses. Watching these heroes of the Canadian west got us all worked up to do battle at the quarry in our improvised costumes, painted faces and homemade weapons.

We took our war-making seriously, as strenuous work, so we never left home on such expeditions without loading up our pockets with apples, raisins and other kitchen goodies. After a hard day's fighting, we straggled home, tired and hungry but already planning the next day's adventure.

Those adventures sometimes involved being mischievous or downright nasty to the numerous tradesmen who provisioned Shaughnessy's households. Bread, milk, fruits, vegetables, ice, all were delivered daily or weekly from the same sort of horse-drawn, rubber-tired wagon, usually black. The milkman came early in the morning, delivering milk or cream in bottles shaped like bowling pins, and butter and eggs according to tickets left for him at the back door. He put his wares in an outside cooler that had a door to it from inside the pantry.

Later in the day the Shelly's bread wagon arrived. The

breadman reached into the back of his wagon with a long, round stick with a nail at the end, dextrously plucked out the loaves he wanted, and off he ran with his wire basket to the back door. Larkin, Asa and I were not above petty larceny if we could get away with it, so we would stand near his wagon watching, our greedy nostrils taking in the delicious odors of fresh-baked goods. But the breadman was wary, and always slammed shut the two big doors of his wagon, so we were never able to make off with even a doughnut.

The iceman and Chinese fruit and vegetable vendor were not so lucky during their weekly visits. The iceman was a stocky rhinocerous of a man, covered front and back by a black leather apron. Sharp steel tongs big enough to pick up a dog dangled from one hip and a long, pointed ice pick from the other. He would glance at the kitchen window for a numbered card, with "25" or "50" on it, the pounds of ice Mother wanted that week, then in a jiffy he chipped a straight crack line along the top and down the side of a huge block of ice, and down flopped the right size block. With lightning speed, he grabbed the block with his tongs, whirled around to position his powerful back under it, straightened his legs, and was off on a trot toward the back porch.

As soon as his back was turned, we crowded up to his wagon, grabbed a chunk of ice as big as a fist and vanished, retreating just far enough so the iceman could not catch us, but close enough to watch him when he returned. He suspected we were stealing, but was not about to waste his time chasing after mischievous boys making off with a cent or two's worth of ice. Nonetheless, having been a boy himself, he played his part in the game, shook his fist, yelled "Thief! Robber! I'll get you!" and pretended he was going to chase after us. Thus he gave us a triple treat; the ice, the exciting thought of being captured by this powerful, hairy iceman with his tongs and pick, and the inflation of our bravado in being able to tease such a dangerous adversary and get away with it.

We added insult to injury with the Chinese vegetable man, reflecting in our unthinking childish cruelty the blatant prejudice of the times. He was such an appealing victim, dressed in black pajamas and huge straw hat. Everything about him was enticing as he walked, bouncing along with two huge baskets, one at each end of a bamboo pole balanced across the back of his shoulders; a delicious target for our mean little minds. Out of sight from the kitchen window, we mercilessly mimicked his walk and mocked him with dreadful racist rhymes such as "Chinky Chinky Chinaman, sittin' on a rail, Hard to make a dollah 'cause you ain't pale." Then we would steal from him; a peach, an orange, a cantalope, even a watermelon one time.

In our snobby Anglo-Saxan minds it was okay to treat Orientals that way, they were "different", probably didn't understand or think the way white people did. We could not understand why our victim never showed anger or took revenge. In fact, every Easter he presented Mother with a lily bulb in a beautiful Chinese bowl.

Perhaps our Chinese vegetable man was a Christian who really practiced our mother's favorite prayer, "Our Father, who art in Heaven...forgive us our trespasses as we forgive those who trespass against us",... or, perhaps he was sustained by some much older Chinese faith.

We finally got our medicine in similar devilry with the junkman, a very special character who came around once a month. We could hear him coming half a block away as he called out in a rusty, sing-song voice, "Rags, bottles, sacks!" As he approached, ambling down the street slower than a funeral procession, his rickety, black, open wagon creaked and clanged. His horse was a skinny shamble of bones, his head drooped so low we thought the poor beast must be walking while sound asleep.

The junkman himself sat high up on a black seat, a long, arching whip beside him, looking every bit like an impoverished gentleman coming to town from the country. He wore a dirty brown wool suit complete with shirt and tie and a black top hat, from head to toe a character out of the Sunday comics, obviously, in our minds, someone made to play jokes on.

And we did, much to our regret.

We had been saving some firecrackers for just such an occasion, and had a plan of attack all organized. We waited until he crossed the street to pick up some junk. Asa's job was to release the brake on the wagon, a long wooden handle by the driver's seat. Mine was to snitch the tin oat bucket that dangled from the rear of the wagon and place it on the ground beneath the nag's belly. Larkin, as the oldest, had the most hazardous and exciting job of all, to place the bundle of firecrackers under the bucket and light the fuse.

Checking to be sure he was unobserved, Larkin lit the fuse, a piece of kerosene-soaked string leading under the bucket to the firecrackers, and we all scrambled behind the Culls' hedge next door. BANG! BANG! POW! The noise was terrific, and the bucket flew six feet into the air. The poor horse arched his bony back, lurched forward on all fours, and galloped wildly down Balfour Avenue. He would have gone all the way to Granville if a car had not crossed his path at the Selkirk intersection across from the Sweeneys' house.

Reappearing from the nearby house, the junkman dropped his load and ran out on Balfour just in time to see his horse, frightened by the approaching car, jump the curb, clatter across the sidewalk and crash into the neighbour's lattice fence, ending up in a jumbled heap of horse, wagon, bottles, bedsprings, pots and pans.

We had sense enough not to stick around. Making off in the opposite direction down Balfour, we sneaked behind hedges, crossed Osler, and hid behind the Mercers' garage until things died down.

Unfortunately, Daphne Christie, a miserable snitch of a girl who lived across the street, saw us take off after the Big Bang. That night after supper we all learned what Dad's leather strap hanging on the bathroom door was really for. He gave each of us five hard strokes across the bare bum as we clung to the edge of the bathtub. That didn't hurt as much as being grounded for a week and being given all sorts of dirty chores. Sadly, the junkman stopped coming down Balfour, and we missed him, not the only price we would pay for the Big Bang.

The junkman caper convinced Mother that we were in dire need of some Christian education. Accordingly, each Sunday thereafter she packed us off to Chalmers Presbyterian Church, just down the hill from Shaughnessy. It was no fun having to dress up in a scratchy wool suit and bow tie, but putting up with this torture had its compensations.

Chalmers Church was a huge, gray, forbidding building befitting the stern Protestant teachings found therein, and our spiritual mentors put much effort into uplifting our heathen minds. Each of us received a prettily illustrated book of Bible stories, and each Sunday we joined the other children in reading these stories aloud; about Joseph and Mary and the birth of baby Jesus, David and Goliath, Roman emperors casting Christians into lion dens, and many others.

Then came singing, our untrained voices bursting forth with more vigour than harmony such comforting verses as "Jesus loves me...Yes, I know... Because the Bible tells me so," or "A sunbeam, a sunbeam...Jesus loves a sunbeam." It was all pretty tame stuff, but we did take some pride in filling our report cards with stars for attendance and singing. The real payoff came in less innocent rewards.

Upon leaving home each Sunday morning, Mother gave each of us a nickle to put into the offering basket. That seemed like very big money to give the whole thing to a rich church, so we readily devised a method for more equitable distribution. On the way to church, one of us was elected to run over to the candy store on Oak Street and change nickle into copper, that is to say, for each medium-sized nickle coin we received five much larger copper coins. The "copper," as large and heavy as a silver fifty-cent piece, seemed, therefore, the appropriate coin for the occasion; two for the collection basket and three for the pocket, or the other way around, depending upon the state of our consciences on a particular Sunday morning.

Thus comforted that we had both given and received, we found the remaining half-hour of doing our Christian duty tolerable.

But as soon as the class let out, we ran back up Oak Street to the candy store for our just reward. My favorite selection was one Sinclair toffee sucker, two jawbreakers, and either a licorice stick or a set of wax teeth; all in a brown paper bag for three coppers.

Aside from this regular petty larceny, another Sunday school escapade made it clear to both God and us that we were not yet ready for Christian salvation. This particular piece of blasphemy required a considerable investment of time and effort before Sunday school, and was decidedly risky. If caught, we would surely make another trip to the bathroom for another session with Dad's razor strap, so we had to be sure to make a clean job of it.

On the way to church, we had noticed that the people in the house right next door put their pet parrot out on the front porch each Sunday morning, and further, that if spoken to, the bird would echo the very same words back. Larkin would say, "Hello. What's your name," then "How old are you?" and back the words came loud and clear. That gave us an idea. What if we said, "You're dumb," or "You're ugly," or even "Go to Hell!"? We decided to find out the next Sunday.

From behind a large hedge separating the house and church we put Charlie through his paces on a trial run. He responded perfectly, even when spoken to in a quiet voice. Loud and clear, Charlie cackled back, "You're fat", "You're ugly", "You're dumb", and "Go to Hell". And all the while he looked so handsome and innocent up there in his cage basking in the morning sun next to the church. We could hardly wait until the following Sunday.

We thought it best to get the attention of a passer-by by starting out nice. Soon our first victims came by, two middle-aged ladies dressed in their finest on the way to church; two absolutely perfect victims to test our new-found form of devilry. As they came alongside the porch, not ten feet away, Charlie greeted them with his most courteous but raucous voice, "Hello. Good Morning".

"What a pleasant surprise!" one lady said to the other, delightedly taking note of this lovely parrot, that is, until Charlie came out with, "You're fat!" and then, "You're ugly!"

"What did that naughty bird say?" asked one lady, and the other replied, "Why, I can't believe my ears!" Needless to say, the two ladies lost no time hurrying to the church door.

Out of sight behind the hedge, we could hardly contain our laughter, and like all wrongdoers left unapprehended, we grew more bold. This time the footsteps coming down the sidewalk were those of a very respectable-looking married couple, and we let go with the cruncher, but not until Charlie got the couple's attention with a polite warm-up.

"Hello!" Charlie cackled, "Nice morning, isn't it?" Well, that got their attention, and they paused to admire this remarkable bird. Then, looking the admiring couple straight in the eye, Charlie blinked and came out with an unmistakable "Go to Hell!".

That did it. The man in spats must have had influence in the church and neignbourhood. The next Sunday Charlie was gone, never thereafter to appear on that porch on Sunday mornings.

Christmas in our family was the most important event of the year, a special time of warmth, love and magic, all orchestrated by a father transformed into the living presence of Santa Claus himself, brimming with good humour and cheer. For Mother, the centre of family life during most of the year, it was a day of rest. She was allowed to idle awhile, receiving such an abundance of gifts and expressions of love from husband and sons that it seemed an atonement for her year-long labours on their behalf.

Like a play of several acts, the spirit of Christmas unfolded by degrees, starting days in advance with Dad's quiet preparations and purchases, all stored in the downstairs den, locked and forbidden territory until the grand day arrived. Thinly veiled questions, suggestions, and hints passed between parents and children, all intended, of course, to be overheard by the mythical Santa Claus.

Dad gave each of us two dollars, a considerable sum at the

time, to "get something for your mother and a little something for your brothers." The night before Christmas, each of us boys hung the biggest stocking we could contrive from the mantel of the fireplace in the living room.

The unmistakable aroma of kippered herring rising from the kitchen was the signal that Christmas morning had arrived, time to get up and open our stockings. Dressed in last year's pajamas and bathrobes, we descended the stairs as quietly as our enthusiasm would allow, remembering what Dad had said, "Remember, boys, this is your mother's day to stay in bed."

The fireplace was already lit, and to more delicious odors of coffee, Johnny cake and maple syrup from the kitchen, we emptied a torrent of small gifts onto the living room rug. From our giant stockings tumbled every small thing a boy could desire; pencils, pens, crayons, a drawing tablet, pocket knife, Boy Scout whistle, wind-up toy cars marked "Made in Japan", or "Made in Germany", candy canes, gold and silver chocolate coins, multi-coloured hard candies, Japanese oranges, figs, nuts of all kinds, and at the foot of the stocking, a potato or turnip, Dad's reminder that greed would not be rewarded on Christmas day.

It was time for breakfast when Mother came down. Like a tired queen, she descended the stairs in her bathrobe, entered the dining room, and took her seat at the oval table, all laid out with a half grapefruit at each place, and the centre laden with dishes and platters of steaming hot kippers, sausage, corn bread and syrup. All through breakfast Dad waited upon Mother as though once again she was his new bride, interrupting his devotion only to retreat to the kitchen to refresh his coffee with a nip of rum.

After breakfast Dad unlocked the den, and Mother leading, the family positioned themselves around the tree, a Douglas fir reaching to the ceiling, all aglow with coloured lights, and at the base a heap of multi-coloured presents of all shapes and sizes.

Dad always commenced the distribution of presents by playing a joke on us, directing Donald to admit the family pets separately, starting with Felix, the black family cat. Upon entering the den, Felix began sniffing about the tree, then catching a whiff of something tasty, stood on his hind legs, reached up a paw and brought down a small white package tied loosely on a branch. Thereupon Dad said, "Larkin, see if he got the right one," and sure enough, there on the tag it said, "To Felix, from Santa Claus," and inside was a strip of kippered herring. Well, it was nothing short of miraculous, and we all thought, "What a clever cat!"

Then Nick was admitted. Straightaway, he too, began to sniff about the tree, reached up with his forepaws, this time a little higher than Felix, and down came a larger parcel. Lo and behold, on the tag it said, "To Nick, from Santa." Another miracle! But this time inside was a meaty bone. Well, it certainly tested credulity, I mean, the same miracles year after year without fail! There was only one explanation; obviously, our family had the smartest pets around!

Taking one parcel at a time from under the tree, Dad would announce, "Well, well, what do we have here? It says "a gift from Santa to Larkin," whereupon all attention would turn to Larkin as he unwrapped his gift. Then Larkin would get up and give a big kiss to Mom and Dad.

Santa's gifts always included practical items like a new sweater, socks and pajamas, along with a favourite plaything; new skates, a hockey stick or soccer ball; and one indoor game, like Chinese Checkers or Pick-Up-Sticks. Mother received a new evening gown or housecoat, slippers, perfume, a huge box of chocolates, and something for the kitchen. Dad usually got a new cardigan sweater, shirt, slippers and box of cigars. When the gifts were all distributed, we all helped clean up the breakfast dishes, then we boys scattered to enjoy our new games while Mom and Dad prepared dinner. Freida and Ling always had that week off, leaving for their own families and friends with a present or two and a cheque for as much as Mom and Dad could afford.

Christmas dinner was a blend of joy, winter birthday party, and a dab of reverence, the one meal of the year that Mother felt moved to open with a prayer. We could tell she was sincere, her voice quivering with emotion as she began, "Let us all bow our heads in prayer. Our Heavenly Father, we thank Thee for Thy merciful bounty", but before long she would choke up, tears coming to her eyes. We waited for her to gather the strength to go on. Heads bowed, we waited, and we waited, experiencing with her a strange, uncomfortable mixture of emotions; gratitude, humility, love, all jumbled together like the presents under the tree, until finally, she came to a fitting place to say, "Amen".

It was a wrenching ordeal, but once Mother said the magic word "Amen", she seemed transformed. Whatever her spiritual burden, it vanished, and she became as jolly as Dad. Christmas dinner was like no other of the year. It started off quite literally with a "Bang!", for at each place there was a Christmas cracker, a roll of coloured paper the size of a napkin, which, when pulled smartly from both ends, opened up with a firecracker "Bang!" and out popped a colourful paper hat in the shape of a bird or animal; a yellow duck, a red rooster, a golden pheasant, a rabbit, a donkey, or giraffe. Around the table the family became a comic menagerie of quacking ducks, crowing roosters and various noisy beasts, all to great laughter and joshing.

Then Dad carved the turkey, dexterously easing one slice after another onto a large platter, and invariably saying to Mother, "Bell, you have done this bird just right", to which she would invariably reply, "I hope you like the sweet potatoes." Her reply was appropriate, as Christmas dinner was the one meal of the year for which she prepared candied sweet potatoes, a fitting dish indeed, with cranberry sauce and giblet gravy. Then came plum pudding and hard sauce. Then cleanup. Then games in the living room. Then, one by one, off we went to bed.

Another Christmas had come and gone. Thus, once a year, year after year, Mom and Dad had attained beloved and heroic stature; we all felt safe and together for another year.

One Saturday a year Dad treated each of us to a day downtown. When it came my turn, Mother dressed me up in my Sunday suit and bow tie, gave me directions, carfare, a hug and a kiss, and off I went to catch the number 22 tram on Oak Street. I was to meet Dad at his office in the Dominion Bank Building at eleven o'clock. "Just stay on the streetcar to the end of the line at the Cenotaph," Mother said, "then cross Hastings to the big brown building with the revolving doors, and get off the elevator on the thirteenth floor."

The instant I pressed the elevator button I felt like a Big Person. Through the glass elevator doors, I watched the black cables moving up and down, heard the rumble of the cage and followed its descent on a dial above the door. The dial stopped, the doors opened, and the prettiest woman in a blue uniform smiled at me and said, "You must be Robin, Mr. Williams's boy. My, what a big boy you are!"

I stepped into the elevator, the operator's white-gloved hand closed the doors, her other hand rotated a handle on a round brass control, and up we went into the mysterious land of grownups. Being with this beautiful, uniformed lady gave me a warm, protected feeling, but also one of strange excitement, and I would not have minded going up like this alone with her forever. So I felt a little lonely when the elevator stopped and she pointed down the hall where I should go. Squaring my shoulders, I walked down the vacant hall to a glass door lettered, "Asa S. Williams, Forestry Engineer".

Opening the door, my loneliness vanished with the familiar smell of cigar smoke. There was my Dad with another man, leaning over a huge sheet of paper spread out on a table. The office walls were covered with brown photographs of logging machinery, of men standing beneath huge trees, and of a tugboat pulling a raft of logs.

As I was closing the door, I overheard the man saying, "Skidder, this is the best way to...", when Dad interrupted him, "Doc, this is my youngest son, Robin." The large man straightened up and looked at me as Dad said to me, "Son, this is my partner, Doc

Cloudy." The huge man, with one enveloping smile and out-stretched hand, chuckled and said, "Robin, I'm sure glad to meet you. I wish I had a son like you!" Then, turning to Dad, he added, "Skidder, you're sure a lucky man!". Needless to say, 'Doc' and I became instant friends.

I was curious, though, why Mr. Cloudy called Dad 'Skidder', and told myself I must remember to ask Dad how he got this funny nickname. Turning to me, Dad said, "Son, you just wait awhile, and we'll go to lunch and a movie." I turned my attention to a seagull on the ledge outside the window. Dad reached into a drawer of a rolltop desk and gave me a handful of soda crackers. "Here", he said, "gulls like soda crackers." I moved a chair over to the window, cautiously opened it, stuck out my hand with a cracker in it, and the gull grabbed it and gulped it down whole.

Before long the gull had swallowed all my crackers, so I turned my attention to the world below. Streetcars clanged down Hastings, a jostle of miniature people moved up and down the sidewalk, and flights of pigeons soared down from the window ledges of the Province Building to Cenotaph Park below. Old or crippled men passed the time of day reading the newspaper, playing chequers or feeding the pigeons. Now and again a peculiarly dressed person aroused my curiosity, but at such a distance I quickly lost sight of the person in the ceaseless flow of people far below. I was glad when Dad was ready to go. I was hungry and anxious to see my first movie.

With Dad following close behind, I pushed through the re-volving door at the entrance to his office building. He took me by the hand, and together we entered the slow-moving crowd as it crossed over Cambie Street and stood waiting on the corner. I felt very good standing next to my Dad waiting for the light. Beside and around me stood many interesting looking people; East Indian men with turbans, beside them women mysteriously attractive with their dark faces, olive eyes, pearl-studded nostrils, and shiny long hair that flowed down the backs of their colourful gowns, and among them, black-garbed Chinese carrying heavily laden grocery bags.

On the street, uniformed telegraph boys pedalled between the curb and passing automobiles and streetcars. On the far corner, a cocky newsboy in cloth cap waved his paper aloft and shouted its headline. A one-legged man on crutches leaned against the Province Building selling pencils from an outstretched hat. All were new and interesting to me, but I could glance only a second at any one of them before being pushed ahead with the crowd as we crossed over Hastings Street.

Noises also clamoured for my attention; streetcars with screeching wheels and dinging bells, honking motor cars and the babble of a dozen foreign tongues. I had many questions I wanted to ask Dad, but the noise was such that it would be foolish to try to talk until we got inside, off the street.

Once we got on the other side, Dad stopped at the Trocadero Café next to the Province Building. Outside it was a plain looking place, but its big window was inviting. In front of frosted pipes there was a display of fish and lobsters, sliced melon, brilliant red apples, oranges and bottles of Orange Crush half submerged in crushed ice. Most enticing was a neon sign above that flickered, making a green palm tree come and go, and curved handwriting spelled out 'Palm Ice Cream' in pink letters.

Inside, the Trocadero was arranged as a cafeteria. A long glass case displayed to best advantage a variety of main courses and desserts, and above, a sign hanging from the ceiling announced the names of the items and each one's price. I decided on fish and chips, a glass of milk and strawberry ice cream. Dad ordered clam chowder, apple pie and coffee. We sat down together at one of the square tables scattered about the white chequered floor. With Dad's chowder came a bowl of marble-sized soup crackers, and I noticed he also slipped some square ones into his coat pocket, undoubtedly the source of the gull crackers.

Midway through the dish of ice cream, the edge of my appetite was off enough to ask Dad about the movie. Dad anticipated me and interrupted his apple pie to say, "You'll like the Walt Disney cartoons, but we'll have to see what the main feature is." On the way out, Dad bought two packs of Lifesavers. I could not have felt more content as we made our way out of the Trocadero and down Hasting Street toward my first movie. Walking down the street with my dad, for the first time in my life I felt what it must be like to be a man.

Down Hastings Street across from the streetcar barn, a sign in coloured light bulbs announced the Rex Theatre. Coming closer, I could make out the main feature, "Treasure Island". As we drew closer still, smaller letters gave the actor's names, Wallace Beery and Jackie Cooper. At the ticket window Dad put down two quarters and received two tickets and a three nickles in change.

Inside, time seemed suspended in the theatre's dark, musty interior. But once we were seated, the darkness faded, and the screen up front came alive as if by magic, with a Micky Mouse cartoon, then the story of Treasure Island; a sailing ship, sword-battling pirates, the evil Long John Silver and the brave Jim Hawkins, as they lived out adventure in the South Seas. It was so exciting I got stomach cramps, just too much for one day, I guess, so I was relieved when the movie ended and Dad and I walked out into daylight and the bustle of the street again.

On the way home in Dad's car, I looked down from the Granville Street bridge to a tug pulling a boom of logs up False Creek. The wharves of Granville Island were piled high with lumber. Black-coned incinerators of lumber mills spewed forth gray smoke. Beside them were rows of long, dark roofs; iron foundries, wire rope factories and warehouses. Here timber was King, and as long as those mills and factories belched forth steam and smoke, the city and my forestry engineer father would thrive. Without them, the city of Vancouver and its inhabitants would stumble and shrivel, a fate which was about to overtake them. In fact, it was just over the horizon as Dad and I turned homeward and climbed the hill to Shaughnessy Heights. It was the fall of 1930, one year into a ten-year nightmare, the Depression of the 1930s that began with the stock market crash of October 1929.

HARD TIMES AND POLIO

By 1931 the effects of the Depression were clearly visible to the residents of Vancouver. The wharves of Burrard Inlet and False Creek were piled high with unsold lumber. The rail yards of the Canadian Pacific Railroad and the Canadian National Railroad were jammed with vacant flatcars, cargo ships lay empty at their moorings in English Bay, and everywhere in the city unemployed men shuffled the sidewalks in search of work. Unable to sell their lumber, logging camps, mills, and related factories and businesses shut down, bringing unemployment and hardship to thousands of Vancouver families, including my own.

However, it was part of the Victorian middle class code not to mix business with family life, nor, even more broadly, deal directly with any of the unpleasant issues in life, such as unemployment, poverty, and gender, racial, or class prejudice. One didn't talk about such things when ladies or children were present, one referred to them only in the most oblique terms or in terms so categorical and final there was no room for discussion. Thus, people referred to the economic turmoil of the Depression by remarking, "money is a bit tight", and an impoverished family was said to be "hard up," or "having a hard time."

Despite my parents best efforts to practice this code of denial, we boys knew something was wrong. Mother seemed pale and tired. Ling, the Chinese cook, was let go. Dad took the streetcar instead of the Studebaker to work. And every week a man or two in threadbare clothes would knock at the back door, ask if there was any work he could do, and Mother would give him a hot meal and sometimes an item of clothing.

At times there was an amusing aspect to this painful situation. The unemployed repeatedly picked our house because, on leaving 1163 Balfour feeling a little less downtrodden, one "bum" chalk-marked an "X" on the driveway fence-post, a signal to the next needy passerby that he would likely also be treated with dignity and kindness at the Williams' household.

Mother felt so sorry for one of these men that she persuaded Dad to let him stay downstairs for a few days in Ling's old room. Part of her liking for Andrew was the fact that he was of French-Canadian background, and she enjoyed speaking Quebecois with him. She had learned the language as a girl on Prince Edward Island by talking with her father's French-Canadian employees and their children. Then, too, she liked Andrew because he played old French folk melodies on the violin he carried with him, and he set to work making miniature violins for us out of Dad's old cigar boxes.

But Andrew had his weaknesses, among them a fondness for the blackberry wine Dad was brewing in the fruit cellar. Andrew would likely have gotten away with his tippling, except that one night he overdid it. Dad was awakened to the sound of Andrew's loud fiddle playing and singing, and the next day Andrew was gone.

Only in hindsight did I come to understand another effect of the Depression on my parents' lives. One day Mother took me with her downtown on Richard Street, where we climbed a flight of stairs in an old wooden building to an office whose door announced, "Planned Parenthood Society." There Mother was greeted in a most courteous and friendly manner by a plump lady about Mother's age and was taken into an inner office while I was made comfortable with crayons and an exercise book in the waiting room.

I didn't know what was going on behind that door, but whatever it was, it must have been important because Mother and the lady were there for at least an hour. At first I heard Mother crying, and this was upsetting, but after awhile she began to laugh a little, then more, as she used to before times got hard. Finally the door opened, Mother and the lady hugged and kissed each other like the best of friends, and we left. But just before we descended the stairs I remember Mother asking, "Now Erma, you're sure you'll come?" and Erma replying, "Of course, Bell, I'll be there."

Many times thereafter, whenever Mother had her monthly ladies' afternoon party, Erma Hatfield was present, and it always seemed that Mother and Erma had a special, secret, and especially warm relationship.

Only years later as a teen-ager did I comprehend the significance of the Planned Parenthood Society, Erma Hatfield, and that rubber bag with dangling tube hanging from the inside of my parents' bathroom door, a douche bag, one of the few methods a woman had for birth control. In that Victorian society, it was illegal, but something Mother needed desperately in those hard times when she was terrified of becoming pregnant again.

The Depression was bad enough, but to make matters worse, on the way home from a picnic at English Bay I caught a chill, that night I had a high fever, and by morning I couldn't get out of bed. I had contracted polio- myelitis, or infantile paralysis, as it was called, and the disease had paralyzed my right leg from the knee down. Mother immediately contacted her sister Flora, a nurse at Vancouver General Hospital, who arranged for an examination by specialists. They all agreed it was polio, common at the time among children under the age of twelve, and likewise they agreed on the treatment, confinement to bed and total immobilization of the affected part.

Not long after, an Australian nurse named Sister Kinny proved that this was exactly the wrong thing to do. What was needed was constant massaging and stimulation of the nerves and tissue to prevent atrophy. Unfortunately for me, however, instead of getting massage and stimulation, I was confined to my bed for many months. Since my five-year-old body was growing rapidly, a long period of enforced bedrest meant that the bones, ligaments and muscle tissue of my right foot and lower leg failed to grow. I was left with a club foot that dangled uncontrollably from a skimpy, undeveloped lower leg.

After weeks of this mistreatment, it became obvious to Mother and the doctor that such confinement of an otherwise healthy child was impossible to enforce, so a special shoe and leg brace were devised, which allowed me to move about the house, at least, dragging my crippled leg behind me.

This was a great improvement, at least I could now join in the household activity downstairs, devise simple amusements, play with the family pets, and hear what was going on with my brothers outside.

It was probably then, at this early period of childhood confinement to the interior of the family home, that I developed a lifelong delight in the simplest pleasures: the morning light coming through the cut-glass panels at the top of the front door and casting a rainbow of colour on the hallway floor, the sun's warmth on Felix's sleek belly, the rhythm of household sounds coming from the kitchen, the clang of pots and pans, click of the icebox door, water running from the kitchen tap, whistle of the tea kettle, patter of Mother's slippers, and the soft swish of her bathrobe as she moved about the kitchen.

Noises came from upstairs, too; miscellaneous cracks, creeks, slithers, bangs, and gurgles as Freida changed bed sheets, mopped, vacuumed, scrubbed and polished the upstairs quarters. Smells were enjoyable too, of morning toast, newly applied wax on the hardwood floors, fresh clothes brought in from the line, and of Freida's warm body as she playfully scrubbed me at the evening bath.

I had my favourite amusements; a wind-up Victrola with records of Harry Lauder singing funny songs in his Scottish brogue, others with singing canaries, Gracie Fields singing "Tiptoe Through The Tulips" or "The Biggest Aspidistra In The World." Then I began to read, first from cereal boxes with puzzles, later from colouring books about animals.

So life indoors had its pleasures, but always gnawing within me was the call of the outdoors. This yearning became particularly acute whenever I heard Asa and Larkin banging away at some building project or Nick's excited bark as they roared down the driveway on their roller skate bugs. Gradually my envy grew into a spirit of rebellion, not against Mother or my body, but against that damnable brace, that steel and leather trap confining me forever as an incompetent cripple. For me, there was only one life worth living, the life of the great outdoors.

I had a problem, however. The doctors had told Mother, "You mustn't let him outdoors or his leg might become worse." But for me, no matter what the doctors said, a life of confinement indoors had become intolerable, and I decided to take matters into my own hands. First, though, I had to devise a strategy, the first tactic of which would be to extract a promise from Mother to let me outdoors to sit on the back porch between the house and the garage so I could watch my brothers and Nick at play. This I accomplished by hiding deep in the linen closet when it came time for my afternoon nap and refusing to come out until she promised that, beginning the next day, I could sit out on the back porch "for just a little while."

So the next day, and the next, all that week, each morning I got to sit out on the back porch, each time a little longer, until Mother began to forget I was out there.

That accomplished, I turned to the next stage of my plan, to observe and arrange in my mind the exact location, timing, and tools for the job. It would have to be in the garage, where hammers and other tools were available, and be out of sight from the kitchen. And the timing had to be right, when Asa and Larkin had left for a morning's adventure, or better still, the day Frieda and Mother went through the whole house vacuuming and cleaning. Then Mother's attention would be directed elsewhere, and the noise from the vacuum cleaner would blot out the noise coming from the garage.

The day to put my plan into effect came, and everything went as schemed. As soon as I heard Larkin and Asa safely down the block on a day-long expedition to Little Mountain and Mother and Frieda upstairs vacuuming, I slipped into the garage. Using a fair sized rock from the garden, I went to work. I had to work fast and make as little noise as possible, just enough to get it over with before I was discovered. Off came the shoe, then the hated brace. Excitement growing, I propped the linkage connecting the shoe to the brace against the rock and hammered with all my might. With a few blows the shoe separated from the brace. With similar ferocity I attacked the middle and upper portions, two flat, stainless steel rods connected to thick leather. Within a few minutes of such warfare, the dreaded brace was a dismembered wreckage. I threw it into a dark corner of the garage.

The deed was done. Both exhilarated and exhausted, I dragged myself into the den and fell asleep on the floor; a brief reprieve before facing the consequences, sure to come, when Mother asked what had become of my brace.

"Where's Robin?" I heard Mother ask Frieda outside in the hallway. Then they both ran outside, not thinking to look in the den, for I never spent time in there during the day. Before long they returned to the kitchen, Frieda crying, and Mother saying, "Oh my God, I think he's run away. Frieda, you stay here while I go out and see if I can find him."

When I heard Mother's footsteps go down the hall to get her coat, I could stand it no longer. I opened the den door, and half-crying myself, blubbered, "Don't worry Mother, I'm here."

Her relief was such that she didn't notice my brace was gone. Then Frieda, joining her from the kitchen, noticed. "You're not wearing your brace. Are you all right?" By then I had mustered enough courage to announce, "Mother, I broke it, and I'll never wear one again."

Mother and Frieda both burst into tears, hugged me, and not knowing what to do about my stubborn defiance, Mother said, "Well, we'll just have to see what your father has to say. But promise me now, you won't go outside until he comes home."

The worst was over. Confident now that I was free at last of that damned brace, I prepared myself for whatever Dad would say or do. I'd probably get a good licking, but nothing could be worse than daily imprisonment in that brace.

When Dad came home, he wanted to know the whole story and where the brace was, but beyond that his reaction was anticlimactic; no harsh words, no strapping. He just shook his head and told Mother, "Bell, we can hardly blame the boy. We'll just have to tell the doctor and see if he can come up with something better. He's not going to change his mind, and we can't keep him in bed." Then turning to me, Dad said, "Robin, you've had your way, but just remember, your mother and I love you and don't want you to hurt yourself any worse than you are now. So stay around the house until we can find out what to do next." Grateful, I gave Dad a big hug, and he grinned, probably amused that his youngest son showed such spunk, a good sign that he might amount to something in spite of his handicap.

Within days Mother found out from one of her friends that the Shriners operated special hospitals for crippled children, one in Spokane, another in Portland, and that her friend's husband, a Shriner, would see to it that I was admitted, provided a local physician recommended it.

Mother's sister Flora arranged a consultation with one of Vancouver's orthopedic surgeons. "Yes", the surgeon said, "Robin might be able to learn to walk without a brace after an operation to correct the club foot, but only a children's specialist can perform that operation on a child so young. Then he will need other services found only in a children's facility. If everything goes well, he will be hospitalized at least two or three months. I will forward my examination findings upon request from the Shriners' hospital."

When all the arrangements were made, Mother and I took the Great Northern to Portland. Mother had chosen the Shriners' Hospital there because Dora Carter, one of her closest friends from her Gleichen days, had married an American and settled in Portland. She and Mother had been the best of pals but had not seen each other for years. Moreover, Dora had never been able to have children of her own and was delighted with the prospect of becoming my substitute mother during my long hospital stay.

Dora and her husband Wilbur met us at the train station. As soon as she saw Mother and me come through the doors, Dora rushed up to Mother, and they hugged and kissed and laughed like two giggly girls. As for me, just the look of Dora and Wilbur put me at ease. Dora was a plump, pink-cheeked lady in a gorgeous flowered hat, and Wilbur a large, portly man with a cigar bobbing between his chin and gray felt hat. Both seemed like jolly, fun-loving people.

Dora interrupted her fun to introduce Wilbur to Mother, then picked me up and hugged me like a Teddy Bear, exclaiming to Wilbur, "Here is our new boy! Oh, Robin, we're so glad you can come to stay with us!"

As much as I enjoyed Dora's effusive attention, I was relieved when she put me down before introducing me to Wilbur. I wanted to shake hands standing up, man to man. From the beginning Wilbur understood this, and we soon became like father and son.

Wilbur carried our bags to a lumbering Pierce sedan and put them in the steamer trunk at the back. Mother and Dora got in back and immediately resumed their laughing conversation, while I sat in front next to Wilbur. He cranked the big old touring car and off we went, Wilbur chuckling and chomping on his ever-present cigar.

After I had spent two days in their home, Dora and Wilbur had become like my favourite aunt and uncle, and when the day came to go to the hospital, I felt a lot safer driving up there beside Wilbur in his big old Pierce. From the outside, the Shriners' Hospital for Crippled Children looked neither threatening nor inviting to me; it was just a big building on a hill, surrounded by large grounds. But once inside, I had no doubt of its nature, a hospital, with that special institution's distinctive smells and sounds.

At the receiving station I kept reminding myself that a hospital's purpose was to heal. But still I was afraid. There was just no getting around it, pain would be involved, probably plenty of it.

How else could they give me a new foot and useful leg without cutting and stitching that part of my body?

But there was more than just the prospect of pain that was scary. I felt helpless, a loss of control in turning my body over to total strangers. Still scarier, this total surrender of myself was not even to a visible stranger, but to an impersonal institution. How could I have faith in anything as anonymous as white walls, black and white checkerboard floors, stainless steel doors, smells of disinfectant, and bustling, starched uniforms called "nurses"?

Fortunately I had little time for such ruminations. Within minutes one of those starched uniforms approached, ordered me into a wheelchair, and took me down the hall. Mother called out, "Don't worry, son, everything will be all right, and I'll be here when the operation is over." The nurse wheeled me down to the end of the first hallway, turned down another, then through a wide doorway into a room as large as a tennis court.

Suddenly, I was in a different world. Sunlight streamed into the ward from the big windows that covered one wall, and all around, the room was lined with rows of white enamel beds. In them I could see boys, some about my age, some older, one or two younger, some lying down with legs propped up in casts, some sitting up and playing games. One boy was hobbling about on crutches.

The nurse stopped the wheelchair beside an empty bed, pulled white curtains around, and told me to remove all my clothes. Soon she returned with pillows and a white nightgown, cranked up the head of the bed to a halfway position, and eased me in. It all happened so fast. Only a minute before, I was in the waiting room with Mother. Now I was in a high white bed, surrounded by other boys in white beds, so fast I had had no time to think about what was happening; just walls, doors, and uniforms whizzing by, and here I was.

I was no sooner propped up and starting to observe my new environment when the boy on crutches came by to get acquainted and show his operation. Then the boys on each side of my bed did the same, and nurses brought lunch trays. By dinner time I had become just one of the gang of two dozen boys on the ward, each as proud of his operation as the other; in fact, the more operation scars a boy could show, the higher his status among them.

So this was how the hospital won the new patient's trust! It came as naturally as learning how to swim by being at the old swimming hole with older boys. The hospital merely placed the newcomer among proud recovering veterans, and he wanted to be one of them. To belong, that most basic need of all living creatures, was mine at last. I had not found it among my able-bodied brothers in Vancouver. But I did here, far from home, among boys who were strangers one minute, but five minutes later, were as close as friends.

Neither I nor they thought or talked about it. It was self-evident. I needed them and they needed me. Like peas in a pod, we all fitted together. That's nature, to be with one's own kind. And it was the same with sharing. If you belong, you share everything; toys, games, books, operations, fears, dreams, schemes, jokes. I suppose that being in a pickle together is how nature developed the thing called 'friendship'.

My education by the ward veterans quickly became explicit, the most vital subject being preparation for my own operation. Well instructed by them, I knew my day had come when, after x-rays and other preliminaries, I was given no breakfast, a nurse gave me a special scrubbing, I was strapped onto a stretcher, and to the cheers of the other boys, rolled down the hall toward the operating room. Halfway there, the nurse clapped a chloroform-soaked wad over my nose, and by the time the stretcher was pushed through the doors and under the bright lights, I could only dimly make out figures in different coloured uniforms. They were all in masks, encircling me and about to perform their grisly magic upon my body.

When I woke up I was back on the ward again, same bed, same companions, but whoosy sick from the anaesthetic. A dull pain came from what used to be my right leg, now encased in thick plaster up to my hip. I felt rotten, but also a comforting sense of complacency. I had made it through my operation and was now a full-fledged veteran.

Soon a nurse came by to take my temperature and give a shot. I asked, "Does Mother know I'm alright?", and she replied, "Oh yes, and she will be able to come and see you in a day or two". Within a minute I was sound asleep, everything right with the world.

The next morning I awoke to the same world, same bed, same ward mates, same tolerable pain, even a little worse, for now I was fully conscious and received only a sedative after supper to help me sleep at night. But the price of a little more pain was worth it, for I could now take in more of my hospital world, in particular what lay outside the ward's big windows. By straining a little, I could make out a large playfield with a circular walkway going all around it. The playfield was bordered with shubs, occasional trees, and beyond, a forest led up a hill. I could easily imagine a path winding up through the forest to the top of the hill, and I resolved that someday, when I had two good legs, I would find that path and climb that hill.

As any person learns who survives a major operation, for a short time during recuperation he becomes more aware of the simplest objects around him, of their shapes and dimensions. Likewise, the other senses become more acute, of touch, hearing, taste, and smell. It is as though Nature heightens these primary means of survival while the weakened body fights its way to recovery.

Thus, as I lay in bed recovering among my veteran friends, everything about me seemed more vivid, even the simplest objects and sensations that one usually hardly takes notice of; the shape and proportions of the white enamel bedstand, its smooth, hard texture, the white bedcover's furrows and stretch, the reassuring firmness of my pillows, and their gentle yield when I rolled my head.

It was the same with the sense of taste, each item of food on the tray at mealtime presenting a more distinctive, heightened flavour, especially the satisfying wholeness of a glass of milk or the sweet crispness of an evening apple. Smells, although often not agreeable, were equally more noticeable.

But most keen of all the senses was that of hearing, for it was by this sense more than any other that I and the others learned of our medical condition and prospects, what was to happen today, tomorrow, next week, or within an hour.

Although the most important, words were not the only sounds we waited for. Each nurse had a distinctive personality and we learned to recognize which one was coming to the ward far in advance of her arrival. Each one's walk was different, in speed, rhythm, softness or hardness of her footsteps, squeakiness of her shoes, and the rhythmic swish of her starched uniform as she moved down the hallway. A few talked to themselves or hummed.

Which one was coming down the hall made a great difference to each of us. Some would tell us all the news, some provide nothing, some only good news, some only bad, some were jovial, some aloof, some pretty, some plain.

My favourite was Miss Andress. Everything about her was right. She was cheerful, motherly, always had something to say, always made me feel special, and besides, was plump, pretty, and smelled as fresh and fragrant as a summer garden. I fell in love with Miss Andress, as much as a boy of six can. Not a night went by that I didn't think of her and hope she would come by the next day. It was not by mere chance that years later my first love was a nurse very much like Miss Andress.

Lying in bed hour after hour, my mind rummaged through its intertwined heap of memories and refocused to see things 'in a different light' as they say. That's natural enough when I was stuck in the same place day after day with nothing to decide about my present circumstances, on a fixed routine, all decisions affecting me made by someone else. All my mind could do was dwell upon the past and future.

But there's something more to it, something about going through a dangerous experience that seems to shake up the brain's stored material and rearrange it into a new perspective. Life doesn't seem the same as before.

Before coming to the hospital I was well on my way to developing a victim outlook. Born as I was the youngest of four boys and raised in a family placing prime importance on the physically vigorous life of the great outdoors, at an early age I was disqualified as unfit to participate.

In theory, I could have adapted in a number of ways. For instance, I could have developed my intellect more, but neither of my parents were scholars and the same was true with music and art. I wanted only to be like my big brothers, joyous outdoor physical creatures, so I rebelled against physical constraints, broke my shackles, and forced my parents to find a different solution than being hobbled with a leg brace the rest of my life.

The availability of the Shriners' Hospital made all the difference, for this environment and recuperative experience encouraged a different perspective. Here, a recovering cripple among my own kind, I received from their fellowship a spontaneous grant of equality, a feeling of pride and status in enduring pain, and the optomistic outlook that being crippled is just a temporary detour on the way to a life as good and free as any other boy.

That's how I felt during daytime. But with the coming of nightfall, after evening treats of orange juice and cookies, favourite radio programs like Gang Busters and the Lone Ranger, when the lights were turned out and all was still and quiet on the ward, I became lonely. The desire to be home again became almost unbearable. It was then that my mind sorted through its closet of memories, picked out the most treasured, and let my imagination soar. As freely as an eagle's flight, my mind soared from one favoured scene of the past to another. Then it continued to soar, into the future, catching glimpses of life's grand possibilities.

This transition was not always easy, and like an actor in need of cues, I reached into the nightstand drawer and brought out reminders of home. I didn't need much light to make out the photographs in the cloth folder. I knew each one by heart. And I always looked at them in the sameorder, first the one of Mother and her four sons on the front porch of the Balfour Avenue home.

Then the one of Dad, strong and handsome when he was in college at Cornell. But best of all was the one with our dog Nick, Asa, Larkin, and myself outside on the back porch.

Each photograph evoked different associations, so I held each up for a moment or two, savouring its richness until the flavour played out. Then I turned to read again the short stories Dad sent me, stories about animals which he illustrated with sketches. To me, they were more enjoyable than Walt Disney cartoons. Each week one came in the mail. One week his illustrated story was about a family of racoons that lived in tree by a pond, and how they caught frogs and fish. The next week another arrived about a cub bear finding a swarm of bees in a tree, and another week about a wise old owl and what he said to the deer in the forest.

I never tired of this nightly ritual of photographs and stories, rather like favourite bedtime stories that a child wants to hear again and again. When they had done their job of reassuring me that I was not forgotten or unloved, I replaced the cloth folder in the nightstand and lay back listening to the stillness of the night. It was then that my mind created pictures and stories of my own, of the future and a new life back home with Nick and my brothers.

Tuesday morning was the most important time of the week, the day the doctors made ward rounds, examined each of us, and decided the treatment regime for the following week. What they had decided was of utmost importance, and each of us hoped to hear directly from the head doctor, a heroic figure in our eyes. But that was seldom the case.

Finally, Dr. De Lahunt came to my bed, merely scanned the chart at the foot of the bed, wiggled the toes protruding from the cast, smiled, made a remark or two to the other doctors, the head nurse jotted notes on the chart, and the powerful retinue glided to the next bed. Only after lunch did I receive the good news from Miss Andress. "Robin, we're going to take your cast off tomorrow. Then you'll get another, maybe two more. By then you'll be able to go outside on crutches for awhile each day."

What the surgeon had done, an operation called a "triple orthodesis", was to shorten and reshape the foot's ligament and tendon tissue. Then the castmaker had done his job of holding the straightened out foot in proper alignment with the connecting ankle and leg bone until the stitched tissue healed. Even if completely successful, the various tissues of cartilage, muscle, and nerve had atrophied so badly the foot would have almost no power to move itself in any direction. But what it would be able to do is rotate in alignment with the other foot, thus allowing me to walk and even ride a bicycle. Running would always be a problem as the foot had no thrust power of its own, but could function as a sort of rotating stick made stable by a sound upper leg, the thrust power for movement coming from the other leg. I would never be able to compete successfully in any sport, except perhaps the one-legged race, but at least I would be able to join in active play with other boys.

Two months after the operation the castmaker peeled off the last smelly cast and the shoemaker measured me for a boot. When it came, the boot was a funny looking thing, built up with cork inside to compensate for a leg two inches shorter than the other. But still it was appealing, this shiny, brown, fresh-smelling new leather appendage, for with it strapped on my skinny new leg I could now get outside and join the world. My new footpiece took some getting used to, however. In fact, it bound and pinched so much for the first several days, I wasn't sure the boot and I were made for each other.

One day, still on crutches, I made my way off the ward, out the door, and onto the cement walkway that encircled the grassy slope outside the ward's windows. Relying less on the crutches with each step, I found the pain tolerable, and upon reaching the end of the covered straightway, I leaned my crutches on a support post and stood up alone. Steadying myself, I took a first step without crutches. Then another, and another, until I was soon several steps away from my crutches.

When I stopped to look back, I realized I was sweating, breathing hard, and feeling a little wobbly, so thought I had better take it easy for awhile. Calmed and cooled down, I scanned the grounds and looked back toward the ward. A feeling of exhilaration welled up in me, of excitement and joy such as I had never known before.

The excitement came in waves, at first small and gentle, then grew stronger and stronger, finally bursting out in words, "I did it!", "I did it!", "Oh, my God, I did it!" Like the feelings that preceded, the words first came quietly, spoken unsurely to myself. Then, with repeating, they grew louder and louder until I was shouting the words aloud. I wanted the world to know, the sky, the sun, the trees, the whole universal garden of life to know. I had been granted a miracle. I could walk again.

Unwinding from this state of ecstasy, I retraced my steps to the crutches and made my way back to the ward. I now knew that in a matter of days I would be on my way back home.

That night in bed I felt no need for my cloth folder of photographs and stories. The triumph of that day was enough. Already I was planning tomorrow, and the next, when by degrees, I would extend my daily walk, first covering the full length of pavement around the grounds, then up the path that surely must exist, leading to the top of the forested hill.

The next morning I found a partner for the adventure in Albert, a skinny freckle-faced redhead from Oregon, another veteran at about my stage of recovery. That afternoon, and each afternoon thereafter, Albert and I hobbled off the ward on our crutches and started around the circle. By making it a bit further each day, we reached mid-point, then the full length. This took us a week or so to accomplish. The staff, of course, had no inkling of what we had in mind.

Albert and I always walked the circle counter-clockwise, and noticed that the three-quarter mark was the closest point on the walkway to the perimeter of the hospital grounds and forest that lay beyond. Furthermore, that location was not visible from the windows of the ward, obscured as it was by bushes on that side of the hospital building. This made it the logical starting point for our clandestine adventure.

We figured that by reversing our habitual counter-clockwise route, we could reach our jump-off point much quicker, thus leaving more time and energy to make it across the uneven slope to the fence line and forest beyond. Once there, we would be home-free, hidden among the trees. If we couldn't make it to the top of the hill the first day, that would be okay; we would just get to know the territory, return before a nurse noticed our absence, and go at it again the following day.

The next morning right after breakfast we left the ward, and everything went as planned. In no time at all we reached the jump-off point, made it across the open grass slope to the treeline, to our relief found no fence, and moved slowly and unsteadily into the forest. The uneven ground and tree branches made it hard going, but breaking these branches to mark our course, we moved ahead in as straight a line as possible. Albert led the way because he was more experienced in the woods. We hadn't gone very far when he stopped suddenly and whispered, "It's clear ahead! Maybe it's a path!" I whispered back, "Let's find out. Then maybe we'd better go back until tomorrow."

Sure enough, it was a path, and not a narrow deer path either, but a gravel one, and wide enough for two people to walk abreast. Up ahead, the path leveled out, and we could make out what seemed like a stone monument. "I'd sure like to know what that is," I said, and Albert replied, "Me too, but we'd better call it quits and get back. My legs are getting sore."

The staff were so used to our being outdoors most of the morning that no one took notice as Albert and I eased our way back onto the ward. Utterly tuckered out, we were mighty glad to reach our beds and stretch out for awhile. That's when our escapade caught up with us. Our new boots would not come off no matter how hard we tried. All we could do was lie down, boots on, and hope the swelling would go down.

Soon the nurse noticed our predicament and helped out, fortunately not inquiring as to its true cause. Like a good nurse, she merely applied a practical remedy, ice packs to our lower legs and booted feet. After awhile the swelling eased, and with some wiggling and scolding, we got our boots off. "Now both of you have been overdoing your walks in the garden. You had better stay on the ward tomorrow or you might be in trouble with the doctor," she admonished. Albert and I didn't need a lecture to decide to take it easy for awhile. The next morning our legs and feet hurt so much we didn't feel like even getting out of bed, let alone resuming our adventure.

Within two days, however, the swelling and pain had gone and we began to agitate each other with remarks like, "I wonder what that monument says?" and "I'll bet there's more like it further up the trail."

Before long we were off again, only now we were a little wiser. We decided we would stop to rest awhile once we made it to the forest, and do the same on the way back.

The next morning we set out, and knowing our way this time, easily reached the path, rested awhile, then started upward toward the stone monument. We could see no evidence of others having used this well-made path, and we wondered why. There was something sort of eerie and suspicious about it, so we proceeded upward quietly and furtively, periodically stopping, listening, and looking down the path to see if anyone was following us. Detecting no one, we continued upward until we reached the monument.

Whatever it was, it was an impressive, beautiful thing standing there all alone in a flat alcove of the path and in the stillness of the forest. As we drew closer to it, we saw that it was a statue of a bearded man dressed only in loose fitting shorts, his arms stretched out in front of him as though asking for something. He wore only sandals on his feet, and below, carved in the stone, were the words, "Christ is condemned to death by Pilate."

"What do you suppose it's here for?" asked Albert. "Gosh, I don't know," I replied, "but it's got something to do with religion, probably Catholic, because an older lady friend of Mother's took me to a big Catholic church one time, and it had statues like this next to the walls. Anyway, I'll bet there's others like it further up the trail."

Albert was eager to find out too, but remembering the painful outcome of our first trip, he replied, "Yeh, but we'd better turn around and get back now, and go up further tomorrow." "Okay," I agreed, "if we feel like it. I'd sure like to know what's up there, maybe more stuff like this, and we can figure it out."

We made it back undetected to the ward, and this time got our boots off without help from the nurse. Lying there on our beds safe and sound, we felt pretty proud of ourselves, so every once in awhile we would glance at each other and grin in satisfaction with the progress of our secret enterprise.

Each morning for the next three days Albert and I left the ward and continued our exploration of the path winding ever upward through the forest, and each day we came upon another monument, always at a wide bend of the path. The second one was of the same man similarly clothed, but now he was bent over carrying a huge cross on his back, and beneath his feet this time the words said, "Jesus is made to carry the cross."

And so it went, on each successive day we made it further up the pathand found more monuments, all of the same man but with different words below. We had made it as far as the fourth monument, still far to go to reach the top of the hill, when our expedition was called to a halt, not because we were discovered, but because I received the best of news from the best of nurses.

I could hardly believe Miss Andress's words, "Tomorrow your Mother is coming to take you home." Did I hear right? Home? Tomorrow? I must have, because there was Miss Andress right next to my bed talking to me. "First she will talk to your doctor about continuing your massages, but that shouldn't take long. The night nurse will bring your clothes, so after breakfast, put them on so you will be all ready to go." She then paused, moved close to me, fluffed my pillow, and with the warmth that made her so special, continued, "You've been a good patient, Robin, and we'll miss you. So have a good sleep tonight and write us when you get home." Then she squeezed my hand, turned, and with a swish she was gone.

That night I could hardly sleep, I was thinking of so many

things. But uppermost in my mind was Miss Andress. She had said good-bye just as she did everything, just right. She knew when and how to give, but also knew when and how to let go. She was the perfect nurse. I would remember and love her forever.

⚬

The hospital staff also knew that the best partings are brief. No sooner had I finished breakfast, put on my clothes, and said farewell to Albert and the other boys on the ward, than I was put in a wheelchair and whisked off the ward and down the halls to the waiting room, as quickly as when I had been admitted three months before. The nurse-powered wheelchair sprang through the swinging doors into the sunlit waiting room, and there they were again, Mother, Dora, Wilbur, all smiles and dressed up like a wedding party.

I wanted no lift-up, Teddy-Bear hugs, so as soon as the wheelchair glided to a halt, I stood up and extended my hand to Wilbur. But it was no use. There came a torrent of hugs and kisses, first from Mother, then from Dora. Finally, when the emotional binge had died down, Wilbur removed his cigar just long enough to say, "Robin, we're mighty proud of you, and we're all going to celebrate with lunch at the Oyster House." That suited me just fine. I didn't care where we went, just as long as we were together again in Wilbur's big old Pierce sedan. And we were, just like before, Wilbur and I up front, Uncle Wilbur with his bobbing cigar, and Mother and Dora in back, laughing and talking as though they had never left off since three months before.

Two days later, on the way to the train, I thought it was a good time to reveal my off-grounds expedition with Albert, thinking Wilber might know the answer to the monuments we had found. He laughed so hard he knocked the ash off the end of his cigar, then explained, "Robin, what you and Albert found were the grotto and shrines where Catholics go to pray as they climb the hill to the cross at the top. These monuments, as you call them, are what they call the "Stations of the Cross", statues of

Christ's life when he was taken away and nailed to a cross by Roman soldiers."

He paused to bite off a piece of his cigar, then continued, "How far up the path did you get, to number four, wasn't it?" And I replied, "Yes, and then I got to go home. But how much further did we have to go to get to the top?"

Still amused, Wilbur chuckled, patted me on the knee, and replied, "Oh, there are twelve or so of these stations, so you were about a third of the way to the top of the hill. Maybe you can come back someday, stay with us and finish the job." "You bet!" I said. Then Wilbur turned his head, and raising his voice, spoke to Dora and Mother in the back seat, "What do you think about that, girls?" Dora giggled, reached up and ruffled my mop of curly hair, and replied, "Oh, I'd like that!", and turning to Mother, added, "Bell, let's plan on that for next summer, shall we?" Mother agreed immediately, and with everyone in the best of spirits, Mother and I boarded the train for the journey back home.

ڲ

We found a seat, the train jerked forward, and we left the station behind. Settling in, I couldn't help noticing that Mother now seemed awfully serious, even sad, more than seemed called for in parting from Dora. It was as though she was keeping something bad to herself. I tried to get her to talk, but she didn't seem to have the energy. She just squeezed my hand now and then and looked out the window, staring, not looking at anything in particular. I called her attention to certain things we passed, but it was no use. She seemed lost in deep and troubled thought. And when she squeezed my hand, she held on awhile, as though drawing comfort from my just being beside her.

When the train reached Blaine at the American side of the border with Canada, I asked her about the words on the white Peace Arch. The words said in big letters, "CHILDREN OF A COMMON MOTHER" on one side, and on the other, "BRETHREN, DWELLING TOGETHER IN UNITY".

She explained what the words meant, that Canada and the United States were both founded by people of British origin, and although the two countries were different in many ways, they didn't fight about it. "Like you and Dad?" I asked. "He's American, isn't he?" "Yes, that's true. Your father and I fell in love and got married," she replied in words that came slowly and quietly, as though she were recalling an event far away in time and space.

I wanted her to go on and explain what nationality that made me and my brothers, things like that. But she didn't want to talk anymore, just resumed staring out the window, and every once and awhile breathed in deeply, then slumped forward as though pulled down by a weight deep inside. I had never seen Mother so upset and was getting worried. I didn't know what to say or do, so I was relieved when she excused herself to go to the restroom. She was gone a long time, and when she came back I could see she had been crying. Her eyes were puffy and red, and she took a handkerchief from her purse and blew her nose.

Now I knew more than ever that something was terribly wrong, that she was in great pain about something, but lacking the confidence to ask her what was the matter, I reached over and held her hand. That seemed to help a little, as she put her arm around me, drew my head toward her breast, and held me, now and again taking another deep breath. After awhile, her breathing became more regular, and awhile later she straightened up, took both of my hands in hers, lifted her chin, and said, "Now let's go and have a nice lunch in the dining car."

A tall, courtly, black waiter seated us at a table, the first black man I had ever seen. He was a splendid looking man, in a white jacket with silver buttons, black bow tie, and a marvelous, warm smile. When he spoke it was in a deep, melodious tone, and he had the manners of a gentleman. Perhaps it was this waiter's gracious manner, the white table cloth and silver service, the whole ritual of being served lunch with such courtesy in pleasant surroundings. Whatever it was, during this brief interlude for lunch, Mother distanced herself from her troubles.

She recovered her smile and twinkle in her eyes as she re-called fond memories of train trips in the past. She told me about the first time she had a meal in a dining car as a girl of eighteen, with her father, mother, and two sisters on the way west from Prince Edward Island to settle in Alberta. Then about going with a group of young men and women from Gleichen to a grand weekend at the Banff Springs Hotel in the days when she had nothing more to worry about than which dress she would wear to the dance that night.

Mother always saw the humour in things, and once she began telling these stories, she began to laugh herself out of her misery, so we had fun at lunch. But when it came time to leave the din-ing car, she became sombre again.

The lunch reprieve apparently gave Mother the courage to reveal part of her burden. "Robin, when we get home, Frieda won't be there. She is getting married to a very nice man, so we should be happy for her." This was very unwelcome news in-deed, delivered in Mother's characteristic way of clothing the unpleasant in some compensating good. Frieda had been closer to me than Mother in some ways. It was she who helped me with my clothes and brace in the morning, gave me baths, and read to me at bedtime. Without Frieda, home just wouldn't be the same. I too, fell silent, staring out the window, biding my time for the pain to work itself out.

The train rolled on toward Vancouver, Mother and I side by side, each struggling in silence with our separate pain. But I sup-pose human beings can tolerate mental depression only so long before, by some protective mechanism, the mind sets the trou-blesome matter aside and seeks distraction. Anything within reach will do; some soothing diversion or pleasure, however trivial or irrelevant, anything to gain a buffer of time until the mind can figure out how to cope with the problem.

Being young, I found this transition easily. I had much to look forward to in returning home besides Frieda; brothers, fa-ther, family dog and cat, the innumerable crannies and comforts of home, plus all the things I could now do with my leg and boot, like learning to ride a bicycle. In short, I had no end of anticipated pleasures to make up for the loss of Frieda. So, as the train rolled homeward, I, too, gazed out the window, oblivious to the passing scene, my mind now focused on such future pleasures. I could afford to let Frieda go, and did.

Growing excited with anticipation as we came closer and closer to home, I turned to Mother to fill in the details. "Is Nick all right?" Does Dad still have his mallards?" "Is he going to meet us at the station?" I had no end of questions, and Mother made an attempt to answer, but her brief, unenthusiastic responses made it clear that she was still deeply troubled, as though she was returning home with dread.

It was good to see Dad waiting for us at the station. We hugged and he complimented me on how well I walked with my new boot. He took Mother's suitcase, led us out to the old Studebaker parked on Main Street, and in ten minutes we were home. My brothers were all off somewhere, and Nick too, but it still felt good to poke around all the familiar places in the house, and garden and garage, my black cat Felix following me everywhere I went.

The house felt rather strange though, empty as it was without Frieda, my brothers, and Nick. Dad just parked the car in the garage and left for his office by the Oak street carline I guessed. When I came back into the kitchen there was hardly a sound in the house, so I went into the den and Mother was there. She was sitting at her little rosewood writing desk going through some papers. She didn't notice me as I stood at the entrance. Bent over at her desk, she seemed totally preoccupied, detached from all her surroundings, as though she hadn't returned home at all. I didn't know what was going on, but plainly it was something bad.

A few days later at supper Dad told all us boys that we were going to move. I didn't know what that meant. This was the only home I'd ever known. And my brothers didn't understand any better than me. It was only years later after we had moved to the North Shore and I learned about other kids having to move too, that I began to understand what Mother was going through that day, and why she seemed so heart-broken and strangely alone.

It was early summer of 1932. The Depression was bullying its way into the lives of everybody in the city of Vancouver, dismembering the economy, spreading unemployment, bankruptcy, and hardship everywhere, including Shaughnessy Heights, haven of the rich. Frieda's marriage to a "good man" was the only good thing Mother could say. Mother would have had to let her go in any case; she had no money to pay her wages. With no orders for machinery from a forest industry unable to sell its product, Dad's business went bankrupt, he couldn't make the mortgage payments on the Balfour home, and he had been served eviction papers. Mother had no home to return to.

From the very start of their marriage, Mother had helped finance the home from the sale of the Gleichen property. Payments from the purchasers stopped coming because Alberta farmers also had little market for their wheat and cattle. She had lost the source of her independent income.

Most demoralizing of all, Dad's Victorian attitude toward marriage got in the way of sharing information about their financial situation and problems. He would not confide in her or seek her advice and so incurred business and personal debts she knew nothing about. Yet he expected her to run the household with no knowledge of where they stood financially.

The lack of sharing and trust upset her more than the frightening financial situation itself. It was a terrible disillusionment to realize that she had chosen a man to be her husband who was not like her father, who had shared everything about business and finances with her, good and bad. Nothing in her life experience had prepared her for her present circumstances. She had always been well provided for, first by her father's enterprise and affluence, then by her own ability to carry on just as well after his death, thus enjoying the same high social status that affluence and her attractive personality allowed.

Her sound Presbyterian rearing taught her not to crave luxury, great wealth or power, but through diligence, careful management, and consideration of others, the good Lord would provide, and sufficiently that she could be generous with others. All this, all that she was to herself and others, all was slipping away in a devastating torrent. She had no home, no money, no partner like her father to share the good and the bad with her, nothing left to be generous with. Her life was thrown completely out of control, and she must have thought also at times, no Lord was watching over her.

She had never really felt much need for Him before, not in a deep, personal way. Saying prayers was just showing gratitude for the blessings she had received. That made no sense at all now; all her "blessings" were washing away, all, that is, except her children. But now they were her greatest worry. How was she to feed and clothe them? She didn't know, but perhaps He did. She now needed His help desperately. That must have been why she was so preoccupied, staring out the window of the train, in a different world so to speak, trying desperately to get His attention, to have Him talk to her, to show her a way out.

And that was probably also why she was gone so long in the train restroom, somewhere she could be all alone for at least a little while to pray. She knew only one prayer well, the *Lord's Prayer*, the one she had been taught as a little girl and had heard repeated hundreds of times in her family home. "Our Father who art in Heaven, hallowed be Thy name. Thy Kingdom come. Thy will be done, on earth as it is in Heaven. Give us this day our daily bread. Forgive us our trespasses, as we forgive those who trespass against us. Lead us not into temptation. Deliver us from evil. For Thine isthe Kingdom, the Power, and the Glory forever. Amen."

Whether God would heed her plea with material help or not, the mere act of saying that prayer to a God she believed was real, freed her from the grip of overwhelming anxiety. She now felt that she was not alone, fatherless,that He, God, the eternal Father, had heard her prayers, and that in due course, He would help her through. Her tears as she came out of the restroomwere not solely ones of desperation. They were also of relief. She was sure He had heard, and that alone gave great comfort. Believing now that He was at her side, she could go forth with greater courage.

That explains why she decided to spend a little of the money she had for lunch in the dining car with her son, a sort of declaration of faith andrenewed hope. The combination of prayer and lunch renewed both body and soul.Now she had time to reflect. What emerged was the unsettling conclusion that she had married a man she never really knew. Only now, under adversity, had the painful truth become clear. She had somehow assumed the husband she chose would be more or less like her own father. He proved to be nothing of the sort. Moreover, she had nobody to blame but herself.

Her friends had tried to warn her. "He is such a gentleman, and he's interesting, but I'm not sure he's the right man for you, Bell." "Why do you want to marry an American, as nice as he is, when you can have your pick of Canadian bachelors, some very rich, or bound to be someday, like so and so..." It was true. She had had proposals of marriage from two of the richest men in Vancouver. "But I don't love....so and so", she replied. "I don't know why, but I'm in love with Asa, and we're going to marry." So what else could they say? Finances were no problem, never had been, so why not marry for love?

She was now paying the price, the bitter, seemingly impossible price.Her only excuse was that Asa was six years older than she when they married,already formed in his ways, and nothing she was able to say or do had any effect in the way he dealt with her. He would listen to her in a barely tolerant or distracted way, avoid responding to whatever question or suggestion she had to offer, then terminate the conversation with an evasive"We'll see." Not that she hadn't taken notice of how some of her women friends got their way with their husbands, and to some degree she was envious. They played weak, were theatrical, and, if necessary, lied, cheated,or threatened. These tactics just were not in her. She had never had to learn how to manipulate men, knew only the kind of open relationship she had had with her father, and had succeeded in business on her own.

Now, for the first time in her life, she found herself in the position of weakness typical for woman of her time, only worse, for she had no experience in the female's manipulatory arts. The closest she could come was to plead and beg, but that didn't work with Asa.

As for divorce, that was easier said than done, a rarity for women of her time, for many and compelling reasons. First, it was "un-Christian." Her marital vows said, "In sickness and in health, in sorrow and in joy, 'til death do us part", and for this vow she was accountable to God.

Second, social pressure, the code being that no decent woman divorced her husband, even a known scoundrel, and this was backed by the force of the law, which allowed a woman to sue for divorce only if she could prove adultery. Being a Protestant puritan in matters of sex, Bell could not bring herself even to imagine her husband in bed with another woman.

And third, what would she do for a living? Outside of teachers and nurses, women were employed only in the lowest, poorly paid types of work, and even in those, a woman was laid off if a man wanted her job.

But the decisive consideration against divorce was her children. It was unthinkable to tell her children that she was leaving their father for another man, even a millionaire who would take children and all. So she had no recourse; she would just have to make it through one day at a time, keeppraying to the Lord, and believe that He would heed her prayers, at least enough to provide her family's daily bread.

The loss of our Shaughnessy home had an entirely different meaning for Mother than Dad or us boys. For her, eviction from the house she and Dad had built was dispossession from everything she had known in life, namely, a comfortable and respected social standing in the solid middle class. That had been her lifelong identity. Now she too, like her sea-faring brothers beforeher, was set adrift, alone and afraid, on the perilous sea of life.

Nothing could be more frightening to a middle-class wife in a society whose outlook was still conditioned by the Victorian Age of a half-century past. For, it will be recalled, she had been taught to believe that whatever came to pass in life was ordained by God. Therefore, with all this misfortune, Mother could not escape the conclusion that she must be guilty of some grave wrong doing.

Was it because she enjoyed her husband's body too much, more than justified by His injunction to "increase and multiply"? Was it because she had been sinfully vain about her beauty and popularity? Or simply that she had taken too much for granted in life and needed humbling?

She didn't know what His reasons were, but had also been taught that they were good and sufficient, and thus, from the day she realized she did not have the trust of her husband and that one of her sons would be a cripple for life, she became burdened with a pervasive feeling of guilt. For that she knew only one remedy, prayer, and it was to that she turned thereafter, at the beginning and end of each day.

She had come to the conclusion that she could no longer predict or control whatever happened in life, that all she could do was pray to God and make the best of what He willed. Such a resigned attitude was foreign to her nature. But she could no longer avoid certain harsh, irrevocable truths; that she was now forty years of age, a mother of four children, bound forever to a failed marriage, and poor.

Henceforth, she must learn another way to live; simply, a day at a time, and to be grateful for each day and whatever little pleasure came her way. Now she understood why her mother became as she was during her declining years, why the Bible became her only constant companion, bereft as she was of husband, home, and children, all alone now except for her Book.

For Dad, the loss of the Shaughnessy house was more on the order of a mere inconvenience, not an overwhelming tragedy and cause for self-recrimination. After all, he was still the man of the house, in charge of at least his own household, and thus did not suffer Mother's terrifying feeling of helplessness.

As for guilt, that he was being punished by a wrathful God, he had never been a believer in Christian theology. Periodic depressions and hard times were not of God's making, but Man's, just part of the ups and downs in life that one had to expect and make the best of until Mankind learned to regulate its affairs more intelligently.

And another thing, the Shaughnessy home was, after all, only a house, one of several he had lived in, then moved on to another as circumstance and opportunity dictated; from New York City to Ithaca, to Maine, the Carolinas, Oregon, Vancouver's West End, then Shaughnessy. He was used to being a nomad. His only permanent home was the great outdoors, mother nature, and for that reason a house out in the country could have advantages not offered by life in the city of Vancouver.

Mother & her four sons,
Balfour Avenue house, late 1920's

My brothers Larkin, Asa, and I with
family pets, about 1928

Lumbermens' Arch in Stanley Park

Granville Island and mills along False Creek, 1920's

Downtown Vancouver, Hastings St., Dominion Bank Building, 1920's

4

NORTH SHORE PARADISE

Dad found the solution on the North Shore, an area he knew well as he had a machinery depot on the waterfront near the Capilano River, and North Vancouver was only a pleasant twenty minute ferry ride to his business in the city. He knew also that the trust company that had foreclosed on their Shaughnessy home had hundreds of other empty foreclosed homes on their hands which they would probably rent out for a nominal amount just to keep them occupied. So he asked the trust officer if he had any on the North Shore. "Oh, yes, quite a few" the agent replied, and described a half dozen. One in particular caught dad's attention. For just $25 a month he could rent a huge house and several acres of grounds away up North Lonsdale beyond the end of the carline.

The next day Dad drove up to look at the house, 230 Carisbrooke Road. "You can't miss it", the agent said, "Just past the corner of St. George's. The driveway is on the left, a long, curving one that leads up to the house. It has two or three acres of landscaped grounds."

The agent was right. At one time it must have been someone's dream mansion; a three story Tudor with granite walls, a tennis court, a stream ambling through a sunken garden into a pond, and in the centre of the pond, an island of pink rhododendrons. By the looks of the grounds, the place must have been vacant a year or two, now overrun with weeds and wild black-berry vines.

Entering the house, he walked out on a veranda overlooking the stream and pond. To the south, a thousand feet below, lay Burrard Inlet and the city of Vancouver. Everything about the place had an atmosphere of mystery that captured Dad's mind. But there was a problem. The house was so huge, twenty-three rooms, that it would take a fortune to heat in the winter, probably the reason it went vacant.

But for that too, he had a solution. Next to his machinery depot was a sawmill where he could get wood and sawdust for practically nothing. He figured that by closing off the top floor of unneeded rooms, about five cords of wood and two loads of sawdust would get them through the winter. A sawdust burning furnace and boiler provided steam heat to all the rooms, and there were fireplaces in the living room, dining room, and den, plus a wood-burning stove in the kitchen.

It would take a lot of work to tidy the place up, but Dad returned to the city, arranged a two year lease, and told Mother that they were moving to the Carisbrooke place as soon as school was out in June. "The boys can take care of the wood and clean up the grounds. They're old enough now, and the exercise will do them good", he told Mother in a matter-of-fact manner. Waxing with enthusiasm, he continued, "It even has a greenhouse above the garage where my vegetable plants can get an early start, and plenty of room for a garden. We can have chickens and fresh eggs. Bantams would be best, they can run wild and keep the bugs down in the garden. And there's a pond for my mallards. Bell, the house is three times as big to keep up, but the boys are old enough to help."

Mother listened without interrupting. Dad had made up his mind without consulting her as usual. Besides, she was relieved. Events were at least moving in a tangible direction, and Dad's enthusiasm gave her hope. She decided to go look at the place the next day.

That night she prayed for God's help to overcome the loss of her present home, so familiar and comfortable, and move into some stranger's abandoned huge old house. It was only a year ago that she had two servants to help her to keep up a smaller home. She felt so tired she didn't know if she had the strength for the move. So she asked for His help to make the move a success, to give her family another home, a home where her boys could grow up to be happy and strong. She felt deep within her, that once the moving van crossed over on the ferry to the North Shore there would no turning back. That would be where her sons would grow up and then leave home.

Dad told us boys just enough about the place to arouse our imaginations; about the stream and pond, the tennis court, the sleeping porch where we would be able to watch the stars from our beds at night, and on the first day of the move he left mother behind to continue packing while he and the four of us went ahead to start cleaning the place up.

The house had been vacant so long there was plenty to do to make it habitable. We swept and mopped the floors, flushed the rust out of the water pipes, cleaned the firebox and smokestack of the kitchen stove, split kindling and filled the woodbox, not the sort of chores boys take kindly to, so in between chores Dad let us explore the house and grounds.

His was a wise strategy, for when we all returned to the city and a very late supper, my brothers and I were all eager to finish the move into our new home. We had decided just where everything was going to be; whose bed would go where on the sleeping porch, where the radio would be placed in the living room, even where to start a vegetable garden and place the chicken coop.

The move had become an adventure, our old Shaughnessy home and neighbourhood receding into the past. "There's got to be trout in that stream" said Larkin on the way back to the city. Don replied, "That's nothing. Dad says big salmon come up the Capilano River, and deer and bear are all over. He's seen them along the waterfront at the mouth of the river." Ace joined in, "Yeh, as soon as we get the work done, lets explore. I bet we'll find a lake or river big enough to swim." I listened closely to everything my brothers said, confident that with my new boot I was going wherever they did.

Mother caught our excitement and went to bed with her mind more at ease. Maybe everything was going to work out. Away over on the North Shore at least she wouldn't have to face the daily sense of inferiority living among the rich of old Shaughnessy, too busy making the new place liveable to dwell upon the pain of losing her own home. She knew she was good at making friends so she would just have to give up some old ones and make some new ones.

It took two trips across the ferry with the moving van and three long days of drudge work before the move was complete and our family gathered around the oval dining room table for our first meal in the huge old mansion. Of course Mother had to say a blessing for our new home, mercifully short, and once done, we were all so tired we paused to look at each other before eating. For no apparent reason we started to laugh; first Don, then each of us, then Dad, and finally Mother. Like firecrackers strung together, laughter ignited and spread around the table until we were all laughing ourselves silly.

I suppose it was partly the sense of relief that the move was over with, partly because the task had brought us together in an unaccustomed way, and partly the incongruity of our new situation. Here we were gathered around our familiar dining table for the evening meal together as usual, but our surroundings so unfamiliar we might just as well be dining together on a boat somewhere rather than in this huge old mansion of mostly vacant rooms.

Probably also, beneath the surface in each of us, there occurred an emancipation of the spirit, a spirit freed at last from the pretence of feeling at home among the cold, formal rich of old Shaughnessy. Now we were safely off by ourselves, no longer having to feel like misfits. The amusing thing was that our new home, acquired only by near impoverishment, was as big and impressive to look at as many of the Shaughnessy mansions we had left behind. So we ate with relief and gladness, and in that mood went to bed for the first time in the old mansion on the hill.

⊙⊚

By the end of summer the place had become home. Mother concentrated her limited supply of rugs and furniture to make a comfortable combination living and dining room off the kitchen and to furnish three bedrooms on the second floor. The rest of the rooms she ignored. She had run out of furniture, had no money to entertain anyway, and by closing them off, could concentrate the heat where needed in the winter. This meant leaving vacant two beautiful rooms on the ground floor; a large formal dining room with chandeliers to the right of the main entrance, and a wood-panelled library and den on the other side, both with impressive fireplaces and perfect for entertaining in style. But mere survival and passable comfort was all that mattered now.

That still left two bedrooms vacant on the second floor, plus the whole third floor. Even the basement had been built in grand style; a gymnasium with hardwood floors, besides the expected furnace room, fuel storage room, washroom, and fruit cellar.

It took my brothers and me all summer to tame the weeds, blackberry vines, lay out a vegetable garden, but in between we found time to explore the neighbourhood, make a few friends, and at suppertime we always had new things to talk about. We found out where the neighbourhood kids congregated. During the day it was either the swimming hole they had made from an old millpond, the playground at North Star School, or the newspaper shack at the end of the carline on Windsor Road. During the evening it was a flat stretch on Carisbrooke in front of the Loutet's house, only a half block down Carisbrooke Road.

⊙⊚

Compared to the Shaughnessy's manicured boulevards, fortress-like mansions, and aloof society, the North Shore was an outdoor boy's Paradise of unrestricted open space and easy friendship. There was no end of places to explore and play within easy distance of the old mansion, nor a shortage of other adventurous boys nearby. We were all in the same boat more or less financially, so we developed friendships rapidly and based upon common interests rather than a division between the haves and have-nots. We needed only one common bond, HAVING FUN TO-GETHER. All that required was a little ingenuity, and we Williams boys always had plenty of that. In a matter of days we were in thick with the neighbour kids and quickly learned the territory.

A prime example of the local boys' ingenuity was the neighbourhood swimming hole. The pond had been formed years before by loggers impounding the flow of Hastings Creek by means of a log and earth dam. In the centre was a sluicegate of planks which could be raised and lowered by a hand cranked winch and cable. The dam's original purpose was to fill the pond with shakebolts, four-foot long slices of old growth cedar, then, by raising the sluicegate, the torrent of impounded water would float the bolts downstream to a shingle mill at the mouth of the creek in Lynn Valley. The dam and sluicegate still being in good condition, the neighbourhood kids merely took over the site and spent days each spring enlarging and clearing winter debris out of the pond.

This took plenty of hard work. We dug out stumps as big as ten of us wrapped together and split them into pieces small enough to burn. All of this we did with only handtools borrowed from home; picks, shovels, crowbars, axes, whatever we could lay our hands on.

Once satisfied we had done enough for a year, we closed the sluicegate, made a huge pile from stump fragments, and as we watched the water rise, celebrated our labour around the bonfire. We whooped and hollered, had mud fights, feasted on roasted potatoes, gorged ourselves on apples and anything else we could sneak from home, did anything and everything to while away the time until the water rose to the top of the sluicegate and splashed into the raceway.

That was the sound we listened for. As soon as we heard the cascading water, off came our swim trunks. Naked bodies caked with mud, we flung ourselves and each other into the virgin pool. A gracefully formed dive wasn't our style, sissy stuff for girls. The 'cannonball' was it, executed by leaping as high as possible off the board next to the sluicgate, tucking one's knees underneath to protect the "family jewels", and plunging bottom-down as ungracefully as possible. The idea was to see who could create the biggest tidal wave.

As uninhibited as we were among ourselves, we had a strict code of propriety when it came to girls. No dirty talk, nor even conversation about girls, was acceptable among us, for we, like our parents, were proper Victorians in such matters. All this was long ago. Sometime after World War II the Municipality took over the pond and surrounding land and named it Princess Park, an amusing choice of names to oldtimers who remember our pond's wild and joyous pagan past.

We applied the same ingenuity to summertime games on the grounds of North Star School, the only large, flat play area in hilly North Lonsdale. Once a week we congregated there to play a game called Peggy, the poor Canadian boy's version of English cricket. We made all the tools for the game ourselves, so that it didn't cost us a penny. Instead of a flat cricket bat, we carved our own sturdy, round bats from freshly cut alder or willow branches, and for a ball, we used short pegs of the same material, hence the game's name.

Otherwise, the game was like cricket. Two holes dug about fifty feet apart acted as wickets, each defended by a boy at bat. As long as the far end of his stick was in the hole, he was safe. The opposing team, one member behind each wicket and others scattered nearby, would pitch the peg underhand from one batter to the other, the two batters taking turns to knock the peg as far as possible, then run back and forth between the wickets, each time being sure to place the far end of his bat into the hole.

A run was earned each time a batter made it from one hole to the other. If a boy at bat swung and missed the peg, if the opposing team caught his flying peg, or if the peg was put into the hole ahead of his bat, he was out. With three outs, the teams changed sides. Like cricket, Peggy could go on for hours. But normally we would play until lunchtime, then meet again at the swimming hole or go exploring, unless we had to stay home to do chores.

Chores were the price we had to pay for a life of outdoor fun, to be avoided if possible, if not, made into a game and gotten over as quickly as possible. Some were unavoidable; taking care of the household wood supply, taking out the ashes, weeding the vegetable garden, picking the fruit, minding whatever goats, rabbits, or chickens the household kept. All these chores went quicker with help, and the same was true with chores that paid, like a newspaper route.

A boy lucky enough to have a *Sun* or *Province* route had no trouble finding a helper to get the job done faster, and of course share in the reward; change for a popsicle, ice cream bar, BB shot for his Daisy air rifle, or a new bike tube. There were harder, less dependable ways to earn a quarter or two; splitting and stacking wood for an elderly person, weeding, or picking and selling wild berries, slim pickings, one might say, so we learned to meet our needs without the use of money and make what little we could come by stretch a long way.

One of the few times boys and girls played together was in the evenings down the street in front of the Loutet house. All these games were variations of the ancient ritual of hide and seek, with one player taking a turn at being IT whose task was to find and capture everyone else. In the variation called Prisoner's Base, whoever was IT stood in a marked circle at an open central location, was blindfolded, then counted aloud to thirty while everyone else hid. Our hiding places were numerous; behind shrubs, trees, garages, anywhere within easy running distance to the base.

Whenever IT caught sight of one of the hiders by venturing

out from the base, he or she ran back to the base, shouted the hider's name and place of hiding, and that person became IT's prisoner at the base. This continued until IT captured all the hiders or one of them beat IT back to the base, shouted It releasing all the prisoners, and the cycle repeated itself.

Other versions were Go-go-go-stop and Kick the Can, all allowing girls to join in these summer evening outdoor games and us boys a chance to be around these mysterious creatures without being teased by other boys. To show anything but the slightest passing interest in a girl until high school was to risk merciless teasing. It was an absolute No-no to be seen alone with a girl. If a boy even talked about a girl except at certain well-defined times and places, he risked being branded either a sissy or dirty-minded.

It never occurred to us to question these taboos. Victorian or not, they served the purpose of holding sexuality at bay, leaving us free to unleash our immense energy for other forms of exploration and fun.

As summer evenings grew short and evenings cool, the urgency of approaching winter transformed the kitchen into a jam and preserve factory. Mother decided how many jars of this and that were to be made and saw to it that each of her sons stuck to his assigned chore until the job was done. Apples were the big thing, boxes and boxes of them; Gravenstein, Winesap, MacIntosh, Russet, all garnered from our own or neighbours' trees. The best, unblemished ones we wrapped in newspaper and stored in wooden barrels in the cellar. The rest we peeled, cored, and made into applesauce or mixed with quince or berry to make jams and jellies.

From after breakfast until suppertime the kitchen stove was covered with bubbling pots steaming and stewing with sauces, jams, and jellies, and on the kitchen table stood rows of shiny Mason jars filled with quartered peaches, pears, and purple cherries or plums.

My brother Don, by now fourteen and allowed to wear long pants, was in a class by himself with good looks, casual self-confidence, and directed ambition. What interested him was geometry, engineering, building things, and he carried himself much like his engineer father, self-contained and following his own agenda. He could be charming when he found female company agreeable, but unlike Dad, he seemed to have little poetic side, not much on dreaming. The oldest, and quietly observant, he was probably the most affected by the unravelling of the family's economic circumstances, painfully aware that while his friends wore new clothes, he had only hand-me-downs from relatives.

So for Don, life was black and white; not pretty, not nice, not easy, and not just. It was simply a problem, something you figured out and made work for you. He wanted some brand new things, too, nice clothes, maybe a car, certainly a university education, and the only way that was going to happen was if he made it happen with his own brains and effort. He hustled any job to be had in the neighbourhood; delivering groceries for Mr. Willcox's Red and White store, splitting and stacking wood, cleaning up yards, anything he could lay his hands on to get enough money to go on in school to become an engineer.

While Don seemed to lead with his brain, doing little without forethought, his younger brother Larkin was just the opposite, a creature of emotion, spontaneously and boldly expressive of whatever he was feeling at the time. Fortunately, he took after Mother's side in having a generous heart and sociable temperament. He too was a handsome lad, darkly attractive with warm brown eyes and open smile, muscular, well-coordinated, and with great physical stamina.

At twelve he showed himself no less intelligent than his older brother, but did not have the patience for sitting still or book learning. His natural bent was to throw himself headlong into whatever interested him at the time. He learned by doing, reaching out with his hands for the feel of things rather than through brainwork at a distance.

Larkin's personality combination did not appeal to grownups

who believed that children are to be seen and not heard, or heard at least only in a manner calculated to receive adult approval. So it was a foregone conclusion that the regimented regime of public school and Larkin were not made for each other.

Asa, or "Ace" as he was called, was in many ways a throwback to Dad's father. Instead of the brown eyes and darkish complexion that the rest of us had, Ace's eyes were hazel, his complexion pale, his physique slender and less robust, and his temperament sensitive and aesthetic. For him, to smile required an effort, his pale aqueous eyes seeming to shroud some secret sadness. Alone among us, Ace would return from his daily excursions clasping a handful of wild flowers or blossoms from a wild fruit tree as a gift for Mother. And he always took note of insects and songbirds, every smallish living thing that crawled or flew.

Perhaps this special gentleness was due to Ace's fragile makeup, prone since infancy to every illness that came along; whooping cough, jaundice, hayfever, whatever it was, Ace succumbed and suffered while the rest of us warded it off. But as he gained strength and stamina in boyhood, perhaps by way of compensation, he became a long distance runner, mountain climber, and played soccer and rugby with great endurance.

I took after Larkin in physique and temperament; muscular, robust, favoured with a luxuriant mop of brown curly hair, playful brown eyes, and happy disposition, in short, endowed from birth with every advantage to bask in my special position as the baby in the family. The attack of polio at age five seemed designed by Providence to exact a price for this privileged position, perhaps to teach me that I, too, must work and persevere as much or more than my older brothers to make my way in the world.

One can almost discern each of our distinctive personalities from a photograph of Mother and us four boys standing on the front porch of the Balfour Avenue home not long before losing it to the mortgage company. Significant is the absence of Dad, the "head of the family", Mother stands alone with her boys. Not that Dad was not a major influence on each of us boys. He was, but his paternal style was akin to that of a referee, counting on

Mother to be the coach in the game of family. He had himself grown up with minimal parental intervention and shaped his adult life around self-centered individualism, so when it came to playing the role of father, economy of effort was his natural inclination.

His was a common attitude among men of his time. Having babies, raising children, managing a household, these were all women's work. Likewise in the social dimension, participation in church, school, and community was in the category of "doing good," best left to women, so long, that is, as men had the say-so in matters of power and property.

Dad expressed no conscious ideology in support of this uneven distribution of responsibility and power. It just seemed to suit his nature, and anyone who meddled with this arrangement was to be ignored or ostracized as a disturbing influence on the natural order.

Aside from benign neglect suiting the complacent man's approach to fathering, there is a certain degree of truth that the most important lessons that children need to learn are not conveyed by explicit, formal instruction, but rather, by parental example that the child will naturally emulate. One didn't lie, cheat, steal, bully, take more than one's share at the dinner table, or avoid one's share of the work necessary for family survival. All these social values were absorbed from the family atmosphere as the natural way to behave. If, perchance, one of us boys failed to grasp such elementary standards, Dad conveyed them explicitly with a little discussion, and if necessary, the razor strap hanging from his bathroom door.

Likewise, the positive virtues and tastes that give pleasure and depth to life were conveyed by parental example, such things as the love of Nature and the vigorous outdoor life, the joys of camaraderie and sporting competition with one's own sex, a protective regard for the opposite sex, and sufficient literacy to make a living and pursue one's interests. Conspicuous diplays of great wealth, power, social prominence, or holiness were not admired, and, by inference, were disdained as so much puffery, proof that man is basically a vain and selfish creature, except possibly when dealing with those he regards as his own.

⚙

Such a laissez-faire approach to the instruction of the young was decidedly not the way things were done at North Star Elementary School. All summer long this plain wooden citadel of learning stood vacant amid its stoney grounds, its broad steps and tall dark windows waiting until the fade of summer days, waiting in stern solemnity until its special day and hour arrived. Then, with a simple tug on a rope, its great iron bell shook the belltower as it tolled out its command. Again and again it rang out in the still morning air, "Come-come" "Come-come" "Come-now" "Come-quick," it seemed to echo across the grounds, "Or you'll be late for schooool......."

And come we did, from every direction up and down the rocky slopes of North Lonsdale, making their way along streets with lofty names like Kings, Queens, St. George's, St. Andrews, Chesterfield, Windsor, St. James, St. Mary's, Osborne, and Carisbrooke. Girls and boys of every size and shape came running, skipping , shouting, teasing, kicking rocks, boisterous children by the dozens with names like Alan, Albert, Alice, Arthur, Asa, Amelia, Bryan, Catherine, Daphne, Edward, George, Helen, Irene, John, Patricia, Roberta, Robin, and Willard, and surnames like Ames, Bevan, Diplock, Galluzo, Hilder, Loutet, Lazenby, McLean, McLennan, Upton, Wallace, and Williams. Most of their parents were of English, Scotch, or Irish origins, but here and there Italian, German, French, or American, and almost all of Anglican or Protestant religious heritage.

Almost all came from homes who considered themselves middle class, many with parents of advanced or professional education, none rich, some comfortably settled in government or other white collar jobs, many just getting by like my family in a precarious state of subsistance and carefully guarded respectability. But the two things our parents all had in common was a strong

84

belief in the importance of education, and that living away up on the slopes of Grouse Mountain was the grandest place in the world.

North Star Elementary School consisted of two buildings, each with its own playground. The lower main building for grades one through five was presided over by the Misses Angus and Hamilton, strict, dedicated missionaries of order and enlightenment, a special breed that was the foundation of public education throughout the province of British Columbia.

For these devoted single ladies the role of teacher was no mere job. It was a sacred calling to which they gave everything of themselves; latent maternal love and stern demand that every girl and boy make the most of God-given ability. Also being eminently practical, they were expert at a well-aimed stroke of a ruler to the knuckles of any of their charges not inclined to sit up straight and pay attention.

Without the inspirational presence of the likes of Misses Angus and Hamilton, the edifice called North Star School came close to resembling a vacant warehouse, a structure utterly barren of beauty, colour, or comfort. Outside and in, its lines were unremittingly straight and square, not a gracious curve anywhere, and every surface painted dull gray, brown, black, or white.

The same barren design, a sort of public school Gothic of the Canadian frontier, was used for Lonsdale School, Edith Cavell on Oak Street in Vancouver and dozens of others throughout the province, so it must have reflected the outlook of the times. One surmises it was the stamp of the Scottish pioneers, builders of so much in Canada, including its system of public education.

They were a frugal, disciplined, and hardy lot, and these austere public school buildings seemed to reflect their strict Calvinist views, as if to say, "All ye who enter here, let there be no distraction of mind from the business at hand. Sit still, obey, listen, and remember well, for the path of a righteous life is hard and straight."

The school day at North Star began with a muster at the foot of its broad wooden outside stairs, girls on the one side, boys on the other. The Misses Angus and Hamilton stood atop the landing eyeing their charges below, a mere glance from their majestic presence sufficient to quiet the boisterous. When all seemed properly submissive, the no-nonsense Misses turned about face, and in total command, strode briskly through the wide doors, down the dark hallway, entered their respective classrooms, and stood arms folded, for their charges to tumble into their seats.

There the boys and girls intermixed, seats being assigned alphabetically by surname beginning at the row nearest the door and proceeding up and down the five rows to the far corner near the windows.

My seat assignment, to the very last seat in the very last row, made me aware for the first time in life that having the surname Williams was a significant fact of life, as permanent a part of myself as my nose, and that for better or worse, I would be forever placed at the end of the line.

Before long I learned that this arrangement was actually an advantage in Miss Angus' class. To begin with, I got to sit next to the windows in comforting proximity to the great outdoors. Without being noticed, I could sidle up to the pencil sharpener, placed on the window ledge up front, and take my time seeing what was going on outside. My manoeuvre was so unobtrusive I could get away with it two or three times a day, thus receiving the additional gratification of feeling temporarily immune to Miss Angus' total authority.

Another unforeseen advantage was that when Miss Angus called on her pupils to recite, her methodical mind always called first upon someone in the middle rows, usually a girl, then worked her way outward and back, giving me the time advantage to prepare for the type of question she was about to ask. Perhaps over time I paid a price of not having to be as sharp-witted as others, but at the time I felt fortunate in having the surname Williams.

Miss Angus had many weapons in her disciplinary arsenal. With girls a simple reproof was usually sufficient. "Now Mary, you're not doing your best, are you? You wouldn't want your father to know that would you?" If this sort of kindly admonition and implied threat were not sufficient to induce a trickle of tears and renewed commitment, being told to stay after school for a little talk usually did.

With others she applied peer pressure, the shame and teasing that accompanied being stood in a corner for a few minutes of exile, or a brief sentence to hard labour at the blackboard; five or ten lines of I WILL NOT TALK IN CLASS, or I WILL DO MY WORK ON TIME. Then there was always the dreaded injunction to stay after school to clean the blackboard brushes, a lonely chore down in the basement while everyone else was out playing.

For the real hard-core offender, usually a large boy with an irrepressible need to show off for a certain girl, the kind of smart-aleck who referred to her as "old lady Angus" out on the school grounds, she could bring forth her ultimate weapon, referral to the Principal.

Just the look of Principal Darwin could strike terror into the heart of the most incorrigible. Although skinny, gray-headed, and not large, Mr. Charles Darwin had the great advantage of his war injuries, one glass eye that could see right through the thickest skull, and in place of a left hand, a large, sharp steel hook that could grasp anything within reach with merciless precision.

Furthermore, out on the school grounds he was as swift on his feet as a Bengal tiger.

Principal Darwin could run faster than any boy in school. From his position of surveillance on the landing of the upper school steps, the minute a large boy dared bully a girl or smaller boy, Mr. Darwin would bound down the steps three at a time, fly across the rocky ground, and before the bully knew what struck, Mr. Darwin had him hooked by the scruff of his sweatered neck while his good hand pinned the boy's hand behind his back.

He then marched the offender to his office for a five or ten minute discussion. Once released, the bullying boy was guaranteed to go forth and sin no more. Furthermore, it took only one such demonstration per year to establish law, order, and good sportsmanship on the playfields of North Star School.

Principal Darwin was anything but a sadistic monster, rather, of brilliant mind and wise to the ways of the world. He knew from his long and painful service as an officer in Canada's military forces during World War I the propaganda value of a theatrical show of force, one well-chosen time and place to set an example that would become firmly embedded in the minds of the troops.

Darwin's office meeting with the offender followed a standard operating procedure. With door closed and bully seated in front of his large wooden desk, he first opened wide a set of windows overlooking the playground. Then, reaching into a desk drawer, he withdrew his strap, a thick strip of leather three inches wide and two feet long. It appeared well used, as though possibly made from a section of his former military belt.

Fixing the lad with his glass eye while standing a foot or so behind his desk, he drew the strap across his upraised arm just above the hook. The strap folded and slithered slowly across his hooked arm as though it were a snake moving across a stout tree limb. The boy sat transfixed as Darwin repeated the movement, slowly, his good eye observing the boy's face and eyes for telling signs of his inner state. If not satisfied, he repeated the movement of the belt again, ever so slowly across his outstretched arm.

Invariably, two or three such exhibitions of the belt were sufficient to induce paleness, perspiration upon the forehead and neck, watery eyes, at times trembling of the hands or chattering teeth. Thereupon, satisfied that he had now gained the miscreant's attention, Darwin brought down the strap upon the desk top with long, swift strokes, not once, but twice, then a third. Each time, the would-be terrorist of the playground before him heaved and winced as though the strokes were landing upon his own flesh.

And each time the leather lash beat upon the desk, the sound resonated like the stroke upon a bass drum. The horrendous sound carried through the windows and out over the grounds from one end to the other. Not a boy missed its message.

The rest was short and simple; a brief discussion about the ethics of proper playground behavior, and the boy was dismissed from the interview. No strapping was necessary. That boy, and all the rest at North Star had been taught a lesson they would never forget. Brains, stern idealism, and the boldness to match were Charles Darwin's weapons, as one might expect of a man with such a name, for he was in fact a direct lineal descendant of the English scientific genius whose theory of evolution stood Christian theology on its head.

⬙

For the first five grades we had our own playground with no bullies to worry about. At the crack of recess out of the bleak building we flew through the wide doors and down the steps like a swarm of multi-coloured bees, then, hardly knowing which game to play first, scattered in joyous abandon all over the playground. Suddenly, with equal spontaneity, we coalesced into small clusters for excited discussion and off we flew again in a dozen directions for endless games of hide and seek.

There was no such state of spontaneous combustion among the older kids of the upper school. Games were more complex and orderly, concerted contests of wit and brawn, usually just for glory but sometimes for wealth, as in the game of marbles.

But in the Fall, the most popular game was soccer, tireless hordes of legs and boots charging up and down the field in ragged formation. We used every trick of dribble, dodge, pass, and kick to bang that leather ball through the opponent's posts, then shout with delirious triumph "GOAL!"

Oh! What a glorious game! There's nothing quite like soccer for sheer barbaric exhaustion; bruised legs, aching shins, scraped knees, scuffed boots, limbs and clothes splattered with mud, shirts dripping with sweat, throats parched for a slurp of cold, clear water. Soccer alone was enough to make me and a lot of fellows eager to come back to school in the Fall.

Knockers was another ideal Depression game for boys. It was simple, violent, and required no capital outlay, merely a large horse chestnut hardened in the oven, and with a hole drilled in it, hung by a two-foot length of store string. The idea was to crack open the other fellow's nut by whacking it with your own, the feat accomplished by a swift, accurate downward stroke upon the defendant's nut as he held it still and dangling from his outstretched arm. As long as the aggressor hit the defendant's nut, he got another turn; if he missed then came the defendant's turn, and so the game went on until one or the other's nut was shattered into bits.

Another game that went on at the periphery of the soccer field was marbles, particularly attractive to boys of an acquisitive bent. You could always tell who was an avid marble player by a bulge in his pant pocket, his sack of prized glass orbs that rolled and clicked whenever he moved. These future bankers and entrepreneurs congregated wherever there was room to draw a circle two or three feet in diameter on the ground and ten or so feet around the circumference for manoeuvring.

Usually only two or three boys competed against each other at a time, just as long as each put an equal number of his own marbles in the circle, or "pot", to start the game. Whoever got to shoot first, decided by a preliminary contest of seeing who could toss his shooter marble closest to a line, then tossed or shot his shooter marble into the circle among the other target marbles from a starter line six to eight feet outside the circle. The other players then took turns doing likewise, maybe even being skilful or lucky enough to knock one of the target marbles out of the circle. That was the whole idea; not only acquiring that marble for his collection but getting another turn, something he could also do by merely touching any opponents shooter marble with his own.

Marble players had to adhere to a few simple rules or the game would disintegrate in quarrels. The main violation was called "fudging", secretly moving a shooter marble into a more advantageous position than where it had come to rest or not keeping knuckles flat on the ground when shooting. The usual way to shoot was to cradle the shooter marble in the index finger, and with hand curled over so the knuckles of the fingers lay flat on the ground, propel the shooter marble forward with a rapid flick of the thumb. But it was also allowed to merely flick the shooter marble with the index finger, sometimes easier when very close to a target marble.

A good marble player could hit a target marble from two or three feet away, and as long as he kept knocking marbles out of the pot, or touched an opponent's shooter, he got another turn. Marbles, being a game of intense individual competition and acquisitiveness, made cheating tempting. But the price of being caught was also high, losing a turn, or, if habitual, finding no one to play with. So the game was good training in civilized business ethics for North Star's future entrepreneurs.

Each of these games appealed to a certain side of any boy's nature; sheer physical vigour, competitiveness with brawn, skill, or wit, camaraderie, and acquisitiveness, and he could play any or all of them at different times if he chose. Moreover, all went on most of the time with little or no adult intervention or supervision. We enforced the rules ourselves, handing them down from one generation to the next.

Wise schoolmen like Darwin knew that not only were they necessary to let boys blow off steam so they would settle down and become educable indoors, but that the lessons learned in outdoor games were in themselves perhaps as important as what they learned in class.

The signs that Winter, not mere darkness and the incessant rains that came in November, but a Winter of snow and fun, usually came in late December after a few clear, cold nights. By morning the outside of our kitchen window had become a white constellation of ice crystals. On the back porch the glass milk bottles gleamed in the cold, their round paper lids popped up with an inch or two of cream. Nothing could be tastier than this poured 'round a bowl of steaming hot rolled oats sprinkled with brown sugar.

And looking out from the back porch, away up Grouse Mountain was the surest sign of all that real winter had come at last. For away up there another two or three thousand feet the mountain, our mountain and its forested slopes were fringed in virgin snow.

My older brother Larkin was usually the first one up to catch this winter sight, and rushing back upstairs, rouse us from our beds, "Heh, get up! There's snow on Grouse! I just saw it! I'll bet there's a foot at the top! We'd better get our sleds fixed up! In a day or two it'll be down here!"

Unimpressed, the ever analytical Don replied, "You're nuts. It'll take at least a week to get down here, and by then it'll be nothing but slush, just enough to get your boots soaked." But Larkin's word was good enough for Ace. "I don't care. I'm going to see for myself", and with that both he and I tumbled out, hurried up to wash and dress to see for ourselves. Larkin did have a tendency to exaggerate.

The trouble was that Don didn't get the point. It really didn't matter exactly how much snow was on Grouse or when snow would arrive at our elevation, or whether it would stay cold enough to stick. The point was that Grouse was our mountain, a very personal and important part of our lives. We regarded it with awe, and anything happening up Grouse compelled our instant attention.

We had a similar primordial feeling about the river, meaning the Capilano River, or the creek, meaning Hastings Creek which filled our swimming hole. We watched and reported about each in minute detail among ourselves; the rise and fall of their waters, first appearance of fish, flooding, whatever occurred.

But Grouse and its sister mountains were invested with a majesty above all. And for good reason even to more mature minds, for back up there in those mountains is where the rivers and creeks were born. No snow on the mountains meant no river, creek, fish, swimming, even fresh water to drink, for from there came the city inhabitants' fresh water supply.

As the snowline crept down the mountain slopes and dark canyons of the Capilano, Seymour, and Lynn, a stillness came with the cold, and life turned inward at the old mansion on the hill. Outdoor faucets were wrapped in remnants of discarded clothes, the outdoor sleeping porch closed off against winter drafts, the furnace sawdust hopper filled to the brim, and the fireplace in the dining room lit before supper. An hour before going to bed we took heated bricks from the oven, wrapped them in newspaper, and slipped them under the bedcovers. And from the kitchen all winter long came the warm smells of simmering soup and fresh baked bread.

And after supper and homework, when all of us boys were snuggled down in bed, we listened to the special sounds of the old house at work against the cold. Its labyrinth of pipes and radiators popped, banged, and hissed as the hot water worked its way upward from the furnace between cold plaster walls.

Still, on a cold winter night, no room far from the kitchen was ever really warm. The house had too many floors and rooms to heat with a single small furnace. So we with our warm bodies helped heat the house rather than the other way around, an irony of spending winter in this former rich man's house.

But for all its winter discomfort and closed off empty rooms, the old house had its own spirit and we grew to love it as if it were our own. It had kept us together as a family with a richness of sharing hitherto unknown, save on Christmas day.

Our first Christmas on the North Shore was slim pickings, what with the costs of moving and settling in. There would have been no Christmas at all if it weren't for Aunt Maisie, mother's older sister in Edmonton married to Gordon Savage, a wholesale grocer. Without fail, two huge brown parcels arrived by railway express a week or so before Christmas.

The heaviest one contained all the ingredients for Christmas dinner; a plump twenty pound turkey and packages of dried and glazed fruits, nuts, and candies, all the fixings for plum pudding and fruit cakes. The second box, larger but lighter, contained gifts to put under the tree; much needed new clothes for each of us boys, always something luxuriously feminine for Mother, and a huge five pound box of chocolates. But most important to us boys was what was in an additional very large, thin box, a mystery until Dad gave Don the signal to go get the butcher knife and open it up, and from inside emerged a beautiful, red, double-barred bicycle, cousin Gordon Savage's old one all fixed up with new balloon tires. To us, it was miracle, for none of us had a bicycle of our own, so we all took turns on it learning how to ride a bicycle until each of us earned enough money for one of his own.

Dad somehow managed to procure all the little things for our stockings, and as before, he prepared breakfast while Mother stayed in bed, then Christmas dinner with all of us in last year's paper hats, and Mother struggling again with thanks to the Lord.

So the magic day of Christmas came and went as before, the family's reassuring ritual of the year. We had made it through the loss of our own home, had learned to make another in another man's house, and thus proved to ourselves that we could survive and thrive as a family no matter what.

🚲

My brothers and I had decided opinions about winter, good if there was a good snowfall that lasted, otherwise we turned our backs on it for fun indoors.

North Star School had no gym, but in the basement of each building there were two large bare rooms, one for the boys, and one for the girls. Skipping rope seemed to be the favorite game for girls, but we devised all sorts of games, usually rough ones leading to many a skinned knee and bloody nose.

In the game of Pile On, two boys of team A would bend over and interlock their bodies, the first boy with his hands against the wall, the second sticking his head between the first boy's spread legs. One by one, team B would vault onto the backs of team A trying to make them buckle under the weight. Whenever team A ran out of backroom to vault onto, it added another boy to its caterpillar line of interlocking bodies. If team A held up under all of team B's weight, they won the Pile On, and it became their turn to vault onto the other team's backs.

In Crack The Whip, one boy, positioned in the centre of the basement floor, rotated, arms stretched out, while one by one, members of opposing teams rushed in, grasped his outstretched hands, extended their arms and hands, and did their best to keep up with the accelerating pace of this rotating spoke of outstretched arms and hands. The further from the centre the faster the pace, and, tougher to hang on. Eventually, of course, it became too fast and tough for an outside man to hang on and he went flying off, slithering across the cement floor or crashing into the equally unresilient wall.

These exhilarating games were hard on knees, elbows, noses, and clothes, but teachers didn't interfere, I suppose, because this recess mayhem served the very useful purpose of discharging pent-up ruffian energy, otherwise disruptive in the classroom.

Whenever there was a good snowfall, the North Star playground became a battlefield of white, snowballs arching and exploding everywhere. Hastily organized armies swarmed and skirmished up and down the field, the goal being to capture the opponent's waist-high snowfort.

Girls were allowed in the fight if they weren't crybabies. But pity the boy who was too rough on one of the girls. He would have to contend with Yvonne Loutet, an Amazon in knee-high leather boots. She was as big and tough as any boy, and, with provocation, promptly wrestled the bully to the ground, and rubbed his face so thoroughly with snow, thereafter he thought twice before taking after another of the fair sex. Yvonne was as bright as she was bold, and with such martial experience on the battlefields of North Lonsdale, well prepared to become one of the first officers of the Womens' Army Corps in World War II.

If the snowfall was a foot or so and nights cold enough so it stayed, bobsledding down Lonsdale at night was the big event.

Like most of our play equipment during the Depression, the bobsled was a contraption we put together ourselves from whatever we could lay our hands on; one boy's Cheesecutter with handles to steer up front, a simple round-runner sled at the rear, and an eight foot plank tying the two together. It was plenty good enough for three boys lying down to career down Lonsdale all the way to 15th, then hitch onto the rear of the streetcar and do it all over again. Not many people had the money to run an automobile in those days, and of course there were no streetlights, so we had clear sledding down Lonsdale, with just enough compaction of the road surface from auto traffic during the day to go like blazes, especially if we could get a fast start by hiking up the steep hill on Braemar and come down the board sidewalk onto Lonsdale.

For the older kids in high school or out working, winter meant exciting weekends up Seymour or Grouse mountains. Many, like Ralph and Hugh Koonts and chums from Ridgeway School built their own cabins up Seymour and so many did the same thing up Grouse that the Ski Village had its own government with elected Mayor, police Chief, et cetera, and many a romance bloomed on those wintery mountain slopes.

🚲

One morning in early April the almost forgotten sun reappeared and stayed awhile to warm the moist air. From east-facing roofs steam drifted skyward, frost-heaved ground melted into soft brown mud, and the morning air came alive with the sounds of birds heralding the coming of spring. "Wake up! Hurry! Fly quick! Fly fast!" the robin and jay seemed to say. "Its time to gather dry sticks and straw! Hurry! Hurry! We must find a good place for a nest before it gets dark!"

Soon blossoms appeared, first the white-petalled wild cherry, then the pink plum, apple, and pear. And on the ground, brave clusters of crocus appeared, yellow, blue, and white, then everywhere the intrusive dandelion. As the sun came earlier a little each day, the morning air abounded in sound, all manner of birds giving voice as they darted and spun through the air. The scent of blossoms brought forth bees and winged ants.

For us inside the old house it was time to move our beds back onto the sleeping porch and submit to the dreaded annual cleansing of the blood. The spring tonic, sulphur and molasses, two tablespoons of the awful stuff, was repulsive to both taste and smell. But Mother thought it was good for us, important enough to set aside two days for it to work its way through the system, two days during which any skunk who might drop by would feel instantly at home. Consequently, this cure for winter's accretion of tired blood was administered on Friday evening to allow the weekend for isolation and recovery, a courtesy to the neighbours.

I don't know whether it was the regenerative power of this folk medicine or the joyous return to sleeping under the stars, but come Monday we raced down the hill to school with renewed vigour. Or perhaps it was Dad's annual spring issue of a brand new pair of high-topped running shoes to each of us, "sneakers" he called them, absolutely guaranteed by Woodward's to make any boy as fleet of foot as a deer in the forest.

Only once a year, in late May, did the teaching staff of North Star feel moved to bring adult organization to the playground. Sports Day required preparatory work in the form of supervising squads of kids to clean up the grounds, spread sawdust in the jumping pits, and lay out running lanes with lime. Teachers looked forward to that special day as much as we did, their chance to escape the dark interior domain of the classroom and play again in the great outdoors.

But perhaps more importantly for our teachers, Sports Day signalled the near end of the school year, the approach of summer's reprieve from their tiring trade. So they turned to the task of organizing healthy competition and good sportsmanship with good-natured zeal, and we, being natural opportunists, thoroughly enjoyed the novelty of their singular display of their attention to our playground world.

As well as supervising races, the teachers joined with us to play baseball. "Look at Miss Angus! Gosh, she can really RUN!" exclaimed Daphne, and Carl exuded in admiring disbelief, "Holy mackerel! Did you see Mr. Ovans hit that ball! Wow! He must'a been SOMETHIN' in school!"

And so it went all afternoon, the fifty yard dash, one legged race, sack race, mixed boys' and girls' relay, high jump, pole vault, broadjump, and more. Everyone went home with a ribbon for something. Larkin jumped a foot longer than anyone else in the broad jump. Even with his flat feet, Ace was so fast he could have walked off with a half a dozen blue ribbons if he'd really tried. And even I, with one strong leg, was a sure winner in the one-legged race.

Sports Day ended as another triumph of leadership psychology for Principal Darwin. Thereafter the classroom behavior of even the most mischievous rebel was noticeably moderated by new-found admiration, even guarded affection, toward those in the position of classroom authority.

۸

By the second summer in North Lonsdale, we knew the territory well enough to dig out whatever paying jobs were to be had in the neighbourhood and contrived to do these in the coolness of morning so that afternoons could be spent at the swimming hole.

Don got the best paying jobs because he was a smart promoter and had earned a reputation as a good worker. He'd see a house that needed a coat of paint or a fence with some boards missing, knock on the door, introduce himself, and offer his services, only of course, if there were indications of affluence about the place and estimating what he ought to get for the job. He had an earnest, competent manner that usually did the trick. Besides, he was uncommonly handsome at fourteen which helped with the lady of the house or if there were daughters in the household.

The rest of us were no less successful in finding employment, albeit less remunerative. Larkin happened upon one of those accentric English remittance men, of whom North Vancouver had more than a few, a fiftyish bachelor doing his best to hack an acre of brush into a homestead. Even at twelve Larkin was skilled with a Swede saw and axe, and noticing the man's amateurish swing of an axe, suggested that for a dollar a day he would guarantee to get the job done by the end of the summer.

"Dear me, I could never manage that," said the tall, slender Englishman in a cultivated voice. "That is all I receive from the old country each month." Larkin rejoined, "Well, how about if I work mornings only for half that much?" He was eager to make the deal, and besides, was finding the old geezer amusing, so the job would also be fun. "Yes, I think that would do" the gentleman replied, and continued, "I can surely see the summer through, not so much for food, kerosene, that sort of thing, and I do want the work completed before winter sets in."

That's the way George Legge talked, one of those loquacious people who think out loud. Also, he spoke with a refreshing egalitarian directness, undoubtedly among the reasons his aristocratic family paid him to reside on the other side of the globe. His father was a bishop in the established Church and his sister a lady-in-waiting to the Queen. George Legge wasn't cut out for pomp and circumstance. He liked roughing it, so he and Larkin got along fine.

While Ace picked strawberries for Mr. Wong in the early morning hours, I became a farmhand for the Monteith family.

It happened in an odd way.

One Saturday morning I was on my way to the swimming hole, late June it was and uncommonly warm for that time of the year, when up St. Andrews came a very stout lady pulling a little red wagon. Her Red Racer was heavily laden, and she was huffing and puffing as she struggled up the hill. Every third or fourth step she paused to wipe her forehead and jowels with a large blue bandana. Her globular face was as red as the wagon as she strained to propel her gelatinous frame up the hill, a pitiful sight.

To tell the truth, it was really her dog which gained my compassion, an old, dignified black and white Border Collie that reminded me of our first dog Nick. This fine old dog followed a few paces behind her wagon, panting and pathetic in the summer heat. So I, doing my best to keep my eyes off the woman's brown stockings as they unravelled down her legs, approached and said, "Let me help you with your wagon. You can't have far to go."

The woman, planted firmly in the middle of the road, for there was no sidewalk, turned about, eyed me suspiciously up and down, then in a voice as mannish as a waterfront stevedore, replied, "Well, if that's what you want," as though she was the one doing me a favour. Not letting her response bother me, I took hold of the wagon's handle and easily kept pace with her rolling gait as we moved up the hill.

Not a word passed between us the rest of way. The road flattened out and we entered a driveway. On the right stood a long, rough board shed, and beyond, a farm gate and green meadow. On the left, a high privet hedge ended in an informal English garden. Tall pastel flowers danced on their stems, and through the garden, a winding gravel path led to the open door of a cottage, the most gracefully formed dwelling I had ever seen, with a curving thatched roof nestled in this lovely garden. It was if they had been born together.

The cottage, garden, rough hewn barn, and sunlit meadow, all together, presented a world of rustic charm I had seen only in one of my storybooks about the Old Country.

Our little procession of exhausted woman, helpful boy pulling a red wagon, and panting dog halted within sight of the cottage door. There, giving herself another good wiping with her bandana, the large woman pointed her fat cheeks toward the door and hollered as if calling her dog, "Elspeth!", paused for breath, and hollered again, "Elspeth!"

She was puffing herself for the next holler, when, from the cottage's darkened doorway there emerged into that lovely garden a person so thin he or she would have gone unnoticed amongst the garden's tall stemmed flox.

This figment of a person came forward as lightly as a butterfly and said, "Yes Olive, what is it dear?" in a pleasant, feminine voice. Having somewhat regained her wind, Olive said, "This young man helped me up the road. Can he have a lemonade?" Despite her diminutive size, Elspeth was plainly in command. "Of course! Of course! Do come in" she said, "And what is your name?" she trippled off in her musical voice as she led the way toward the door.

"Robin", I replied, following the lively little lady into the cottage. "Robin, oh that IS a nice name", she exclaimed. "And do you live nearby?" she queried as she placed parcels from Olive's wagon on a long, sturdy table in the centre of the cool, dark room.

I surveyed the room. Its walls were lined with cupboards and shelves, and beneath a double window, a sink with large double basins and taps, then a white refrigerator. Momentarily checking my curiosity, I replied, "Not very far. In the big house on Carisbrooke and St. George's, but I have never been up here before."

Following Elspeth's lead, I placed some parcels from the wagon on the other end of the long table and continued my inspection of the room. Opposite the window side, among more cupboards and shelves, was a shiny cream-coloured electric stove, upon it two huge blue enamel pots. On the wall toward the door hung rows of long-handled metal dippers, various beaters, and long wooden spoons. Walls, cupboards, utensils, all except the wooden spoons were cream, white, or blue, spick and span, not an unclean thing anywhere. Even the floor, large squares of black and white linoleum, was sparkling clean.

This unusual kitchen had a peculiar odor, not unpleasant, even fresh, and I wondered why. One doesn't ask questions about odors upon first entering a house, even pleasant ones, so I bided my time until I found out.

The explanation wasn't long in coming. First Elspeth had to satisfy her curiosity about me, this curly headed little boy, evidently used to being crippled, as it didn't seem to bother him, hardly noticeable except he wore short pants and one leg was plainly thinner than the other.

Turning toward Olive, Elspeth said, "He must mean Thomas Nye's house", then turning back to me, asked for more details. "Robin, do you mean the big house of gray granite with stone steps and a tennis court?" I replied, "Yes, that's it. We've lived there a year."

Turning again to Olive, Elspeth said with a note of surprise, "That's it, the Nye place. Malcom told me he thought it was up for taxes, poor man, like so many others, what a pity", then turned to pursue her curiosity further. "And how old are you Robin?" I replied, "This September I'll be eight", hoping that Elspeth would say how big I looked for my age.

Instead, Olive, seated on a stool by the table, restated her interest. "Elspeth, are we going to get a lemonade?" "Oh dear. I AM sorry. I'll make it right away" replied Elspeth, smiling indulgently toward Olive.

I was equally curious about Olive and Elspeth. What an odd pair I thought, each the fattest and skinniest women I had ever seen, and here they were talking like they were husband and wife, but of course that would be impossible, yet surely they couldn't be sisters they were so completely unlike.

It wasn't just that Elspeth was all bones and Olive all fat, but their faces, colour of hair and eyes, speech, absolutely nothing was the same about the two. Well, I thought, that's just another thing I would just have to wait to find out. Besides, I had more practical considerations to keep in mind, maybe a job at their place, because it did appear to be some sort of farm and I had always dreamed of working on a farm among animals and sweet-smelling hay.

Presently Elspeth brought the lemonade, freshly made with a round glass squeezer, placed the tumblers before Olive and me, poured herself a tumbler of milk from a white pitcher from the refrigerator, and perching herself lightly upon another stool, resumed her interrogation.

She wanted to know what grade I was in school, how many

brothers and sisters I had, and whether my father worked in the city. Evidently satisfied, she shifted ground, "Robin, would you like to see our goats?", and I replied, "Yes, I sure would. How many do you have?"

Pleased with my interest, Elspeth grew more descriptive. "Not counting our billy, we have twelve milking and six kids, all Taagenberg, perfectly beautiful animals. Then we keep bees. It's great deal of work, but we love it, so healthy, isn't it dear?" she said turning toward Olive.

Olive, of less poetic mind, replied in her usual blunt manner, "Can I have more lemonade and some graham crackers?" Elsbeth, evidently accustomed to such conversational deviations from Olive, placed a plate of graham crackers on the table, rinsed out our tumblers, and reaching into the refrigerator, filled each tumbler with milk. "Much better for you", said she in a sweet, maternal tone.

She then resumed my education about the farm. "Robin, you would be surprised at how much our animals provide; six gallons every day. Of course some is for the kids, but that still leaves enough for our regular customers, and the rest goes for cheese. We make our own you see, right here in the kitchen. That's why it must be kept so clean. One must be careful with milk. Doctors prescribe goat's milk for sickly babies. It's richer and far more digestible, you know."

Aha, I thought, that's why this kitchen has such a funny smell! It was not any ordinary kitchen, but a creamery and cheese factory for the goat's milk, too!

Rising from her stool, Elspeth opened a door to a small, cellar-like room off the kitchen, and continued my orientation, "This is our cooling room where we bring the milk after milking, twice a day, you know", and pointing to an oblong basin in the corner of the cement floor, continued, "Those cans of fresh milk are kept cool by refilling the basin with fresh, cold water, two or three times a day, according to how warm it is."

Elspeth led me back to the kitchen table where Olive had remained hunched upon an invisible stool staring at the empty cracker plate like an entranced Buddha. Then Elspeth, noticing that my tumbler was still half full of milk, inquired, or rather stated, "It's good, isn't it?" Not pausing for my response, she answered her own question, "And goat's milk is so good FOR you too" with evangelical certainty.

I wasn't sure at all. In fact, I was quite sure I DIDN'T like the taste, or smell, no matter how good it was for me. I was very fond of milk, the kind of milk I was used to, cows' milk, and it had never occurred to me before that there was any other kind. And certainly not something that tasted and smelled as oddly as this goat's milk.

I had managed to down half the tumbler and was in no hurry to finish the rest for fear Elspeth would fill it up again. I couldn't possibly make it through another tumbler, in fact was secretly cogitating how I might get rid of the rest of this one without Elspeth noticing.

I was caught in a crisis of conscience. I wanted to get rid of the remainder of my milk, but also I felt uncomfortable about dumping it somehow, down the sink, perhaps the toilet, I didn't know exactly how, but that would not only be sneaky but wasteful too, pretty near a mortal sin with something as valuable as milk. On the other hand, I didn't want to tell Elsbeth the truth, that I didn't really like her goat's milk, because it was plain that with her it was like a religion and for darn sure she wouldn't offer me a job on their farm if she knew I loathed her goat's milk.

In short, I had never imagined that a simple glass of milk would ever pose such a complexity of practical and ethical problems. I wasn't sure what to do.

Thank Heavens, Elspeth changed the subject, giving me a brief reprieve. "Now, Robin, how would you like to see the farm?" Again assuming she knew my response, she turned to Olive and said, "Now dear, while I'm doing the separating, why don't you show Robin around, then come back and we'll all have a bite of lunch?"

"Great!", I thought, and rose quickly from my stool to move out the door. But, rotten luck, Elspeth rose just as swiftly, and, smiling at me maternally, said sweetly, "Now finish your milk before you go, Robin."

Trapped, I sat down again eyeing that half tumbler of goat's milk. There was no way out. Raising the tumbler of awful stuff, down it went in one long draft. Elspeth looked pleased, Olive managed to pry herself off the stool bearing down on the table like a Japanese wrestler, waddled out the kitchen door, and I followed close behind.

She did her best to give me the grand tour; barn for storing grain and machinery, milking shed, kid's corral, gray-bearded Billy in his special pasture, all very interesting, but I had difficulty absorbing it all. My mind kept thinking of lunch and the possibility of having to cope with another tumbler of the dreaded milk.

Thinking I might avoid it, straightaway upon re-entering the kitchen, I asked Elspeth if I might have an empty tumbler, and just as hastily, filled it to the brim with tap water and took my time just sipping on it to keep it more or less full.

Olive planted herself firmly on a stool and I did likewise, noting with relief no signs of further milk. Elspeth inquired, "Aren't our goats beautiful?" and reached into the refrigerator. I was stunned. What she brought forth was an oblong tray, and upon it a plate of sandwiches, and spaced evenly around, three tumblers of milk.

"I know you'll like the sandwiches, Robin, made with duck eggs, so much better for you. Would you like a dozen to take home to your mother?" she said. Rendered temporarily speechless, I gulped, then stammered, "Oh, yes, yes. Thank you very much."

Elspeth gave us each a plate, and passing the sandwiches around, placed the tumblers of milk beside each plate. It was plainly time to capitulate. Personal preference is no match for religious zeal. It was either a job with goat's milk or no job at all. So, staring at the tumbler of milk, I placed the water aside, smiled weakly at Elspeth, and said, "Oh, the sandwich IS good."

Elspeth smiled with particular maternal warmth and said, "And now Robin, after lunch would you like to help Olive take the goats to pasture?" I replied, "Why yes, that should be fun", glancing at Olive for some sign she approved. No sign came from her stolid face.

After lunch, Olive belched, levitated her huge frame from the stool, and moved toward the door. As we departed, Elspeth waved and called out "Malcolm should be home by the time you get back and we'll all have tea together."

I walked beside Olive at first, then rushed ahead to open the pasture gate, a two-by-four with a handle that slid between two posts. After passing through, Olive grasped the top of the gate and pushed it back into place, saying, "Robin, never forget to lock the gate."

With that one simple command Olive became a different person to me, a thinking, decisive adult, not the dull, dependent, sort of overgrown child that she seemed hitherto. More importantly, I gained the feeling that she not only liked me, but the idea of me working with her around the farm. From then on I felt a new sense of respect and camaraderie with Olive, something I could not have imagined before.

As we proceeded down the fenced lane toward the milking shed, the goats in the pasture followed Olive along the fenceline, clamoring to get as close to her as the fence would allow, each seeming to beg for her attention with raspy-voiced Baaa-ing. And Olive spoke back to each by name, "Come Dorothy. Come Betty. Come Annie. Come, come.."

Each had a bell hanging from a leather collar that clanged in pleasant concert as they hurried along together. I couldn't tell one from the other at this stage of our acquaintanceship; all had white, course hair, very large floppy ears, gray-green eyes that shined like marbles, long noses, and a bulging milk bag with two plump pink tits dangling down between their hind legs. To Olive, each of her goats was evidently an individual, much cared-for creature.

Upon nearing the end of the lane, Olive disappeared into the milking shed, returned with two rough-hewn shepherd's staffs, handed one to me, slid open the gates from the pasture and at the end of the lane, and motioned to me to follow as she strode behind her daughterly herd.

Upon reaching the meadow, Olive's new persona took on an even more assertive tone. Staff in hand, she walked firmly, decisively, sure of her command and ground, not at all the ambling, wobbly sort of gait she displayed upon first acquaintance. In fact, her whole manner changed. In place of her usual sullen glower, she smiled as she looked upon her family of goats. She hummed. She talked to each individually now and then, sometimes softly, at times firmly if one strayed too far.

Old Jamie, the handsome old sheepdog, had followed us along too, and now and again she ordered him to chase after one or the other, and he obeyed Olive, quite dutifully nipping at the errant one's heels and rounding it back to the flock.

Olive settled upon a round, comfortable rock on the high slope of the meadow, staff tucked under her chin while I sat nearby. The goats' antics were endlessly amusing, not at all like dairy cows content to mow hour after hour upon dull level ground. For goats, the higher up the better the fare; they were forever rearing up on their hind legs to reach a branch, especially of wild berry or the sweet leaves of a vine maple tree.

Soon I was reaching up with my shepherd's staff to bring more branches within reach, then shinnying up a large springy vine maple, and working my way out on it hand over hand, bending it down with my weight. When the goats had nibbled their fill of the leaves, I let go, and with a WHOOSH the branch sprang skyward, and I to the ground.

It was great fun, but tiring too, so for intermission I lay on the grass and watched the kids play. They were natural comics chasing and butting each other, scampering sideways, and skittering over and around large rocks playing tag.

While the goats nibbled and crunched, a host of smaller creatures moved about. Swallows played in the sky, their sleek black and yellow bodies swooping close to the ground. Bees flitted from daisy to dandelion. Orange and black Monarch butterflies drifted by. Occasionally from afar came the drumming of a grouse upon a log, then the rhythmic cooing of wild pigeons high up in a hemlock tree.

All too soon Olive called her family together. It was time to go. "Come Betty. Come Dorothy. Come Jennie" she called, and Olive and her flock of tinkling bells and Baa's set forth on the homeward path. Behind came Jamie, roving and circling, then I. In contented procession, we moved homeward in the late afternoon sun.

Olive led the flock into a small pasture next to the milking shed and together we walked up the lane toward the cottage, Olive in silence as usual. "Gee, that was fun", I said. Olive turned and smiled, her silent signal that she was pleased with my company and wished me to stay.

I thought to myself that it mustn't be easy for her to always be under Elspeth's command. Now she had shown me her other self, when she was in command. Like a secret held between two friends, this afternoon Olive and I had formed a bond needing no words.

No one was in the kitchen and the clock on the wall said four. Elspeth called from another room, "Olive dear, after you wash up, do bring Robin in for tea." Olive turned on the warm water taps at each of the sinks and handed me a yellow bar of soap. While drying my hands on a teatowel I overheard a man's voice, a pleasant, cultivated voice, say, "Well, that IS interesting."

Olive led the way into a large, sunny room. It overlooked a small lawn framed in a free-spirited English garden of multi-coloured flowers. Were it not for the window casements, the room was like an extension of the garden itself; a sofa of pastel flower designs, gracefully curved wicker easy chairs with rose or peach coloured cushions, a rich toned mahogany tea table set upon an oriental rug, and here and there small tables with olive shaped vases of flowers.

As I entered this exquisitely beautiful room, Elspeth turned to her husband and said, "Malcolm, this is Robin." Malcolm stood up, a good six feet two, slender, tanned, with laughing eyes, a handsome, inviting man. Shaking hands, Mr. Monteith motioned me to be seated in the chair nearest him.

"And did you like it out with Miss de Wolf?" he inquired in jovial tone as Elspeth poured tea. "Oh yes, I certainly did. I wouldn't mind doing that every day" I replied. Laughing, he glanced at Elspeth, then replied, "Well, we'll have to see about that."

Elspeth served each of us a small plate of sandwiches, cucumber and watercress with just a touch of mayonnaise, and the conversation turned to bees. "Tomorrow I'm going to extract a hive or two. Would you like to see how it's done?" asked Mr. Monteith. "Yes, that sounds interesting. What time should I come?" I replied. "It's best done when it's cool. Could you come at seven?" he asked, and so it was agreed.

He then went on, "Robin, you might be interested in a little history of the house you live in", paused to see if I was, then continued, "That house is probably the grandest one built in North Lonsdale, certainly the biggest, over twenty rooms wouldn't you say, Elspeth?", turning to his spouse for confirmation as married couples seem to do.

"At least", she replied, and Mr. Monteith continued, "Tom Nye and each of his two brothers got a hundred and sixty acres of Crown land for service in the South African War. One brother settled in Lynn Valley, I don't know about the other, but Tom decided on North Lonsdale, partly, I suppose, because he and Jack Loutet came out together from Montreal. You know the Loutet family of course."

Mr. Monteith paused to sip his tea, then resumed, "That was about the turn of the century. It was a good time to come to North Vancouver. It was booming, with hundreds of new settlers coming from the old country. So Tom sub-divided his land, made a great deal of money, and built his dream house on a choice five acres he kept for himself. That was about 1911 I think, a year or so before the Great War."

He paused to sip his tea, and seeing that I was listening intently, continued, "He spent so much money on it, more rooms than he ever needed, and expensive to keep up, that people came to call it Nye's Folly. That proved to be true. When the building boom ended, then a Depression came along, he couldn't afford the taxes, and probably a mortgage payment too. So, Robin, that's how you came to live at 230 Carisbrooke Road. You should tell your parents, as it might be of interest to them."

Elspeth got up to take the tea tray out, so I knew it was time to go. In the kitchen she handed me a shoebox wrapped with twine, saying, "Do be careful with duck eggs. They're wrapped in newspaper, but all the same I wouldn't run." Walking with me to the driveway, she seemed pleased with the day's events, and said in a self-assured voice, "So we'll see you in the morning."

"Where have you been?" Mother asked in worried tone. "At the Monteith's away up St. Andrews", I replied excitedly, handing her the box. "Here mother, these are duck eggs for you from Mrs. Monteith. And I think I've got a job."

Reassured, she gave me a hug and said, "I was beginning to get worried. Ace said he hadn't see you at the swimming hole."

She wanted to know the whole story, and I told it again at supper to the rest of the family. When it came to the part about having to drink two tumblers of goat's milk, Mother laughed longer than one would ordinarily expect, then explained, "Robin, you are the only one of the boys not raised on goat's milk! When I stopped nursing, that's all your brothers drank for a year or so, then I switched to cow's milk because it was easier to get."

That WAS good news, just what I wanted to hear; if goat's milk was good enough for them, from now on it would be good enough for me.

The next morning I was up early to have cornflakes and milk with Dad and arrived at the Monteith's before seven. As I came up the driveway a strange sight was going on outside the shed. A ghostly figure moved about amidst barrels, boxes, and puffs of smoke.

Coming closer, I could make out detail; the ghostly figure was a man dressed in an African safari pith helmet and from it's rim a veil of mosquito netting obscured his face. The figure moved slowly among the barrels and boxes, baggy coveralls tapered tight at the ankles with rubber bands and hands concealed within long gloves.

Mr. Monteith, the beeman, was at work. Clusters of fat yellow honey bees crawled drowsily upon his draped figure, sedated by periodic puffs of smoke from his billows. Stealthily he extracted the bees' golden treasure by rotating flat trays of comb in a barrel with an eggbeater sort of device, then slid a fresh tray into the bee box.

I watched and waited until Mr. Monteith was done, not daring to approach until he beckoned. Removing his hat and gloves, he invited me to dip my finger into the barrel of fresh honey for a taste. I sucked my finger and said, "Gosh, it's darker than any honey I've seen and sure has a rich flavour."

He seemed pleased with my remark and explained, "You see Robin, the colour and flavour of each batch is different. It depends on what blossoms the bees are feeding on. Just now it's a blend of clover from the pasture, wild foxglove, blackberry, daisy, dandelion, and some trees in the forest, particularly dogwood, cascara, and poplar, as well of course, from flowers in the garden."

Mr. Monteith didn't seem to mind answering my questions about different aspects of bee keeping, in fact, seemed amused at the working of my young mind. Placing his hand on my shoulder, he grinned and said, "Well now we've done our bee work, so let's go in for tea and breakfast before we tackle the chores." So through the garden and down the cottage path we went like the best of pals returning from a morning's hunt.

I stayed all day helping with all sorts of chores, and at afternoon tea, Mr. Monteith said, "Robin, how would you like to help us out on the farm the rest of the summer, say weekdays from nine until three? We can't pay you much, let's say a dollar a week, a dozen duck eggs, and a gallon of milk? You discuss it with your parents, and if they agree, you can start tomorrow."

Of course they did, and all summer I worked on the Monteith's farm, mostly tagging along with Olive as she tended the goats, and the hours were such that I could go swimming in the afternoon. One day I even got an extra dollar for discovering a missing swarm of bees that had settled up in a tree instead of the boxes where they belonged. But mainly I learned many different things. Do you know, for instance, that it's easier to carry two pails than one? Or that it takes strong hands to milk a goat, and with a massaging kind of rhythm or the goat won't cooperate?

I also learned about this wonderfully different, hospitable family; that the reason Mr. Monteith got up even earlier than Dad was because he was an accountant in the city, that they never ate meat because they were Buddhists, and eventually, that the reason Olive and Elspeth were so different is that they were only half-sisters, something I had never encountered before. But then I was only eight or nine at the time and had a lot to learn.

The smartest of North Lonsdale's outdoor boys was Alan West who lived up on Osborne on the way to the swimming hole. He was the informal leader of a pack that included his younger brother Leonard, Dave and Walt Blair, Bill Hilder, Larkin, Ace, and sometimes me. We went on expeditions all over the North Shore; to Lynn Canyon to slide the rapids and swim in the deep pools when things got too hum-drum at the swimming hole, fish for trout along Hastings and Mosquito creeks, or in the early Fall, to make the long trek trek to the Capilano to jig salmon as they idled in deep pools below the suspension bridge.

Alan knew a great deal about Nature, particularly fish and game, partly because his father was a commercial fisherman, but also because he was just darn smart about figuring things out, like coping with the game warden.

It was illegal to jig salmon as they moved upstream in the shallow water of the river, good for a ten dollar fine or a couple of days in jail. But times were so hard during the Depression that many North Shore families wouldn't have had any meat to eat without salmon from the river and an occasional deer.

Alan figured that just as long as the gang took only one salmon each, didn't make a hog or nuisance of ourselves on the river, that the warden would look the other way. And he was right. More than once we caught sight of him at his lookout high above the riverbed. He could easily have caught us as we climbed up one of the narrow trails along the canyon wall.

He never bothered us just as long as we kept to that silent understanding between us, but Alan knew that if we showed up on the river more than once a week or started selling salmon he would be down on us like a hawk. He knew this because items appeared in the *North Shore Press* saying "So and so sentenced to one week in jail, convicted of illegal possession of salmon taken from the Capilano."

Alan said, "He got what he deserved, made a hog of himself, was probably selling salmon door to door cutting into the commercial fisherman's livelihood. The warden was just doing his job to protect the salmon run for next year."

Sensible warden or not, jigging salmon from the Capilano wasn't all that easy. It involved several risks to life and limb plus considerable effort and skill, in short it was an adventure. I felt lucky to tag along whenever Alan and the gang set out for the river.

Provisions for the expedition were simple; a six foot bamboo pole with a large cod hook attached to its thin end with cod line, a gunny sack to carry the fish home, whatever we could put together for lunch, and six cents for carfare in case we were too tired to trudge back home. That was a good three miles, and all up hill.

Getting to the Capilano early in the morning was nothing, but once there, we had to be mighty careful descending the narrow trail along the canyon wall. It would mean certain death if you slipped and tumbled over the side. And it was essential to approach the riverbank with stealth. Any noise or quick movement, anything out of the ordinary, and our salmon quarry would slide sideways into the river's current and disappear downstream.

I made the mistake of making too much noise crossing the

rocks along the riverbank. "Dammit, they're gone!" Alan whispered, then forgiving me for being such a greenhorn, said, "That's okay. Just be quiet for awhile and they'll be back." While saying so, he crawled, jig pole in hand, out on a cedar log that protruded into the river, laid down with his legs spread out straddling the log, and slipped his pole into a dark pool. He held the pole firmly against the log and waited, eyes focused on the business end of the pole with mercilessly sharp hook lashed to its side. Waiting, his pole rested motionless in the deep pool, so motionless it could be taken for a branch from the log.

I watched Alan's every move from the bank above.

All was quiet but the sounds of nature along the river. High above the soothing tumble of the river's current, a lone herring gull skulled its way upriver between the dark canyon walls. The caw of a raven echoed up and down the canyon in the still morning air.

In the stillness, Alan's ears picked up a familiar sound, the unmistakeable SWISH-SWISH of a salmon's powerful tail propelling it upstream through the shallow rapids. Soon its sleek body would drift unsuspecting into his pool.

Alan's pole-holding arm arched upward in one powerful stroke. Simultaneously, his legs hinged forward, knees locked against the log, and as swiftly as an acrobat, he leapt to his feet and ran shoreward along the log, fish writhing desperately at the end of his bamboo pole.

"What a beauty! Not long from the saltchuck. Firm. Eight to ten pounds" Alan whispered, jumped off the log, thumped his prize on the head, and slid him into his gunny sack. Then, laughing, he turned to me and said, "As easy as falling off a log. Now its your turn. I'm going to see how the other guys are doing," and promptly disappeared downstream.

All alone, I thought, "Sure looks easy to me", crawled out on the log, and laid down just as I had seen Alan do.

Straddling the log with my legs, I gingerly slipped the pole into the pool, and surveyed its depths for any lingering fish. Seeing none, my eyes followed the length of the pole to make sure my hook was facing in the right direction. The part under the water looked crooked, going off in a different direction as soon as it entered the water. At first I thought I must be 'seeing things', lifted it slowly out, then just as slowly, returned it to the pool. The same thing happened. Alan didn't say anthing about that, and I wondered how the heck did he know just where down there his pole and hook were.

So I thought about it, and it finally dawned on me that it was a natural thing called refraction, that things look different under water because of the effect on light when it enters water. Alan was so used to this phenomenon, he'd learned to accommodate to it, and took it for granted that everybody knew a simple thing like that. Well, that was just the first of a number of simple facts of life and jigging for salmon that I would learn that day.

I waited for the tell-tale SWISH-SWISH sound of another salmon coming up the rapids and practicing in my mind what Alan told me to do once a fish glided into the pool.

"Don't be in a hurry. Just enjoy watching him for awhile. Let him come to you. He doesn't know the difference between your hook and a stick unless it moves suddenly. Then he'll move out quick. Let him get right up against the pole, so you can even feel him brush up against it. Then when he's settled down and just idling there just above the hook, pull straight up, not down and up, but straight up quick and strong, and don't let go, because when he feels that hook slicing into his flesh he's going to fight like heck to get away and head downstream, pole and all."

My fish soon came along and everything went right, "as easy as falling off a log" I remembered Alan saying. And boy, was it ever exciting lying there just watching that beautiful fish, as big as Alan's, right there where it ought to be next to my hook. Just like Alan said, he didn't seem to know the difference between it and a piece of bent stick.

But my fish wouldn't idle there forever, so I said to myself, "Now's the time," and with all my might pulled straight up, and by golly the fish was on! I could feel the weight, and terrific tugging and wiggling as he tried to wrestle the pole out of my hands.

But before I knew it, I was floundering in the river flat on my back waving my pole, fish off the hook. The upward momentum of my thrust had sent me flinging like a cartwheel off the log and into the far-side of the pool. Fortunately, on that side the pool wasn't so deep that I couldn't stand up. Shocked, I stood there in the cold water trying to figure out just exactly what had gone wrong. I was glad that at least no one was around to see me standing there so foolishly.

Clambering ashore, then back along the log for another try, I experimented with different positions that might avoid the same mistake; sitting, lying down across the log, and finally, lying down facing the other way. All felt awkward until I tried the latter.

That position felt more secure, with my strong leg on the far side of the log bracing me to prevent another cartwheel. That way I could lean on my left forearm, and with the pole in my right, hold it straight down against the side of the log. It was a good position for pulling straight up instead of the sideways movement that had propelled me into the drink.

After awhile, another fine fish drifted into the pool, I waited enjoying him just as before, then decided 'here goes', and with one swift, clean uplift, had him on the hook. He pulled, wriggled, thrashed, did everything in his power to wrestle the pole from my grasp. But I managed to hang on, and to my amazement, I was still on the log.

My heart was pounding. I shinnied my knees forward on the log, and not daring to stand up for fear of losing my balance again, I crawled, fish still firmly on my hook, back along the log to shore. I was not a graceful sight, I'm sure. But I made it. And none too soon, for just as I slipped my salmon into the gunny sack, the rest of the gang showed up, gunny sacks full, and ready for lunch and a swim.

After gutting and wrapping our fish in ferns, we stashed our fattened gunny sacks and poles under a log, and headed for our favorite pool. I was wide and deep with a rocky ledge from which we could dive. Each of us peeled off our clothes in a hurry so as not to be the last one in. "Last one in is a dumbbell" shouted

Ace, and off we went thrashing our way wildly across the pool to the diving ledge.

Almost imperceptibly, the shadows of tall fir trees closed in upon the river. It was the end of another day of adventure along the Capilano. Driven home by hunger and approaching darkness, we reluctantly put on our clothes, gathered our salmon, and headed up the trail. We decided to take the streetcar home, so we left our gaff hooks under the log. There they would remain safely hidden, waiting for our return, eager again to wrestle another salmon from the cold, clear waters of the Capilano.

晳

Despite the hard times of the 1930s, each of us boys in the family found ways to earn money for school and still have fun. It was a good thing Don was ambitious as well as brainy because North Van High was full of brainy kids, and having been pushed ahead a year when we moved to the North Shore, he had to study hard to qualify for the university. Dad was helpful in coaching him in algebra and trigonometry and in getting him summer jobs in logging camps so he wouldn't have to carry after-school jobs.

Don's first summer job away from home at age fifteen was as a cookhouse flunky at Campbell River. Each summer thereafter he advanced himself a little more, becoming successively a spark chaser, whistle punk, and finally, after taking special courses, a log scaler and first aid man.

From these jobs he learned there was more danger than money in logging, so after graduating from high school in 1937, he switched his interest to mining. That summer he spent at an Army-run outdoor placer mining school near Hope, then went on to finish first year at U. B. C. He was then only seventeen, but, eager to both learn more about mining and earn more money to complete university, he went to the goldfields of Alaska and stayed for two or three years.

Larkin was so drawn to the outdoors, he was usually up and

gone by sunrise. This suited his restless temperament, but was practical too. If not fishing for trout in a nearby creek or stalking grouse with his BB gun, it was working at an early morning job like tramping through the dew to deliver the *Vancouver News Herald* or to help Johnny Hanum with his milk route.

Johnny used to pick Larkin up at home while on his route, sometimes while it was still pretty dark, and it was on one of these mornings that an accident occurred which nearly broke Larkin's heart. They were careering down the driveway when they heard a thump up front. They stopped the truck, got out to take a look, and there was Nick, our family dog laid out on the road, stone dead. Nick was getting old, deaf, and couldn't get out of the way in time.

Larkin broke down and bawled, so Johnny parked the truck while Larkin picked Nick up, took him up to the house to show Dad, together they buried him in the back garden, and Dad promised to get another dog as soon as possible. That very evening Dad kept his word, bringing home the funniest looking spaniel we ever saw, a brown curly-haired rat-tailed water dog famous for duck hunting. We named him Buster, and he became the best retriever we ever had.

Larkin was incapable of staying indoors once the sun was up. So it was not for lack of brains or ambition that Larkin kept getting into trouble at school. Regardless of its value, school was after all, a place of confinement during daylight hours.

Neither Larkin's seventh grade teacher, Mr. Charles Ovans, nor the school system of the time had any comprehension of boys like Larkin. Educators like Mr. Ovans thought it normal that education was something found only within the dark confines of a classroom, and by inference, associated the outdoors with ignorance and sloth.

Larkin had no trouble learning while in school, in fact by the seventh grade was quite competent in reading, writing, and arithmetic, and eager to learn more, provided it went on outdoors and about things that interested him; animals, both wild and domestic, the forest, fisheries, and machinery of any kind.

This Mr. Ovans failed to understand, instead labelled him an incorrigible rebel and "dumb". "Do you want to be a ditch-digger all your life?" he'd say, revealing his contempt for any student not aspiring to become a white collar worker like himself.

Lest I be too harsh on Mr. Ovans, he reflected the culture of his time. In North Vancouver, the manual worker, however skilled and essential to society, was regarded with little respect, not at all on a par with the merchant, clerk, teacher, doctor, anyone who wore a white shirt, a tie, and worked indoors. Of course it was class prejudice at work, something teachers like Mr. Ovans were loath to admit, however damaging to a pupil's spirit.

Larkin wanted to quit school but couldn't, because the law said that at age thirteen, he was a year too young. So, when Mr. Ovans had tallied   enough inattention and minor mischief to warrant expulsion, he marched Larkin down to see the terrible Mr. Darwin, then still principal at North Star School.

As the reader will recall, Mr. Darwin was no fool, and decided more strappings would be futile with a boy like Larkin. This lad took pain like a Roman, was stubborn as an ox, plainly not stupid or lazy, just not made for indoor school. So with voice that could be heard down the hall, Principal Darwin announced through his open office door, "Larkin Williams, we have had ENOUGH! You are EXPELLED from school, FOREVER!"

Larkin understood. Darwin had a slight grin on his face, the grin just between them. Needless to say, Larkin could not have been happier than if the Principal Darwin had presented him with a spotted pony, which is exactly what he had, all his own, within a year.

Principal Darwin was a man vastly underemployed in terms of intelligence and worldly knowledge for the head of a grade school of the times. But that's another story which we shall come to later on. Larkin immediately got a job on a dairy farm in Langley through his friend Johnny Hanum. The Thompson family treated him like a son. He received free room and board, thrived on the rich food, and working like a trooper, was paid ten dollars a month, and soon had his first brand new suit of clothes.

But after a few months of milking cows twice a day he became bored, so saying farewell to the Thompson family, he got a more interesting job on a cattle ranch near Golden. There he proved so good with horses, he soon had his own, then moved to an even more interesting job at the fanciest ranch in western Canada, the famed Prince of Wales in southern Alberta.

That job proved to be highly educational in more ways than one, even being assigned to help show off the ranch's prize livestock at the Toronto Exhibition. The only drawback was the pay. Larkin had an appetite for good-looking clothes and girls. At sixteen, he was a grown man physically, close to six feet tall and strong as a moose. So, following family tradition, he came back to the coast and went to work in a logging camp.

His first job was setting chokers at Union Bay. Like Don, he learned the ropes fast, and by time he was old enough to enlist in the army at eighteen, he had worked his way up to fireman on a steam donkey.

Love of reading and athletics kept Ace in school. He read anything he could get his hands on, particularly adventure stories of the sort found in *Chums Magazine*. He was forever running, never walking if there was any possibility of moving faster, and he put this love to profitable use delivering his *Province* route in record time and caddying at the new British Properties golf course.

Saturday mornings at six Ace and Buster would take the streetcar to the end of the Capilano line and hiked up Taylor Way to the golf course. The new Properties course had replaced Shaughnessy's as the rich man's, so the tips for doing a good job of caddying were worth the long trip. And it was here that our new dog Buster proved worth his weight in silver as a retriever. All Ace had to do was pretend to heave a golf ball into the rough at a likely spot, say "Fetch!", and Buster would return time after time with lost balls, worth a dime apiece at the pro shop, sometimes more in a private sale.

↺

The *Province* newspaper shack on Windsor near Lonsdale was the year-long hangout of neighbourhood boys, located there because this was the end of the B.C. Electric carline and the trading centre for North Lonsdale. Besides the post office just up from Kings, there was Shirran's Drug Store, Willcox's Red and White grocery store, and the all-important Confectionery, source of penny candies, Pep Chews, popsicles, and ice cream bars.

Attached to the back of the Confectionery was a tiny separate shop where Mr. Watson repaired shoes while his wife kept an eye on him from their house on a hill not a hundred feet away. Mrs. Watson seemed to maintain an incessant surveillance of her husband as he worked at his trade, always looking out the kitchen window and every so often running down to the shop. As far as we could tell, Mr. Watson was a darling man. He never turned us out of the waiting room of his little shop where we newsboys kept warm waiting for the papers to arrive on cold or rainy days.

Mr. Watson seemed to enjoy our company. Perhaps we reminded him of his youth, but also, we suspect, our banter afforded him a brief reprieve from his wife's extreme religiosity. All day long from the house came an outpouring of hymns, prayers, and sermons from her radio. If it wasn't Canada's own Amy Semple McPherson holding forth life and direct from Los Angeles, it was the Full Gospel Tabernacle from downtown Vancouver, or the Pentecostal Hour of Decision bellowing forth God's word from Seattle.

One thing these radio broadcasts all had in common, aside from a thumping preacher and tremulous electric organ, was the absolute certainty that Judgement Day was coming, and the Mission needed Money, lots of it, and NOW, to save as many souls possible before the arrival of that dreadful day.

So we felt sorry for Mr. Watson. He had no bad habits that we could see; didn't tipple on the job, cuss, chew tobacco, entertain fancy ladies, even have bad breath or B.O. that we could tell. He just pounded, stitched, and glued shoe leather all day long, and put up with his wife's blaring radio.

Perhaps she feared that her husband would become contaminated from some of the games we played outside the newspaper shack, or merely that we were having so much fun. No doubt about it, there was tempting, devilish hilarity going on, gambling even. In Pitch Penny, we'd draw two lines in the dirt about ten feet apart and toss pennies from the starting line to see whose penny landed closest to the other line, the winner picking up all the pennies.

We had all sorts of games; playing darts against the shack wall, yo-yo and bat-ball contests, and others, all accompanied of course by the usual whistling, howling, loud laughter, the noises boys always make whenever they gather to have fun. There wasn't a thieving delinquent among us. But there's something about boys in groups that strikes terror into the hearts of some elders, especially those of an extreme religious bent.

☙

In the summer of 1938 someone bought the old mansion on Carisbrooke and gave Dad a month or so to find another place. Naturally the news was unwelcome, but Dad soon found another big old house in North Lonsdale at 606 Windsor Road, about the same distance to the carline, and $10 per month less to rent. Dad rented it directly from its owner, Mr. Wonder. The builder of the house, a Mr. Kerr, didn't have the means of Tom Nye, so the property had no impressive granite stonework, wood-panelled rooms with fireplaces and chandeliers, no such frills at all, just a big, square, two-storey house with an earthen floor basement and an acre of land.

But it would do, especially as it would be economical with a wood-burning hot air furnace, soil good enough for a kitchen garden, several apple trees, and a chicken house. So Mr. Kerr's house became home and remained so until all us boys completed school and went off on our own.

As plain as it was, the Kerr house had two advantages over the Carisbrooke mansion; it was much closer to the swimming hole, and not much of a walk to the Spendlove farm in Lynn Valley where I got a job that made me feel like a real man.

Mr. Spendlove cleared land for a living, a stocky, barrel-chested Dutchman who moved rocks as big as his belly as though they were soccer balls. Soon after we moved into the Windsor Road house I watched him as he walked behind his Belgian draft horse clearing a lot across the street. His horse was pulling a stone boat, and seeing how often he had to bend over to pick up sticks and roots to put on the sled, things that even I could handle, I asked him if I could help.

He grinned, stopped his horse to look me over, wiped his forehead with a red bandana, and nodded his head.

All that day I followed Mr. Spendlove and his horse filling the stone boat with wood debris and small rocks. At the end of the day he paid me a quarter, and I had a Saturday job. I figured that as I got more useful he'd pay me more, and that's what happened, first a half dollar, then a whole one, as each Saturday I proved my worth. "Robbie, you'd better put on long pants though, you're down on your knees so much" he told me, so Mother patched a pair of Larkin's old work pants. With them on hitched up with a set of bracers, I went to work for Mr. Spendlove feeling like a real man.

Saturday morning, as soon as the sun was up, I ran down the hill to the Spendlove place on Royal Avenue, knocked on the back door, and Mrs. Spendlove told me to sit down for breakfast. She was just as big around and good-natured as her husband, with rosy cheeks and short, fat hands that she often wiped on her apron.

And talk about cook! I'd never seen a breakfast like the ones she prepared for Mr. Spendlove and me. They had their own milk cow, pigs, ducks, and chickens, and it seemed as if they all contributed to those heaping bowls and plates she put on the kitchen table, even a bowl of steaming hot oatmeal among the plates of fried eggs, sausage, home-made bread, and a big enamel pitcher of fresh milk. On the stove rested a blue enamel coffee pot, and she took it for granted I was used to coffee, filling a thick mug beside my milk tumbler without even asking.

After breakfast I followed Mr. Spendlove out to the barn to hitch up the horses, two stocky brown Belgians named Dolly and Ben. We then loaded the tools we'd need for the day on a rubber-tired wagon; the stone boat, a plow, harrow like a bedspring with six inch spikes to loosen up roots, two sets of block and tackle for pulling out big stumps, several sets of rope and chain, two crowbars, saws and axes, a peevee, rock drills and three pound hammer, picks and shovels, water buckets, half a box of dynamite sticks, canvass bags of oats for Ben and Dolly, and two black lunchboxes Mrs. Spendlove put up for us.

Mr. Spendlove hitched the team up to the wagon, climbed up on a wooden seat, and I beside him, commanded "Gee", and with a slap of the reins, off we went out of the yard, Mrs. Spendlove waving and ducks and chickens scurrying every which way. Just as we entered the roadway, Mr. Spendlove's little black dog ran lickedy-split down the driveway and leapt upon the rear of the wagon, and off we went to the next clearing job.

Mr. Spendlove was very systematic in the way he went about clearing for a new homesite, first walking over the land with the owner and marking it off with stakes; the boundaries, where the driveway and house would be, and which trees and large boulders were to to be left. He then cleared the unwanted trees to one side, piling the limbs where he could use them to cover rocks and stumps when he blasted. Then out came the stumps, little ones first to get them out of the way so the horses could maneuver when he tackled the large ones.

The big ones needed uprooting and splitting with blasting powder, and sometimes he had to use block and tackle to increase the horses' pulling power.

He didn't touch any big protruding rocks he didn't have to because they were the dickens to split and get rid of. It took a lot of tedious work pounding on a hand drill to make the dynamite hole, then pile on brush to keep the rock fragments from flying everywhere when he set the charge off. That and seeing a red hot fire lick its way through a pile of stumps was the exciting part of the job.

But the most rewarding time came at the end of the day. Back at the farm, Mr. Spendlove would say, "Robbie, you've done a man's work today" and handed me my pay. Tired as I was, I ran all the way home to show mother the dollar bill I'd earned that day.

In the spring was the only time I didn't like working for Mr. Spendlove; mornings when we'd load up from Ben and Dolly's huge pile of accumulated winter droppings and deliver the steaming heaps of manure for people's gardens in his old dump truck. Silly as it was, whenever we would drive by a friend's house, particularly where there was a girl that I was sweet on, I would scrunch down in the truck's seat so that they might not see me going by with that stinky load of manure.

But times were hard, and I couldn't turn down a chance to earn another dollar no matter how embarrassing the job was.

Tom Nye mansion, 230 Carisbrooke Road, North Lonsdale

North Vancouver ferry dock, 1920's–30's.

North Star School classroom, early 1930's

L to R: Dave Lawrence, Ross Johnson, Harold Dyer, Hugh Lawrence and Harry Chisholm.

5

CLOUDS OVER PARADISE

The Depression of the 1930s cast a dark cloud of fear over every North Shore settler's little piece of Paradise. Tom Nye was only one of hundreds who lost their homes for taxes; three-quarters of the property in the City and District of North Vancouver was foreclosed for non-payment of taxes during the depressions of 1912-14 and the 1930s.

My parents no longer had a house of their own to lose. Now renters, like hundreds of other North Shore families, they could be chased from one rented place to another with little notice. "Home" was now merely a state of mind, where one's family lived at the moment, not a particular piece of property endowed with deep special meaning to its occupants.

For persons accustomed to a nomadic way of life this probably poses no problem to their sense of well-being; they may feel equally at home in several different locations. Perhaps this is the case with certain North American native peoples who migrated back and forth following the seasons and their sources of food. But such was not the case with white residents of North Vancouver. They came to settle down in one place, one little plot of ground in which they invested all their savings and hopes.

Living in one such place for any length of time becomes almost akin to an enduring marriage, a deep and dependable bonding, reassuring in its continuity, a safe refuge from the world and the vicissitudes of life. Dispossession from such a home place is thus akin to a divorce from a seemingly permanent relationship, a traumatic disruption of one's sense of well-being. Such was the wrenching experience of families by the hundreds in North Vancouver during the 1930s.

With sales of new machinery almost nil, Dad moved his office to less expensive space in the Shelly Building on Pender Street across from the Vancouver Sun tower, and took to selling used machinery from closed down camps, even their cookhouse utensils and dinnerware. Still money was tight, so he took the streetcar instead of the Studebaker to work, gave up the *Sunday Times*, and bought cheaper cigars, thin King Edwards in a pack of five instead of fat Havanas in a cedar box.

He still had his *Saturday Evening Post* and *Country Gentleman* for weekend reading, an occasional matinee at the Rex, and every Saturday afternoon he trudged up the hill and through Carisbrooke Park, walking backwards to catch the view, with the week's groceries from Woodward's, including a fat Sunday roast. In his fifties now, Dad seemed to believe that mankind and the so-called civilized world was sliding back to barbarism. Disorder and decline were everywhere; Canada, the United States, England, Europe, all over the world, there was depression, riot, or war.

None of the politicians or "isms"; Fascism, Socialism, Communism, Townsendism, Social Credit, Technocracy, all doctrines of desperation and despair, seemed to provide a satisfactory explanation. So he turned as always to the realm that did make sense, that followed laws with absolute regularity, and likewise never failed to provide pleasure and satisfaction; to Nature, to his garden.

Mother, too, accommodated to a simple country life, that of mother, holding things together until her job was done. At that, her ingenuity showed everywhere. She was not content to bake just plain white bread; by adding raisins, nuts or cheese, she gave the family a variety of the staff of life. It was the same with soups, cookies and cakes; with a little of this and a dab of that she invented all sorts of tasty delights.

On birthdays she would come up with something new; chocolate cake with date and shredded nut filling, date bars with a crust of rolled oats, apple sauce cake with raisins, nuts and caramel icing, or an all-time favourite, pineapple upside-down cake with thick slices of pineapple and cream cheese topping.

In summer there were always freshly baked apple and berry pies. One of her small pleasures was picking wild berries from the vacant land behind our house. First came the little blackberries from vines that creep along the ground; then yellow and orange salmonberries, too juicy by themselves, so she would add gelatin and apple to thicken them; then the plump black Himalayas; and following them, the red huckleberry and its cousin, the blue.

Summer or winter she wasted nothing. Fat from the roast went into gravy, or with lye added, was made into soap. She sent away for a pattern, and from that, turned flour sacks into curtains and tablecloths. But she did acquire one bad habit, cigarettes. Even there, with Zig Zag paper and a little rolling machine, she made one pack of Players long cut last a week. To pay for that little sin, she took in roomers, Bill and Francis Just. Bill was a well-educated Englishman in his early forties, a teacher at Kingsley, the nearby private boys' school. And Francis, well, they weren't married, but still, they were very nice, so "it's nobody's business but their own" was Mother's attitude.

The winter of 1937 was particularly severe, day after day of freezing cold, more than the water pipes in the old mansion could stand. Joints froze, ruptured, and sprang so many leaks that Dad had to call a plumber. Mr. Legros, a short, stocky man in coveralls, rolled out of his truck and with a loud knock at the kitchen door, unceremoniously entered, glanced at Mother's careworn face, demurred at her offer of a cup of tea, and surveyed the rooms with leaking pipes. Following several hours and frequent trips back and forth to his truck, he presented Mother with the bill, $100, saying he expected payment the next day, or he would have to take legal action.

"I have bills to pay, too. I'll come after dinner tomorrow to see Mr. Williams" he said, then left through the kitchen door as unceremoniously as he had entered.

Mother broke out into a cold sweat as she looked again at the bill. She set it on the kitchen table, reached nervously for the teapot at the edge of the kitchen range, filled her cup, and sat down. Despite the kitchen's warmth, her whole body felt cold. Hands trembling, her tea spilled into the saucer. She put it down.

Of course Mr. Legros had every right to present his bill and insist on prompt payment. He had done his work. She was grateful he had stopped the leaks. But they simply did not have the money to pay him, could barely scrape together the $25 to pay the rent each month. And she knew from her business experience that Mr. Legros was also right about taking legal action. He could file a mechanic's lien and demand an auction of their personal property within ten days of their failing to pay his bill, jewelry, furniture, everything could be sold to pay his bill.

It was a devastating blow. She didn't know what to do. She would have to tell Asa as soon as he came home. But what good would that do? He had let her down so often in business matters. He would just put it off until it was too late, as he always did.

She got up, walked into the living room and looked briefly at each piece of furniture in the room; the oval dining room table, chairs, radio, buffet. She opened the drawers and inspected the silverware, did the same with the china closet, inspecting the chinaware and vases. She did so quietly, mechanically, as though a ghost anesthetized to the fond feeling normally aroused by each object, counting, but with no precise numbers summing in her head. So little was left from her Shaughnessy home, barely enough to call a house a home. The plumber could take every bit of it, even her silver, and could even take the beds and linen to pay that $100 debt.

The thought struck her of how many times before she was married she had reached into her purse and brought out a crisp, new hundred-dollar bill to pay a hotel bill or her fare on the C.P.R. on holidays from Calgary and had thought nothing of it.

In those days she had plenty in the bank, not to worry. Now she had no bank account, and looking in her purse, counted $11.31, all the money she had to run the house for a week or so.

The strange reality of her present situation jarred loose her latent sense of humour, and she even mustered a smile. Slowly the coldness left her body. She returned to the kitchen table and lukewarm cup of tea.

She thought of relatives who might help. There was sister Maysie in Edmonton, who had always provided for Christmas. No, that would be asking too much, the shame of it to admit that Asa was in such desperate straights, especially as Maysie had not approved of the marriage in the first place. Then, sister Flora, nursing at Vancouver General, but no, Flora could barely survive on her low wages. It was the same with cousin Edna, divorced and raising two teenagers in a rented flat near King Edward High School on a salary of $12 a week as a bookkeeper at Mac and Mac, the city's largest wholesale hardware dealer. No, friends and relatives were out of the question. All had troubles of their own.

She warmed her tea, sat down again and came to a decision. Tears welled up in her eyes. Trembling, she removed a diamond ring from her left hand, her Tiffany engagement ring. She set it next to the saucer on the cold table top, then quickly retrieving it with her right hand, held it up to the winter light of the kitchen window. She rotated it slowly back and forth, noting the rainbow shafts of colour it cast upon the table's plain white surface. For a minute or two she relaxed in reverie.

Strangely, she thought first of her mother in her dying days, frail and wordless, then of Asa's mother Clara and of the deep love they had shared, and only then of Asa, so handsome and charming as he asked her to marry him, and later, of the deep joy she felt when he slipped this sparkling ring on her finger.

She dwelt fleetingly on her wedding day, the delicious intimacy of celebrating with a few close friends and relatives, then the minister's words, "Do you take this woman, Eliza Bell Larkin, to be your wedded wife, to cherish and protect, to have and to hold, in sickness and in health, in joy and in sorrow, until death do you part?" She remembered Asa's "I do," but more vividly, a feeling of transformation, new to her, as she looked up into his soft brown eyes and repeated the same simple words, "I do."

Two simple words, but with them alone, a God-fearing woman of the comfortable middle class abdicated her fate under God and law, forever. Christian doctrine and the laws of the land vested the male with all the power.

Her tea grew cold. The rays of the morning sun broke through the frosted window. It was getting late. She had business to do. Taking a square of orange tissue paper marked Sunkist, she wrapped the ring and tucked it inside the zippered pocket of her best dress purse. It was a luxurious purse, of brown crocodile leather. Dressing to match, she boarded the streetcar for the city. She knew exactly where she was going, to Birk's jewelers, corner of Granville and Georgia, the city's best.

She knew the store well, swept through the revolving door, passed by rows of display cases, went straight to the repair counter and asked for Mr. Firbank, buyer of estate jewelry. Mr. Firbank appeared promptly, as dapper and courteous as a Church of England usher, and recognized her instantly. "It's so good to see you, again, Miss Larkin," then corrected himself, "Oh, I mean, Mrs. Williams, of course."

Getting a grip on herself, Bell looked to see no one else was around, reached into her purse, unwrapped the ring, and placing it on the counter, said, "It's a very good diamond, as you can see, from Tiffany's in New York, but something has happened, and I must sell it. What would you give me for it?"

Mr. Firbank straightened up, looking a bit shocked. He was a gentleman, with years of experience dealing with the ups and downs of the rich, but he had the same warm feeling toward Bell as almost anyone who encountered her. With discerning compassion for her obvious distress, he looked Bell straight in the eye and said gently, "Mrs. Williams, I am so sorry. I'll see what I can do."

He placed the ring on a black felt tray, retreated to the examining room and reappearing within minutes, leaned over the counter to speak in confidence to Bell. "There is no doubt about it, Mrs. Williams. It is a very fine stone, one and one-half carats, and set perfectly, as one would expect of Tiffany. But I'm afraid we can't pay what it's worth. Nobody's buying today. I don't know when things will get better."

Bell listened intently, torn with desperation and embarrassment.

Mr. Firbank paused momentarily, then resumed in a quiet voice. "However, I do have a suggestion. Suppose you just left it for cleaning and minor repair. The stone is just a little lose in the setting. We'll see it's done right. In the meantime, I'll see if I can find the right buyer, someone who would really appreciate this ring's quality. I'm sure I can. But let's say I won't let it go for a year from today. In the meantime, let's just say Birk's will give you a security deposit. How much would you say would be sufficient? And may I ask that you keep the arrangement between us? I will give you a receipt, of course."

Bell knew she could trust Mr. Firbank and was immensely relieved. With some embarrassment, she replied, "Would it be too much to ask for $500?"

The jeweler paused a moment, then looking at this obviously careworn woman whom he remembered as one of the most beautiful and genuine he had ever met, replied, "Well, if that's what it takes, we'll just do it."

With that, he carried the ring away and reappeared shortly with a cheque and receipt for the exact amount. He then reached across the counter, clasped his hands around Bell's right hand, and said gently, "Now, Mrs. Williams, don't forget. Your ring will be in safekeeping for one year. It will be all cleaned and repaired. There will be a small service charge, of course. I do hope things work out for you."

Bell could not help herself. Tears came to her eyes. Reaching into her purse, she dabbed her eyes with a small handkerchief, took a deep breath, paused until she got a grip on herself, then replied, "Mr. Firbank, I shall never forget your kindness." She lifted her head, straightened her shoulders, snapped her purse, and mustering the bravest smile she could, passed by the counters, through the revolving door and out onto Granville Street.

Mission accomplished, she felt unaccountably tired, so wrung out she thought she had better rest awhile. The answer came with one glance down Granville, to the sign opposite the Bay, Purdy's Chocolates. Within two minutes she walked through the door of this elegant shop. Sparkling showcases displayed row upon row of chocolates, showcase tops shone with beautiful ribboned boxes, and well-dressed ladies moved about enveloped in the aromas of peppermint and expensive perfume.

She was greeted by a very attractive saleslady dressed in a black and white starched uniform. It was her cousin Elsie, partly raised by Bell as a girl when her parents were having some troubles. Bell was like her second mother, and arms interlocked, together they climbed to the upstairs tearoom. Once seated, Bell waited until Elsie returned downstairs before removing her dress gloves. Sooner or later Elsie would notice that her ring was gone, but now was not the time. Elsie, too, had not made the best marriage, to one of Vancouver's best-looking men, bright, fun-loving, and from one of the province's oldest, most prominent families, the McBrides.

Len McBride turned out to be an unambitious playboy who could not keep a dollar in his pocket, so Elsie had to go to work in a chocolate shop. Elsie would understand the problem with Asa, but Bell had been raised not to advertise one's problems. When the time and place were right, she thought, she would tell Elsie the whole, sorry tale. Right now, though, she needed a hearty lunch, and that's what she had; sandwiches and a hot cup of tea. Then she put on her gloves and went home, that is, after cashing the cheque at the Bank of Commerce and pinning the ten fifty-dollar bills firmly inside her purse.

When Asa came home, she told him about the plumber's visit, showed him the bill, told him matter-of-factly that she had got a loan on her ring at Birks to pay it, and handed him the two fifty dollar bills to pay Mr. Legrosse. He responded, "Too bad, but you did the right thing." And that was that. She deliberately avoided mentioning the remainder of the $500, which she hid in a secret compartment at the back of her father's writing desk; her "rainy day" fund for future emergencies. Then she turned to preparing dinner.

The following summer, 1938, someone with more money wanted the old mansion on Carisbrooke, and we had to move.

Dad somehow found another big, old house at 606 Windsor Road, probably paying $10 or $15 a month rent. It was a much simpler house, a square, three-story box with an earthen basement and wood-burning, warm air furnace. Its advantages were an acre or more of ground, an orchard and chicken coop, and it was several blocks closer to our swimming hole. This drafty old house remained the family home throughout the war.

⚲

Many families with kids in school were worse off than mine. Ed Carr, his parents and two older sisters got by on his father's war pension of $56 a month, reduced to $36 when the father left the home, and the pension was taken away entirely upon his father's death. Apparently that was government policy in the 1930s; no surviving war veteran, no money for his widow or his children.

War veteran Carr's son was 14 and in grade eight at Keith Lynn School. Suddenly, he had to leave school and become the "man of the family". He got a job in Vancouver delivering telegrams for the C.P.R. on his bicycle, bringing home about $40 a month, enough to sustain the family, with the help of a vegetable garden that Ed cultivated in a neighbouring vacant lot. Within a year he got a job at the North Vancouver Ship Repairs as a fitter's helper, earning $80 a month, and by the time he was 18, he had saved enough to help his mother buy her own house. Then Ed left home for the merchant marine, did so well that he was sent for officer training, and despite his limited public schooling, was soon an officer aboard ship.

Many fathers had to leave their families in North Van for a job somewhere else. One boy's father, a baker by trade, had to go to a logging camp up coast, and to make ends meet for his mother, a sister and himself, the boy took two paper routes and delivered groceries on Saturdays. Needless to say, with a furnace and kitchen stove that consumed many cords of wood a year, he had no time for sports.

In homes fortunate enough to have a father with a full-time job, his hours of work were often so long he had little time at home. The common work week was six days, 10 hours a day. Throughout the Depression Pete Moffat's dad had a job all right, but as a night watchman in Vancouver's business district, he worked seven days a week, 10 hours a night. With the coming of World War II, Pete's dad could finally return to his blacksmith trade in a North Shore shipyard at decent hours and pay.

Gerry Green's father was in a similar situation, working the night shift as a B.C. Electric carman in Vancouver, and many a foggy winter night Gerry's mother waited anxiously for her husband to trudge up the hill from the late-night ferry because the North Van streetcars didn't run that late.

In those pre-war years, there was no unemployment insurance or sick leave, to say nothing of days off for vacation, and with jobs scarce, men didn't dare miss a day's work.

For women who had to work outside the home, conditions were even tougher. There was a general prejudice against a woman occupying a job that a man might do, regardless of the fact that she might be the sole support for a family. If a teacher, she was automatically paid less for equal qualifications, as much as 20 or 30 percent less. Such was the case with women clerks and highly trained bookkeepers, typically paid $10 to $12 a week. There was no legally established minimum wage. Whenever a position was listed in a Help Wanted ad in the *Province* or *Sun*, women would line up for blocks, competing for one opening.

Taking advantage of this situation, Vancouver's largest wholesale grocer used such applicants to get clerical work done for nothing under the pretext of "testing" them until what the company was doing became so flagrant that the law stepped in.

It wasn't only "plain folks" like shipyard workers, longshoremen and mechanics who lost their homes, but also engineers, accountants, teachers and even bankers. Such a family was that of Ailsie Falkner, daughter of the assistant manager of the local branch of The Bank of Commerce, graduate of Cambridge, decorated officer of World War I, and a highly respected member of the community. When Ailsie was just a girl of seven her father died, leaving her mother with two children to raise on a modest bank pension. It was not enough to keep their family home, and the Falkner family joined the ranks of renters, temporarily occupying some stranger's house.

From a social standpoint, North Van was also probably a less disturbing place to endure the Depression than the congested city of Vancouver. The entire population of North Vancouver in 1931, City and District combined, was only 14,000, a fraction of Vancouver's, and it was spread out from the First Narrows to Deep Cove, a huge expanse of mostly unoccupied land. Dwellings and people, then, were hardly ever crowded up against each other. Almost all housing was made up of single-family dwellings with front and back gardens, even in the most populated neighbourhoods within easy walking distance of the Lonsdale streetcar line.

Moreover, the residents of North Van were widely dispersed and intermingled in terms of income levels. There were no exclusive enclaves of the wealthy, such as Vancouver's Shaughnessy Heights, or strictly working class neighbourhoods with no mingling between people of differing economic circumstances or educational and cultural backgrounds. Certain geographical areas, usually on the higher slopes of ground such as Templeton Heights, North Lonsdale, and bordering the Grand Boulevard, tended to be occupied by the more affluent, but not exclusively. There was no clearly visible line of demarcation between these areas and the surrounding territory.

In short, there were no visible "rich" versus "slum" neighbourhoods. Instead, there was a diverse mix, so that class distinctions were not much in evidence, and kids could make friends with anyone they chose.

Small neighbourhood markets survived by knowing their customers, offering home delivery, and extending credit. They also had no competition from chain stores like Safeway, which was not present in North Van until after World War II. They did, however, get a lot of competition from the block-square Woodward's Department Store on Hastings Street in Vancouver. Woodward's could back up its motto, "The Best For Less", because of its huge volume, and for many a North Van family, a Saturday trip to shop at Woodward's was a special event. Still, many families would not have had a Christmas turkey or anything else special for that important holiday if it were not for relatives with a store or farm, or hampers sent around by the Salvation Army.

So few homeowners could pay their taxes that by 1933 both City and District were unable to pay their bonded debt, and thus, under law, were forced into receivership under the sole authority of a person appointed by the Provincial government to administer their affairs. Commissioner Charles E. Tisdall, a former Mayor of Vancouver, took immediate, stern measures to cut public services to the bone.

Public school courses were reduced, teachers were laid off, and those who were retained took drastic pay cuts. A woman primary school teacher with twenty years' experience received $1360 per year in 1931, but was cut to only $1030 by 1933. Not until ten years later, when World War II was well under way, did she get back to where she was in 1931.

If she was a married woman she took double punishment; first for being female, second for being married. The theory behind the two pay scales was that men were "heads of families" and that a married woman was not the main breadwinner, both wrong assumptions in many cases.

Naturally this led to considerable frustration or duplicity among women. If she was single, a woman was paid substantially less than a single male teacher, and if she married she risked losing her job altogether. A few brave souls took the risk of getting married secretly. One can only imagine the tortured feelings these women must have endured in having to keep secret the supposedly sacred institution of the Christian marriage.

Men teachers fared considerably better, although they also took whopping pay cuts. Charles McIntyre, honors graduate of U.B.C. and with two years' experience, started teaching at North Van High in 1931 for $2100; in 1933 his salary was cut to $1700.

In addition, teachers often did not get paid at all, sometimes for two or three months, so anyone who was determined to be a teacher would do well to be on friendly terms with a banker. Miss Mollie Nye, a grade school teacher for many years, tells of the start of the school year in 1935, with no money, no paycheck, nothing for carfare to get from her home in Lynn Valley to the primary school where she taught. Fortunately, the manager of the Bank of Montreal was an understanding man, and like everybody in the community, knew the pioneer Nye family. "Oh, Mollie," he said, "for Heaven's sake, pay me back when you can," as he reached into his pocket and produced a ten dollar bill, all she wanted to borrow for a three months' pass on the streetcar to her teaching job.

Not until World War II put people back to work and they could pay their taxes did teachers get a raise, and not for fifteen years, in 1958, did the B.C. Teachers Federation succeed in getting equal pay for women, married or single.

As for the general population of the City and District of North Vancouver, about one-third were on relief, receiving the grand sum of $5 a week and $1 or $2 extra for each dependent up to the maximum of $12 per week per family. As one North Van grocer put it, "Folks on relief never bought toilet paper; they didn't have use for it on what they got to eat!"

For those who had a job, a little money went a long way. They could ride the streetcar from Capilano, Lynn Valley or North Lonsdale for 6 cents, take in a movie at the Lonsdale Theatre on Fifteenth for 15 cents, treat themselves to a hamburger and milkshake at Johnny's Inn or the Tomahawk Barbeque for 25 cents, or ride the ferry to the city and back for a dime. If they were really flush, they could go dancing on Saturday night to a live band at the Swedish Hall or Dundarave for all of 50 cents.

Families with children looked forward all year long to the summer church picnic at Eagle Harbour, Horseshoe Bay, or Deep Cove. All would pile into a wood truck, for there were no school buses then, and off they would go for an afternoon of swimming, races, ice cream and soda pop.

☙

One reason people liked living on the North Shore was because it was a place apart, the trip across the inlet induced a feeling of safe removal from the tumult of the city and world beyond.

The feeling was a comforting illusion, for no short stretch of land and sea was ever more dependent on forces and decisions made somewhere else. The North Shore's lumber mills, shipyards, real estate, all thrived or went bust according to the ebb and flow of world commerce or war. The North Shore's first industry, Moody's mill, built in 1865, thrived because it shipped lumber to Australia, Europe, all over the world. The same dependency on foreign trade was true of the shipyards, which flourished on orders for naval vessels during the first World War, and the residential development of North Vancouver in the early 1900s was largely due to English investors.

And so it was again in the 1930s. With war clouds gathering in Europe, Guinness Stout money scurried to move funds out of England, and in 1931 acquired 4,000 acres of view land on the slopes above West Vancouver for a pittance and a promise or two. The promise was to spend $400,000 on roads and improvements, employ West Van's unemployed for 40+ an hour, and build a bridge across the First Narrows to link the British Pacific Properties, Vancouver's new Shaughnessy, to the city. This they did. By Armistice Day of 1938, the Lion's Gate Bridge, with a suspension span of 1550 feet and 200 foot clearance for ships, was completed at a cost of less than $6,000,000 and dedicated by King George VI and Queen Elizabeth in May, 1939.

West Vancouver was so grateful that it gave the Properties another bonus; no taxes on improvements, and only $175,000 on six square miles of prime building land. With the right to collect tolls for the use of the bridge, Guinness recouped its investment many times over within a few years after the end of World War II.

By 1932 about one-third of North Vancouver's 14,000 residents were on relief, but in Vancouver things were even worse. Not only did the city have about the same percentage of established residents on relief, amounting to 34,000 people, but hundreds of unemployed single men roamed the streets, not just laid-off loggers and mill workers from B.C.'s defunct forest industry, but people who poured in by freight train from all over Canada. Cardboard and scrap lumber shantytowns sprang up along the shores of False Creek and Burrard Inlet. Federal, provincial and city government argued interminably about whose responsibility they were, and, if they were to be helped, in what form and how much.

Married men with families and single men alike, all wanted meaningful work and sufficient wages at least to put a roof over their heads and food enough to survive until better times. They needed public works, if necessary, on roads, schools, forests and parks. But the Conservative government of R. B. Bennett did not agree with this. They preferred the simple dole, which reflected a lack of respect for the dignity of the unemployed and was in contradiction with conservative creed that any grown, able-bodied man must work for what he receives.

So there was trouble. In March of 1932, 15,000 of the unemployed marched through the streets of downtown Vancouver, demanding work and wages instead of the hated dole. City and municipal government, being closer to the people, understood this fundamental need to work for what one receives, and contrived all sorts of work projects in spite of the prevailing federal policy. For the single men, the federal government set up quasi-military camps far removed from the city and paid them 20 cents a day to stay. That did not solve the fundamental problem, meaningful work at decent pay, so men drifted back to the city.

There were more demonstrations, parades, illegal begging on the streets, 'tin canning', it was called. To draw attention, some broke into downtown department stores; Woodwards', Spencer's, and the Hudson Bay. In short, there was increasing turmoil and attacks on property until, in 1935 there appeared the commanding personality of Gerald Gratton "Gerry" McGeer, newly elected as mayor.

A lawyer, largely self-educated, a spell-binding orator and natural politician, Gerry won election by an overwhelming vote. Although he did not solve the problem of unemployment and dispossession of citizens from their homes, he brought order, civility, excitement, and pride back to the life of the city. McGeer was imaginative, vain, bombastic, and not above duplicity if it served his ends. He grabbed the spotlight of publicity and turned the public's attention from the misery of the situation to what could be done in spite of the odds.

He was a great showman, and as a symbol of hope, he built an illuminated fountain, rainbow coloured at night, in the middle of Lost Lagoon at the entrance to Stanley Park. He then organized a gigantic parade celebrating the Silver Jubilee of King George V and Queen Mary, a parade of marching bands and fireworks that wound for hours through the city and down Georgia Street to more gala events at Brockton Point.

Next he built a new city hall on the most prominent piece of high ground he could find, a hill overlooking the city to the mountains of the North Shore. Day after day, with boisterous energy, charm, guile and wit, he battled, bullied and boasted for his city, Vancouver, to him the greatest city on earth.

But first he had to bring order, and although he agreed publicly with the unemployeds' basic position of work instead of the dole, he would not tolerate conspicuous illegal begging, looting, occupation of buildings, or mass marches through city streets. Such things scared the daylights out of downtown businesses and authorities in Victoria, who looked across the water at Vancouver and thought they saw a Red revolution in the making.

Despite Gerry's popular rhetoric, he was solidly a member of the propertied establishment, having married one of David Spencer's daughters, thus enjoying the advantage of a "no charge" account for many of his needs at a Spencer store. So, on April 23, 1935, the new Mayor McGeer read the Riot Act to hunger strikers assembled at Victory Square: imprisonment for life if they failed to disperse within thirty minutes. It worked, they dispersed, the problem still unsolved. Thenceforth, however, the unemployed directed their protest away from marches and demonstrations in downtown Vancouver toward Ottawa, and into the arena of political education, organization, debate, and hopefully, a change of government to one that had some remedy for seemingly endless suffering and turmoil.

⚛

The Depression persisted, not for lack of the materials of wealth; fertile land, timber, fish, livestock, gold reserves, skilled workers eager to be employed, but for lack of leadership. Those with power, private and public, lacked the knowledge, and in some cases, the will, to exercise their power by taking remedial action, however experimental.

The study of economics was in its infancy. The prevailing doctrine of those in positions of power in Canada, the United States, Britain, most of the western world, was that of Adam Smith, who, in his monumental work, *The Wealth of Nations*, written in 1776, propounded the philosophy that "the hidden hand of private gain", if left alone by government, would, by private initiative and investment of capital, assure high productivity and the wide distribution of wealth. For a hundred years and more this approach to wealth, government, and human well-being shaped Canada, the United States, Great Britain, and, indeed, much of the world. It seemed well suited to the rapid discovery and exploitation of the world's natural resources.

Then came the 1930s, when year after year things did not work as they had before. Productive facilities far exceeded the populations' ability to purchase goods and services. Wall Street, banks, the whole financial structure was in disarray. The result was massive unemployment, dispossession of farms and homes, and the ridiculous spectacle of farmers dumping their milk, vegetables and meat while thousands went hungry in the cities.

In Canada, as in Britain, the main political party of the Adam Smith doctrine called itself "Conservative", a name appealing to most people's desire for stability and continuity. When translated into economic policy, it meant rigid resistance to any use of government to restrict or control private ownership of property and wealth.

By the middle of the 1930s it was becoming clear to most people that this theory of unbridled private ownership and management of virtually all economic resources was not trickling down to the majority of Canadians, and, just as upsetting, that many well-off Conservatives didn't seem to care.

A striking exception was their leader, the brilliant lawyer and orator from Alberta, R. B. Bennett, who saw a chance for the Conservatives to retain power if they adopted a platform borrowing some ideas from the American politics of Franklin D. Roosevelt's New Deal. In the United States, with an overwhelming electoral mandate, Roosevelt took bold measures designed to reduce farm debt, regulate banks and business, establish unemployment insurance, minimum wages, protect workers' rights to form unions, and other measures to make the private enterprise system function more effectively.

Too many of Canada's Conservatives these remedies were seen as too radical, and Bennett's program split their ranks, so in the election of 1935

Canadians turned again to the Liberals and William Lyon Mackenzie King, who had served as prime minister from 1921 until 1930. He was neither radical in political outlook nor a dramatic personality, but he was an extremely knowledgeable and astute politician.

Throughout King's many years of experience in government and private industry, he acquired an extraordinary grasp of the practical workings of both realms. Remaining a bachelor, he devoted himself entirely and doggedly to keeping Canada from splitting apart, with its various internal conflicts of race, region, religion and economic interests, while getting the best deal possible for Canada in dealing with Britain and the United States.

King had a keen understanding of Canada's dependance on these two powerful nations' influence over Canada's future; for investment, markets and military protection. His strategy was to watch and wait, court the powerful, be obsequious if necessary, and gain maximum room for movement. Then, when the timing was right, he would seize as much tactical advantage as possible to enhance Canada's economic and political position as a geographically vast but relatively new, sparsely populated, and economically undeveloped country.

Once elected again as prime minister in 1935, King set aside Bennett's version of the New Deal as too divisive of Canada's business leadership and too threatening to foreign investors. He carefully cultivated those in power in the United States and Britain, invited F.D.R. to Canada in 1937, and visited him in Washington. He was equally solicitous of the Crown and British establishment. Quite naturally, many Canadians, in dire circumstances year after year, were not content with King's seeming complacency and inaction, regardless of the fact that Canada was a minor world power. Some concluded that Adam Smith's doctrine, which glorified private ownership and gave it control of virtually everything, while reserving an almost negligible role for government, resulted too often in ignoring the interest of the vast majority of the population.

For some, the frame of reference for their set of values was Christianity; for others it was simple humanistic concern for their fellow man; while for others it was some variety of socialism.

What they all had in common was a belief that moral values, not the property rights of a privileged few, must be the dominant force in any civilized society, and hence, that it was the responsibility of representative government to control economic affairs accordingly. Their objective was the well-being of the whole community; useful employment for all with adequate reward, affordable housing, education and health care accessible to all, and special protection for children and the elderly, in short, a more secure and abundant life, with no sacrifice of civil rights and representative government.

Among these Christian or social democrats there was much discussion of just how the government was to bring about such a society. Some thought government control of the financial system would suffice; others, that this must be extended to natural resources, utilities and essential public transportation. Still others thought that outright public ownership of all means of production, including factories and banks, was necessary to achieve their goal of a more humane society.

Whatever their individual point of view about the kind and degree of intervention required, this broad range of reformers all agreed that whatever changes were necessary must be accomplished by lawful, orderly means. Although their change-resistant opponents tried to paint them otherwise, they declared themselves clearly to be believers in evolutionary, democratic government, fundamentally opposed to violent revolution or an authoritarian state.

The Depression of the 1930s probably hurt most the four western provinces, and it was they who took the lead toward economic reform. First they developed cooperatives to market their wheat, the United Farmers Organization. Later, they combined with a large segment of organized labour to form the Canadian Commonwealth Federation. Many of the Federation's early leaders were ministers of the Christian faith, who saw that their parishioners would certainly not be able to practice Christian morality in an economic system that seemed indifferent to human need and suffering. Such was the case for the organization's national parliamentary leader, J.S. Woodsworth, a Methodist minister turned reformer and an M.P. from Winnipeg.

The C.C.F., as the Canadian Commonwealth Federation was

called, was Canada's version of Britain's Labour Party, believing in the British parliamentary system and in gradual, peaceful progress toward socialism. It turned its back on communism, and the tiny Communist Party made only minor and temporary gains in Canada during the Depression. At the political extremes of right and left of the C.C.F., there were those who believed that the end justifies the means and who preached revolutionary violence and an authoritarian state. The few, but vocal, Fascists and Communists shared this belief, but otherwise their values and objectives were miles apart.

Fascism, as in Mussolini's Italy, and Nazism, as in Hitler's Germany, both came to power in the 1930s as a result of the same economic breakdown that wreaked havoc in much of the world. Both Fascism and Nazism posed as a brand of socialism, but in truth, both were exactly the opposite. They were alliances of the largest landowners and businesses with the authoritarian military to defeat democratic or socialist regimes. Moreover, they were dangerous even to English-speaking conservatives because they fully intended to conquer the world and parcel it out to their favourites, members of the fictitious Aryan race and authoritarian allies in other countries, including Spain, Portugal, and Japan.

Communism's goal, on the other hand, was to bring about an ideal, classless world, where there was complete equality of races, colours, sexes, and where all property was held in common. It was to be a blissful, unselfish Heaven-on-Earth governed by the creed "From each according to his ability, to each according to his need". The trouble with this Promised Land lay in how to get there. The Gospel according to St. Marx declared that revolutionary violence and a "dictatorship of the proletariat" were necessary transitory measures to achieve complete abolition of both private property and the political state, seen as a mere tool of the capitalist class and unnecessary in a classless society.

The faithful in the Communist Party regarded Karl Marx's *Das Kapital* as an unerring scientific interpretation of economic history, and the Communist Party, according to their *Manifesto* of 1848, was the only legitimate leader of the "working class". To these few but fearless zealots of Paradise on Earth, the Christian and social democrats who rallied around the C.C.F. were self-deluding reformers, destined to fail because the "ruling class" in Canada or anywhere would never yield control over the country's wealth to a government it did not control, even if it were elected by an overwhelming popular vote.

This proved to be true in Germany, Italy, Spain, and a few other countries, but not so in Canada, the United States, Britain, Scandinavia, the Netherlands, Belgium, France, in short, in countries with deep traditions of representative government and civil rights. Thus, as desperate as the Canadian people were for a remedy to their ills, only a small minority succumbed in desperation to either the Fascist or Communist view.

Residents of the North Shore were as diverse in political views as other Canadians in groping for answers during the 1930s. They ranged from traditional Conservatives or Liberals, to C.C.F., Townsendites, Technocrats, even Communists.

One to whom Communism appealed was my brilliant, fearless and beloved principal of North Star School, a sign of how desperate people were at the time. Even a decorated war hero of such ability and family name as Charles Darwin was risking his job to express such views. He did so openly and actively, not on his job, of course, but he made no bones about where he stood after school hours.

How could this be? I wondered until I was in high school and got to know Mr. Darwin better. Then I began to understand why he held such extreme views. His background set him apart from ordinary people. He was, after all, a descendant of the English scientific genius after whom he was named, but also a battle-scarred soldier, used to danger and trained to take bold action against whomever he saw as the enemy in war or peace. He had become disillusioned with the Christian frame of reference by his experiences in World War I, when so-called Christian nations fought each other to a standstill, then joined forces to turn on a worker revolt in Russia which had overthrown an extremely backward and despotic royalty, who also claimed to be Christian.

Darwin had adopted a creed that seemed to make sense of the situation. Karl Marx saw the common enemy as the capitalist class in all countries, those few who controlled the economies and governments in every country, who resisted any attempt to restribute their wealth and power with military repression at home and wars among themselves for resources and markets regardless of their supposed common Christian faith. The problem was the "capitalist system", according to *Das Kapital,* Marx's ponderous analysis of the evolutionary relationship between economic and political forces affecting human societies.

Marx's attempt to explain the human social organization was an obvious counterpart theory to Darwin's *The Origin of the Species and Descent of Man,* explaining human evolution in the natural world. Both Darwin and Marx developed their theories after years of travel, observation, research and reflection, the original Charles Darwin in world-wide study of plant and animal life, Marx after years of study in Germany and London's British Museum. Both men developed sweeping analyses of history that would have revolutionary impact on western civilization.

According to Marx's 1848 political statement, *The Communist Manifesto,* reform movements like the C.C.F. were mere "stretcher bearers" for a capitalist system on its deathbed, whereas Communist parties in all countries were supposed to be the only political force capable of introducing a whole new stage in human history, the classless society. But this would require a new kind of warfare, a war of class against class, supposedly inevitable, for humankind to evolve to the next level of social organization.

Principal Darwin was a decent, kind, civilized man, but also a fearless, seasoned soldier, willing to sacrifice all for what he believed in. He believed that Marx was right, and as far as he was concerned, he was just doing his duty working for the Communist Party, just as he had done for King and Country during World War I.

History has proven since that Marx was wrong. Revolutions of the exploited masses were supposed to occur in the most advanced capitalist countries like Marx's Germany. Instead, the Nazis took over, capitalism survived, harnessed to a pathological, anti-Christian form of racism, and in backward Russia the Communist Party took over, only to perpetuate despotism in the name of the working class.

The citizens of the North Shore learned for themselves that popularly elected government ceased to exist if it failed to pay its debts. This happened when City and District affairs were taken over by a Commissioner approved by its bondholders in 1931. But that did not stop intense debate about the fundamental economic, political, and social issues facing them, their country, and the world. Arguments, theories and remedies were bandied about in families, among friends, neighbours, occupation groups, church members, and to some extent filtered into the public schools.

There was no doubt where the school system administration stood; squarely on the side of the established order and Commissioner Tisdall, their new employer. His job was to serve the bondholders, and to them the enemy was socialism in any form. It threatened to meddle with the rules governing investment capital and the banking system.

Thus, each year the grade-school pupils of North Vancouver were encouraged to write an essay or story about the perils of Bolshevism, the idea being to link any thought of fundamental change in the established order with violence and anarchy, thus stultifying any attempts at reform. The best story was selected from each school, and the pupil rewarded with a $5 prize from the Canadian Legion.

So I, eager for approval as much as for the money, conjured up a tale about an Alexandrof family escaping from Bolshevist Russia by way of Alaska to the blessed freedom of Canada, and I won the prize. Of course, I was completely oblivious at the time of how even grade-school children were manipulated for adult propaganda purposes during the Depression.

ᛞᛟ

Not long thereafter my youthful idealism put me at odds with the established order. The occasion was the constitutional crisis posed by Edward VIII, the handsome, adored Prince of Wales, who threatened to give up his throne to marry the American divorcee, Mrs. Simpson. The scandal shook the British Empire. A photograph of Edward VIII in full military uniform stood at the place of honour of every classroom in Canada's public schools, including my North Star Elementary.

The year was 1936, and the news was full of stories about the spreading menace of Nazi Germany under Adolf Hitler to everything Britain stood for; individual rights, representative government, Christian civilization itself. Yet we had a King who thought so little of his position and duty to his subjects that he would desert his post in time of increasing danger, merely to marry a divorced woman that took his fancy, not even a British one at that. How could I, or any Canadian schoolboy, respect a King like that? So I started a campaign among my classmates to take a vote on removing Edward VIII's portrait from the front of the classroom.

When my teacher, Charles Ovans, heard about it, he decided I was getting too big for my breeches and that an example had to be made. He knew my father was American, and probably suspected I was lax on respect for royalty in general. Punishment was swift and sure, a trip to the office of Mr. Terry, the new principal. In the august presence of the district superintendent William Gray, Mr. Terry administered three hard lashes of his leather strap to my outstretched right hand, presumably in the name of God, King, and Country.

I took my medicine bravely, but without contrition. As far as I was concerned, it was the Prince of Wales who was the spoiled brat and should receive a thrashing for deserting his country in time of peril, to say nothing of going against church law to marry a divorced woman. However, I apologized out of respect for Mr. Gray, who seemed an honourable and fair man just doing his duty. But far from reinforcing my obedience to authority, the episode had the opposite effect, spurring on my seemingly independent and combative spirit to find out about different systems of government and resolve some of the confusing contradictions I was beginning to notice in the world around me.

At suppertime I had to "spill the beans" about the strapping, but it was not too bad. Dad and Mom agreed that the King was behaving badly and should either give up Mrs. Simpson or abdicate the thrown in favour of his younger brother. But Dad lectured me, "That's up to the British parliament, not for boys like you to take matters into your own hands. You need to be careful not to do things that bring shame on the family name. You should apologize to Mr. Ovans."

Fortunately, he did not demand that I do so. I did not think much of Mr. Ovans as a teacher. His mind seemed to be somewhere other than on his pupils. And I had never forgiven him for labelling my brother Larkin a "dumb ditchdigger" just because he was restless in class and wanted to be doing something outdoors, like working on a farm. I also had a sneaking suspicion that he had something to do with Mr. Darwin's being replaced as principal by Mr. Terry, a nice enough man, but nowhere near the heroic proportions of Mr. Darwin.

My interest in public affairs began to surface in grade school, inordinately early for most boys, and probably began to develop unconsciously years before as a way to adapt to the challenge of competing with three older brothers. Most likely, too, I was influenced by the fact that in my early years we lived in Shaughnessy Heights, a neighbourhood in which our family was distinctly inferior in economic and social status. Thus, in my earliest years I became acutely aware of differences among people; physical, economic and social; sensitive to inferiority and inequality. "As the twig is bent, so grows the tree" was certainly true in my case, and inevitably, as I went on in grade school to learn more about the world around me, my interest in social and political issues came automatically, then fed on itself.

Dad certainly did not encourage my curiosity. He was either indifferent or discouraging, saying to me once in seeming exasperation with my questions or opinions, "Son, you think a lot, but you don't often think right." Dad was a conservative fatalist when it came to public affairs, reacting automatically to avoid, deny or minimize social problems, scornfully rejecting any proposed intervention as meddling in the natural order of things.

Not that he was uninterested or ignorant. He loved to read, habitually taking in the daily *Province* and thoroughly enjoying his weekly reading of the *Sunday New York Times, Saturday Evening Post* and other magazines as he could afford. He also regularly followed the news on the radio. But he had no sense of personal connection or responsibility for public affairs.

Just as my early childhood influenced me to be very sensitive and prone to activism, his, with a mother whose activism in public affairs he disliked, bent him in a negative, isolationist direction. Natural temperament, however, probably set the stage regardless of his mother's activism, as both he and his brother took after their father in temperament, shy, sensitive and private by inclination.

As Dad went on in life, both these influences were reinforced by his choice of occupation. It combined engineering, forestry, and business. His career associations were with business and professional men like himself. They were men of power and property. Their vested interest was in the maximum control of private business with the least governmental interference.

The fact that his business went bankrupt in the Depression of the 1930s, during an almost total breakdown of the prevailing economic system, altered his isolationist mind-set not in the least. Mother, even with her much broader sympathies, continued to support the Conservative Party, not because of what economic policy it represented, but out of a feeling of loyalty to its' leader, fellow Albertan, R. B. Bennett.

ᘓᗝ

The family radio was probably the most powerful bearer of news during the 1930s, grabbing the attention of everyone in the family with a dramatic immediacy unmatched by newspapers and magazines. Broadcasters like H. V. Kaltenborn, with his rich voice and scholarly presentation, dramatized events as though he was the voice of truth itself. The same was true of Edward R. Murrow, the voice of an American network every weeknight from London.

Even on Sunday night, news of the world penetrated the normally quiet family atmosphere with the strident, partisan voice from New York, "Good evening, Mr. and Mrs. America. Let's go to press!" And Walter Winchell was off to a run, dramatizing the latest news like a gossip columnist, with the "exclusive, inside" story of international events and personalities, gripping the listener with blow-by-blow descriptions of epic battles between good and evil. No ifs, ands and buts with Winchell. According to him, Communists were "Commies". Stalin and Hitler were ruthless maniacs sworn to enslave or bury us all. Secret agents of the Nazis and the Commintern had infiltrated the top echelons of the British and U.S. governments. Fifth columns were organized in key cities to sabotage our defences. And the only man to stop them was Winston Churchill, gallant descendant of the Duke of Marlborough, one of Britain's greatest military leaders.

Dad liked Winchell in spite of his New York brashness. He was all for letting the "Commies" and "Fascists" fight each other to death, leaving good and decent people to live in peace. That's how Dad saw world problems; get rid of the radical troublemakers, no matter where, in Germany, Russia, Japan, yes, and Canada and the United States, too. It was evil, ruthless leaders exploiting natural disruptions in man's affairs who were the problem. He saw no causal connection between the rise of such leaders and the failure of established leadership to resolve basic economic and social problems prevalent throughout the industrialized world.

My reaction was, sure Hitler, Mussolini and Stalin were bad men, but they had no say-so in Canada, Britain and the United

States, where conditions were terrible too. So it couldn't all be caused by a few evil men. There had to be more to it than that. But Dad didn't want to discuss it further. I was dumbfounded that a man as smart as Dad was not interested in the whys and wherefores. I was determined to find out more anyway I could.

That meant reading, more education, high school, then university, where surely I would find out the answers to all these perplexing events and problems. It meant earning and saving money, and toward that end I took any job I could lay my hands on. I hung around the *Vancouver Province* newspaper shack on Windsor Road as a helper until I got my own route, 32 customers along Windsor west of Lonsdale and around North Star School down to 27th between Mahon and Chesterfield. The route was all downhill, perfect for a bike, so Dad let me sign a contract to buy a new C.C.M. from Haskins and Elliot in Vancouver for $5 a month for three months, and I had a nifty blue, double-barred, balloon-tired bike with carriage rack up front.

The paper cost 75 cents a month for home delivery, of which I got 25 cents and sometimes a tip or two if I did a good job and put the paper where the customer wanted it out of the rain. That meant $7.50 or more a month, enough to make my bike payment and have some left over for an occasional five cent ice cream bar or candy. Then I got another route delivering the weekend edition of the *Toronto Star* on Saturday evenings to homes and apartments in Lower Lonsdale. That was a long way from home, but I solved the problem by grabbing onto the streetcar for a free ride back up Lonsdale when I had finished delivering the route.

It was tricky business holding onto the window screen with the left hand while guiding the bike with the right, particularly when the streetcar started ahead with a jerk and on dark winter nights. It was the dickens to hang on with fingers numb with cold. But the *Star* route was worth it, bringing in another $6 a month and a free copy of the paper. And sometimes when I had a few cents extra, I would stop into Mrs. Hanson's bakery on Lonsdale at 15th to get two of her big, puffy sugar donuts to warm me up and give me the energy to make it home, all in a brown paper bag for 5¢.

I kept the *Province* route until the second year in high school, when I got a better job at Shirran's Drug Store, on the corner of Lonsdale and Windsor. For $2.50 a week, after school and all day Saturday, my duties called for keeping the store clean and making home deliveries, prescriptions and books from Mr. Shirran's lending library, mostly mystery stories like Agatha Christie's. On Saturdays I was busy all day long, first sweeping the wooden floor, using a long push broom after sprinkling with Dustbane, a mixture of sawdust and oil, dusting the counters and shelves, and burning cardboard packing boxes in a barrel behind the store.

At 6 o'clock Mr. Shirran would say, "All right, laddie, you've earned your pay," hand me $2.50 and sometimes a chocolate bar, and I would push my bike up the hill and home for supper.

Mr. Shirran was a short, middle-aged, kindly Scot who must have received a very sound professional education in the old country because most of the prescriptions he prepared himself in a back room laboratory, its walls lined with row upon row of large glass jars lettered in Latin script. Beneath ran a long counter with two sets of scales, various sized mortars and pestles, beakers, rows of test tubes and a Bunsen burner.

Despite being surrounded with all this learning, I had little interest in becoming a pharmacist. About the only thing I learned was that the proper name for aspirin was acetylsalicylic acid. I worked for Mr. Shirran until better paying jobs showed up in war industries along the waterfront.

🚲

The British parliament finally recognized Edward VIII's behavior as intolerable, forced his abdication in December 1936 and passed the throne on to his younger brother, George. George VI was an unglamorous, decent man, safely married to Elizabeth, of well-trained royalty. Knowing by now that war with Hitler and his allies was inevitable, the Commonwealth reacted with relief and rallied around the new monarchs. The British government promptly put their new King and Queen to work solidifying the Commonwealth in preparation for war. Canada's wealth, manpower, potential as a training ground for military forces, and geographical proximity to the powerful United States, all placed her as a top priority for a royal visit. Accordingly, the new King and Queen arrived with much fanfare at Quebec City on May 17, 1939 and Vancouver on May 29.

I must have been well liked by the other kids at North Star, as they elected me president of the school's Red Cross chapter, and evidently restored to trustworthy status by the school establishment after the Prince of Wales affair, I was chosen to greet the new Queen on behalf of the school children of North Vancouver at a show-piece ceremony at Queen Mary School. I was probably chosen also because at age 13 I had some resemblance to the English boy movie star Freddie Bartholemew, with my mop of curly brown hair, winning smile and a spirit that did not let my crippled leg get in the way of being a regular, athletic kid.

At any rate, the big day arrived. I had been trained beforehand on the etiquette involved; bowing, kneeling, kissing the Queen's hand, saying my short speech of greeting, and presenting her with the traditional bouquet of flowers. All went off in acceptable fashion. I felt proud to represent my school, but to me the whole affair was less exciting than scoring a soccer goal. Underneath I had philosophical reservations about the institution of royalty. Apparently, though, I concealed my mental reservations well enough to win praise for a convincing performance. My reservations, however, remained unresolved. Belief in royalty is akin to belief in God, a matter of faith. You either have it or you don't. Either way, it is a lot easier than being unsettled about it.

Part of being involved in the Junior Red Cross was training in elementary first aid at the St. John Ambulance Corps. For several Saturday evenings in the winter of 1938 I took the ferry to the city, boarded the B.C. Electric at Hastings and Carrall to get to corps headquarters on Davie Street. There I climbed the wide, creaky stairs of the two-story gray building, entered a gymnasium-size room and joined a throng of other teenaged boys from Vancouver's public schools.

The three instructors, senior members of the Corps and dressed in the black and gray corps uniform, lined us up for roll call, handed each of us a copy of the pocket-size first aid handbook, seated us before a large blackboard, and began our orientation for the ten-week course. It covered emergency treatment for shock, asphyxiation, cuts, bruises, and broken bones.

There was no doubt about who was in charge, Captain Austin, a slender, slightly graying, fortyish man, precise in every movement. He addressed us in a dry, measured voice that seemed to emanate from his colourless uniform. Standing next to a life-size male human skeleton, he held our attention by constantly manipulating the skeleton's limbs, dangling them up, down, sideways, this way and that way, as he reviewed the various bone fractures.

Successive lectures, illustrated by similarly life-size diagrams of the adult male body, enlightened us about the other anatomical systems. The circulatory system was indicated by red lines for arteries and blue for veins; other colours indicated the respiratory and nervous systems. Following every lecture we had a one-hour practice session, folding and applying bandages and splints and tying various knots. That was the fun part, pairs of us spread out all over the gym floor, one acting as the patient, the other his rescuer, as we took turns practicing for working on the real thing; broken arms, legs, ribs, or artificial respiration.

It was a very systematic course of instruction, practice and homework sessions all laid out in the little black Handbook. On the tenth week came the examination, with a short written part, followed by the main test, an inspection of our expertise as we, again in two-man teams, responded to a range of first-aid situations. No granny knots or floppy, loose bandages, or you would flunk for sure. Each of us did a reasonably good job, we all passed and received our reward, a certificate with our names and the corps insignia, saying we had successfully completed the first course in first aid.

We were presented with a gray cloth armband with the corps emblem to be worn over a white dress shirt, then were assigned to a team and given our first written orders. Mine were to cover one of several strategic points on the royal parade route as King George VI and Queen Elizabeth made the grand tour from New Westminster to Vancouver.

The day of the grand procession was blessed by a clear, sunny morning. I was posted on the Patullo Bridge as it slopes northward toward New Westminster, a perfect place to view the royal parade as it came over the crown of the arching bridge from the south. By 9:30 a.m. both sides of the bridge were jammed to the siderails with people, all in a joyful, excited mood, some waving flags, others carrying small bouquets of flowers.

Everything went off like clockwork. The crowd waited expectantly behind an invisible sideline indicated by uniformed officers stationed every 50 feet along the route. As the hour approached, from the south, up and over the bridge's slope came the advance motorcycle escort, handsome police officers astride their shiny, powerful machines; then the rolling thunder of the first military band; then another, a Highland regimental band, splendid in their flaming red kilts, bearskin hats and shrieking bagpipes.

Slowly, majestically, the royal vehicle approached. It was an open touring car, and there they were, the new monarchs, side by side. The King sat on the right in a simple blue suit, smiling and waving in leisurely strokes. The Queen, adorned as colorfully as a fresh flower, waved and smiled as warmly as a soft breeze in the morning sun. The bands and royal coach drifted by and disappeared as though merely a dream. Everything was so orderly and splendid. A magic wand had passed before my eyes, leaving something substantial within.

The King and Queen must have felt strange that sunny morning in May, 1939, as they passed over that bridge spanning the wide Fraser River where it enters the Pacific Ocean. Strange, because on the bridge, along both sides, the crowd looked as though they must be somewhere in the Orient rather than in western Canada. Swarms of young children waved little Union Jack flags. But their bright, shiny faces were plainly Japanese, all from the nearby fishing village of Steveston at the mouth of the river. Within three years all would become dispossessed outcasts, labelled potential traitors to their adopted country merely because of their racial origin.

By September of 1939 Hitler and Stalin had signed a secret pact not to turn on each other but to divide up Poland and the small Baltic states of Latvia, Lituania and Estonia. This freed Hitler to unleash his full military machine on France and Britain, in no way prepared to withstand the onslaught of Hitler's mighty war machine.

Britain was in a jam. She had promised to come to Poland's rescue if Germany attacked, and attack Germany did, overrunning Poland within weeks after signing the Hitler-Stalin pact. Europe was running headlong into war.

6

WORLD WAR II: WATERBOY
TO SHIPFITTER'S HELPER

On Sunday evening, September 3, 1939, the voice of King
George VI went out by B. B. C. radio from London to British
Commonwealth nations around the world announcing a state of
war between the United Kingdom and the Nazi regime of Adolph
Hitler of Germany.

Within a week, on September 10, the Parliament of Canada
under the leadership of Prime Minister MacKenzie King closed
ranks with the mother country to fight a war that lasted almost
six years, until Germany and her European allies surrendered on
May 8, 1945, and Japan on August 14, 1945.

King George's announcement came as no surprise to Canadians gathered around their radios. War with Nazi Germany and
its Fascist allies in Italy and Spain was regarded as inevitable as
the world watched while Hitler gobbled up Austria, Czechoslo-
vakia, attacked Poland, and prepared to invade France, the rest
of western Europe, then turn on Britain and the Soviet Union.

Canada's involvement in World War II largely determined
what went on in the lives of everyone in North Vancouver for
those six years, including those at North Van High, which I entered in September 1939 and graduated from in June 1943.

I remember that first day at school after Britain declared war.
All over the soccer field boys gathered in excited knots. "At last
we're going to teach that maniac Hitler a lesson, and his strut-

ting puppet Mussolini. We'll teach them a thing or two!" Another chimed in, "My dad was in World War I. When I get to be eighteen, I'm going to join the airforce. Mr. Freedman says maybe we're going to start a cadet corps and learn Morse code."

There was talk that Wallaces' shipyard might start building ships for the war, and maybe there'd be summer jobs for us in the shipyards. It all sounded so good. Excitement. Adventure. Duty. A Righteous Cause. We all wanted to DO something; as if starting the first day of high school wasn't enough to get our adrenalin going.

Three Canadian divisions were rushed overseas to defend the mother country, among the few battle-prepared troops available to defend the British Isles, and, unlike World War I, this time Canadian troops were under Canadian command, recognition of Canada's coming of age as a strong new nation with huge resources to help win the war.

Then came the letdown, the "phony war" of stalemate in Europe through 1940 and into 1941 except for the aerial Battle of Britain. France thought it was safe behind its Maginot Line of underground fortifications until overrun by Hitler's hordes of mechanized barbarians in a matter of weeks. Air raids rained death and destruction on British cities. German submarines and pocket battleships raised havoc along Britain's sealanes. We cheered each other up with songs like "We're going to hang our washing out on the Siegfried Line". Britain prayed for time to shore up its fragile island defences against a German cross-channel invasion.

Nazi Germany's blizkrieg type of warfare demonstrated the new importance of air power. The vast open spaces of Canada became the training ground for the British Commonwealth Air Training Plan, training thousands of pilots and air crew members from all over the Commonwealth. That meant hundreds of huge hangars and other facilities, and for that B. C. had the lumber and skilled manpower. The Vancouver Creosoting Co. plant near the First Narrows bridge went into high gear.

It was there that my brother Asa and I got our first war industry jobs in the summer of 1940, two of a half-dozen North Shore boys hired as water boys. At two dollars a day, our job being to keep the huge stacks of lumber, acres of it, dampened down to prevent fire. I think it was Mr. Blair who got us the job, so besides Ace and me, the water boy gang consisted of Dave and Walt Blair and Alan and Leonard West, pals together at the Hastings Creek swimming hole up in North Lonsdale.

Two bucks a day was darn good money in those days, enough to pay for a new bike with a week's pay, and besides, the job was lots of fun. Each of us was assigned an area of the lumberyard reachable from a hydrant and hundreds of feet of heavy duty garden-size hose afixed at the business end with a sturdy brass nozzle. With forty pounds pressure, the cold, clear water shot out of our nozzles fifty feet high before splashing and dripping down the sides of lumber stacked thirty feet high, row upon row of it, at least twenty acres.

We did our job well; not a pile but was sopping wet by noon. But boys being boys, we figured we deserved some play too. So as soon as each of us had completed the first wet-down, usually about noon, we dragged our long hoses up and over the outside piles leaving the nozzle end dangling deep within each of our assigned areas, a distance just too far for our boss to track us down. Being careful to stay out of sight, we made our way down to the log boom on the waterfront. There, under the wharf where we couldn't be seen, we ate lunch together, maybe took a puff of a cigarette, talked about the war, fishing, and planned the day's fun.

We always packed a big lunch; a half dozen sandwiches made with thick slices of home-made bread lathered with home-made mayonnaise, and filled with slices of tomato, bacon, or salmon spread, and our paper bags bulged with packets of raisins, at least a half dozen apples or plums, and sometimes a chocolate bar like an Oh Henry, Mackintosh's toffee, or licorice whips.

There were no end of things to do at the booming grounds. We fashioned crab nets from barrel hoops and thick cod line. First we'd catch shiners with a small hook baited with a sandworm, then cut the shiners up and use them for crab bait or to catch a rock cod or flounder with a bigger hook. To catch the bigger fish we slithered out between the piling to deeper water in a battered old dugout canoe. We were all pretty good swimmers, so our only danger came from our best friend, a noisy harbour seal who loved to follow us, barking all the way, a racket that might draw the attention of the boss from the mill at the land end of the wharf.

We risked being detected also by our favourite sport, burling competitions. Rolling and spinning a log with our feet, a boy at each end of a long log, we would try to knock the other off balance and into the saltchuck. With one bum leg, I was no good at this and lost a new Micky Mouse watch before I had sense enough to quit.

But we never got caught, and liked to think that we did such a good job the boss didn't mind us having a little fun. What's more, by the end of the summer we all had new bikes, pocket watches, school clothes, enough spending money to see us through the school year, and pride that in our own way we were helping the war effort.

As vital as airplane hangars were to Canada's war effort, North Vancouver's greatest contribution came from its shipyards; the Wallace family's Burrard Drydock and Shipbuilding Co., and North Van Ship Repairs, both located next to the ferry landing at the foot of Lonsdale Avenue.

Between the two yards, they built 4 corvettes, 17 minesweepers, 161 Victory class cargo ships, and returned to service many other vessels damaged at sea.

By the summer of 1941 these shipyards employed several thousand men and several hundred women working three shifts. Some were highly skilled, experienced shipbuilders and metalworkers, most just adaptable workers from other trades, and even farmers from the Prairies who came into the yards for the steady work, better pay, and to be more useful in the war effort.

The first ships built by North Vancouver's shipyards during World War II were fast little corvettes and minesweepers to defend convoys of cargo ships on their long and perilous voyage from Halifax to the British Isles, and they were built the time-honoured way, stitched together with rivets.

Thousands and thousands of rivets were required to fasten together the components of even a comparatively small ship; its hull, ribs, crossbeams, decks, housing, machinery, armaments, everything. It was an exacting, time-consuming process requiring a large work force, all specializing in one aspect of the work or another, and all working under the supervision of master shipbuilders responsible for seeing that the ship fitted together as designed.

Within a year the two yards also undertook the construction of large cargo ships, the Victory class and others. German U-boats were taking a terrible toll of Allied shipping and a faster method had to be devised to   replace and expand the merchant fleet. That method was welding, the fusion of a ship's components by the intense heat of high voltage electricity generated by the welding machine, a method successfully demonstrated by Henry Kaiser's shipyards in the United States and transplanted to the North Vancouver yards. With welding, a huge cargo ship could be put together in a few weeks, rather than the months required to build a ship with rivets.

Old time shipbuilders like Mr. Williams were sure that a ship put together by welding was not nearly as strong and resilient under the battering of heavy seas as one built with rivets. But with cargo ships the need was for shipping tonnage and quick, not quality to last, and North Van's yards quickly adopted the new technology of welding for cargo ships.

But we're getting ahead of our story about building ships the old fashioned way.

The process of putting together a steel vessel with rivets is a complex, noisy enterprise. It demanded brains, precision, coordinated teamwork among the many specialists involved, and immense stamina and physical strength. But it was also exciting to put together a new ship. The shipyard was like a sprawling theatre stage of shops, wharfs, warehouses, lofts offices. Men and machines rushed everywhere, a drama in which each shop and trade played its indispensable part to the incessant ratta-ta-tat of rivet guns hammering together cold slabs of steel.

The process began with transposing a blueprint onto a wooden template, a precise, full-size pattern for shaping each metal component of the ship. From the template raw plates and beams were cut, shaped, and drilled with holes to fit adjoining members. Starting with the raw material of straight, flat steel, huge presses and the blacksmith shop folded, bent, and shaped them into precisely the right configuration. It is then the head fitter's job to fit them together in the right order.

First he laid the keel, the new ship's long thick backbone stretched out down the centre of launching way on large wooden blocks. Then came the ribs and crossbeams to form the skeleton of the emerging ship, all bolted together with exacting precision before being hammered together with rivets.

The ship's dimensions and shape had emerged, to which were then attached the ship's skin or hull, interior compartments or bulkheads, and surface decking and housing. With the addition of propeller shaft, propeller, and rudder, the ship was still nowhere near complete, but as soon as she could float, down the ways she went into the saltchuck and out of the way for the next newborn.

Once launched, the mere shell of a ship was tied up at a wharf for all the intricate finishing work; installation of her electrical nervous system, engines, stearing, navigation and communication equipment, crew quarters, and armaments.

Building ships took a lot of kidpower too, for jobs like rivet-passer, chalk boy, and helpers for various trades like draftsmen, pattern-makers, fitters, shipwrights, drillers, blacksmiths, tinsmiths, machinists, and steamfitters. And these shipyard jobs paid better than lumber mill or other woodworking places like Vancouver Cresoting, 29+ an hour and time and a half for overtime, so every kid in North Van hoped to get a shipyard job.

I was lucky. One of my best friends was Murray Williams whose dad was a 'bigshot' at North Van Ship Repair, an old time shipbuilder from the Clyde in Scotland. So one day I asked Murray's dad about a summer job and he said in his Scotch brogue, "Why sure laddy. Show up at the personnel office at seven sharp tomorrow and I'll see if I can get you on."

There was nothing to it. I showed up the next morning in work clothes with my lunch bucket. The man at the counter had a work slip all made out in my name directing me to report to the yard boss in charge of rivetting crews. Mr. Williams had "greased the ways", a shipbuilding term for when the shipwrights slather thick grease on the keel blocks so when they knock the wedges out, the newly built ship will slide down the ways into the saltchuck.

Slip in hand, I reported to the rivetting crew foreman. "So you want to be passerboy eh sonny? You'll have to step lively in that job, melad! Here, follow me, we're short a hand on Hank's crew."

I followed the burly man down the gantry to a set of plank stairs that stretched up several stories through a maze of planks and crossbeams, the scaffold skeleton surrounding an emerging ship's hull. The noise of rivet guns was deafening, thick rubber hoses ran everywhere, and the scaffolding shook and swayed as we mounted the stairs to the top level, walked across a couple of springy planks and onto the top deck.

The foreman pointed. "You see that fellow with a pair of tongs and charcoal pot? That's the heater for Hank's crew. Go tell him you're their new passerboy. He'll tell you what to do."

I approached the tall, lean, young fellow with a red bandana across his forehead. His arms were bare except for a pair of long leather gloves, and in his gloved right hand he grasped a pair of yard-long tongs. His left hand reached into a gunny sack and plopped a couple of sooty charcoal briquets into a round iron pot. Beside the sack of charcoal stood three five-gallon wooden barrels, his source of rivets.

The rivet heating pot rested waist high on a tripod, and when the fellow pumped a foot pedal beneath the tripod, puffs of acrid gray smoke and sparks whirled skyward. As I came closer the heat and smoke made me cough. Thin black lines of sooty sweat ran down the fellow's stringy neck and his eyelids and cheeks were black with soot.

I interrupted. "Hi, I'm your new passerboy. The foreman told me to report to you." I was relieved when from his blackened face he gave me a toothy grin, wiped his left arm across his bandana, stirred his pot with the long tongs, and said, "Yeh, that's swell, we can sure use you. The other kid took off, couldn't stand the height of the scaffolding I guess. My name's Jim. Just a minute and I'll show you what to do." He grabbed a white hot rivet out of his pot, ran over to the edge of the deck, yelled to someone below, paused a couple of seconds, opened the tongs, and the rivet disappeared below.

"You gotta move fast, get the rivet in the hole while its still white hot or its no good, too much work and lost time for Hank to hammer it in if it turns red. We're paid piece work. The more rivets we bang in, the more we make, and you gotta work your ass off to make more'n wages. You see there's another guy inside. He's the holder-on. Hank and he jammer the piss outa the rivet 'til its tighter than an old maid's twat. If they aren't, we don't get paid, gotta ream 'em out and do 'em all over again."

Jim took a swig of water out of a canvas bag, ran over with another white hot rivet, then explained my job. He held up a cone-shaped sheet metal scoop the size of a rugby ball with a handle half way down. "This is your bucket. When I toss a rivet, you catch it in this bucket, grab it with these short tongs, run over as fast as you can and stick it into the hole next to the one Hank just pounded in. Here, come with me and I'll show you where I want you to stand. I gotta know you'll be there because I'm goin' to toss 'em from where I'm standing by the pot and can't see you over the side of the deck. I'll toss a few slow 'til you get used to it, but then we've gotta speed up or we'll never make our quota." He paused a second for breath, then said, "And for Chris'sake, try not to miss 'em....a guy down below ain't too tame if he gets a white hot rivet down his neck."

I liked Jim and the way he explained things, but when he led me over to my work station I wasn't sure I could handle the job. Up there on the scaffolding the dock looked a hundred feet down. I was scared, so scared my knees began to shake and buckle. It wasn't just the height, but the planks laid parallel to the hull bounced with every step throwing me temporarily off balance and making me dizzy and sick at the stomach.

I wanted to grab onto something to hold me steady, but nothing was within reach, just a layer of two inch thick planks, three of them wide and space wide enough to fall through between them and the hull.

Oh God, was I scared, but I couldn't let on to Jim lest he think I was a sissy. So following him toward Hank I walked slow, feeling my way on the planks with each step, legs spread apart, and bent over like an ape. Trying to get the hang of the springing planks, I felt my way toward where Hank was kneeling, rivet gun cradled in his arms.

Thank God Hank had a grin on his face as I caught up with Jim and he introduced me to the crew chief. Noticing sweat running down my face, Hank said, "Got the shakes, eh kid? Well, give it a try. We'll take it slow for awhile, 'til you get used to the height. Just don't drop any." He stood up and continued, "Here, I'll show you how to handle the bucket. Think of it like a catcher's mit and you're goin' to catch a fly ball. Sorta ease back with the bucket when the rivet comes flyin' in, so it don't bounce out. And hold it about a 45 degree angle like this, the same direction the rivet's comin' in." He turned to Jim with another grin. "Jim, why don'tcha just plop the first few over the side 'til he gets the hang of the bucket?"

God, was I ever grateful for Hank's attitude! He could see I was scared to death, but willing to give it a try. He needed a passerboy and I needed the job.

Jim handed me a pair of long leather gloves and the bucket, I stationed myself about eight feet from Hank, and waited for Jim to drop the first rivet. Pretty soon his tongs poked over the side between me and Hank, the rivet dropped, it clunked into my bucket, I reached in and grabbed it just behind the head, and shuffled squat-legged toward Hank, shoved it into the hole, and Hank's gun exploded with a violent ratta-ta-tat-tat-tat-tat-ta-ta-tat. His gun fell silent just as soon as I had worked my way back to my station, still squatting like a wounded chimpanzee.

I got there just in time. Jim's tongs poked over the side again like a tropical snake, opened up, and the second white-hot rivet clunked and sparkled into my bucket. Again I made it over and back dripping with sweat and breathing like I was pumping my bike straight up Lonsdale. It went on like this for the next half-dozen rivets. My upper leg muscles quivered with strain but I was still too scared to stand up straight, and I didn't dare look over the side, just concentrated on getting from here to there and praying to God I was doing it right. Hank kept banging them in, so I guessed things were going all right. But I didn't know how long I could keep it up. I was tired as the dickens and the nausea in my stomach told me I was running out of energy.

I tried to think of what was in my lunch bucket, a black metal one with a place for a thermos bottle inside the lid, the sign of a real workman if you carried one of these. I visualized opening it up to get a couple of oatmeal cookies and pouring a hot cup of tea from my thermos. But I couldn't remember where I'd left it. I remembered checking into the shipyard with it, but from there it was a complete blank. That made me feel even more hungry.

The next rivet, white hot and sparkling came arching over the side about an arm's length in front of where I was waiting. Bucket in hand, arm stretched out as far as I could, I lurched forward, but not quite far enough. It bounced off the rim of my bucket onto the scaffolding, rolled, smoking a brown streak to the edge, and dropped out of sight.

I expected all Hell to break loose. Jim had picked up the pace, tossing this one from his pot to just in front of where I usually stood, exactly the way he should, only I wasn't prepared. Hank hadn't noticed either, until the next one came sailing through the air. Meantime I had sense enough to move up the plank about a foot, and when it came I was ready. Into my bucket she went sizzling hot, I grabbed it, poked it in the hole, and retreated trying to remember exactly where I waited the last catch.

Jim really knew his stuff. He knew I'd missed the first toss; no banging of Hank's gun. But he'd broken in a lot of passerboys and figured if I was smart I'd be ready for the second long toss. And the third, and on and on until it was time for lunch. One time he tossed it just a little too hard, it arched so far out I lost my balance reaching and thought for sure I was going to fly over the edge. Instead, I flopped forward on my knees, and still hanging onto the bucket, rivet inside, crawled like a baby up the planks and put it into the hole.

From then until the whistle blew for lunch it was back and forth dumb and numb as a pit pony. I was past the point of feeling hunger, or the pain in my legs. Or thinking. Or fearing. I had become an unfeeling, unthinking gear in the shipbuilding machine. It took just half a day, and like a malleable fresh rivet out of Jim's barrel, I was pounded into shape, turned into an obedient shipyard worker.

The noon whistle blew, Hank's gun rattled off a special ratta-ta-ta-dum-dum signal to his holder-on deep inside the ship's hull, and I followed him through the maze of scaffolding and up the stairs to the deck privy, then lunch beside Jim and his coke pot.

A short barrel of a man with a head just as round and fleshy rolled in, wrapped his short bow legs around a rivet barrel, lowered his massive frame, and bending forward, opened his lunch bucket and shoved a thick sandwich into his mouth. Hank joshed, "Heh kid, meet Meatball, the meanest hanger-on in the yard." Meatball retorted, "Heh Hank, ain't we goin' to step it up a little? It's kinda slow down there." Thankfully Jim interceded. "We're doin' okay. I'm keepin' count. Gotta take it a little easy with the new kid. We'll pick it up pretty soon."

I too was perched on a rivet barrel deep into my lunch bucket, which I retrieved from behind a coke sack, scooted out of the way by Jim. He was a methodical, decent guy, like seeing that the crew always had cold drinking water, two canvas water bags hanging from a steel pipe nearby. Hank trusted him to keep the count and set the pace. And Jim knew it was better to have a passerboy who was a little slow to start than none at all. He was forcing me about as fast as he figured I could stand. Being part of a small crew like this was a new experience for me, and as much as my legs ached, I wanted more than anything to belong.

Getting started after lunch I went through the same scarey feelings and shakes, only I got over them quicker, and by the end of the week I was even standing up straight instead of shuffling bent-over like a frightened ape. Knowing I would never be able to run along the bouncing planks, I devised a method of moving fast by taking long swooping strides to cover the distance to the hole without wearing myself out. I'm sure my strange gait looked oddly out of place for a passerboy, but no one on the crew made fun of me; they now had a passerboy making money for them.

It was only at the end of the shift when I lined up to check out at the gate that I really felt that I had become a qualified member of the shipbuilding fraternity. Like joining any new outfit, you only learn the ropes by getting in line and following those who do.

I watched those in front of me as they passed through the narrow opening single file. Each paused beside a huge wheel with numbers on it, rotated it to a certain spot, and punched in a sort of handle. This device was the shipyard's timeclock, each man punching in his number to verify the time he checked in and out of the yard. But I didn't have a number that I knew of so I asked the man in front of me. "New eh?" he said, and pointing to a little office window and sign saying "Timekeeper", directed me, "Go over there and get your tag."

From behind the high glassed-in window the bespeckled time-keeper peered down at me and said, "What's your name, laddy?", and I replied, "Robin Williams, new this morning." He reached over to a slotted board on the wall, glanced at a slip of paper, then at the curly-headed boy looking up at the window. "So you are" said he, sliding the slip and pencil through the opening. "Sign your name on the line", he said, then placing a small brass tag on the counter, directed "That's your number. Now don't lose it or you won't get paid."

Picking up the precious tag, I looked at the number, "3608" it said, stamped into it in black. I was now # 3608. Robin Williams, my name, was merely incidental to North Van Ship Repairs.

I repeated my number several times to myself, slid it carefully to the bottom of my left front pocket, went through the line, rotated the huge dial to click-stop at 3-6-0-8 punching in each number, and walked out the gate, head up, chest out, black lunch bucket swinging by my side.

I didn't mind being now merely #3608. Quite the contrary. With my new numerical identity I was now a member of the shipbuilding fraternity and on the streetcar all the way up Lonsdale I dwelt on my new status; how I would tell Mom and Dad, how much my first paycheck would be, how to overcome my fear of scampering along that scaffolding, whether Hank thought I was good enough to keep me on, and more.

The streetcar came to a halt. It was the end of the line. Windsor Road. Only then, when I stepped off to begin the walk home, did I again notice the pain in my legs.

Mother took care of that with a hot bath and supper. But before going to bed with the alarm set for six I threaded a shoelace through the hole in my tag and tied it to a beltloop on my work pants.

I made it through the next day, the rest of the week, and the remainder of the summer. But I could never get the hang of the bouncing planks anymore than burling logs at the booming grounds. And passing rivets all day long got boring. I wasn't learning anything new. So about the fourth week I punched in a half hour early each morning to check on getting a helper's job in one of the skilled trades lined up for the following summer.

Again I was lucky. As soon as school was out for the summer of '42, I went to the personnel office and told the man I wanted a helper's job so I could learn a skilled trade. "Well, I guess you proved to be a steady worker by your time card last summer, so I'll send you to the fitting foreman. Here, take this slip to the Fitter's office next to the tool shed."

The fitting foreman turned me over to the sub-foreman in charge of drillers, who in turn directed me to a driller who needed a helper, and boy was I ever lucky! George Wilson was the slowest walking and talking driller in the yard, but highly respected for his experience because the head fitter always insisted George do the drilling for the most exacting assignments, like drilling the holes to fit the plates at the ship's stern for the propeller shaft and rudder.

Working for George was the softest job in the yard, the same pay as a rivet passer, but instead of being stuck in one place all day I got to walk all around the shipyard following him with his long wooden toolbox, run errands to different shops, and watch other trades as I waited on my new boss. And George Wilson was a darling man for a boss, a quiet little Welshman who hummed wherever he went and forever studiously examined a particular drillbit he turned over in his hand.

I thought I had it made for the summer. George said I was a good helper, always there when he needed me, quickly learned the names and sizes of the different drill bits and other tools of his trade so I handed them to him as soon as he called, even got to anticipate what he would need next and have it ready so he didn't have to ask, so I could see no reason why anything should change.

But the fitting foreman thought otherwise. His head fitter, a master shipbuilder off the River Clyde in Scotland, needed a new helper, and the foreman thought I was a smart enough kid to meet this man's exacting standards. A head fitter is one of the few elite craftsmen who build ships, the man who oversees fitting all a new ship's components, exactly how, where, and when to put them together according to design and blueprints. So in importance and status he is right up there close to the Superintendent of the whole shipyard, and when he wants something he gets it.

George had his orders; let me go and take me over to meet my new boss. He had his own office next to the fitting foreman. On the way over, George said, "You'll learn a lot more about shipbuilding from Mr. Churchill", paused, then added, "I wish you luck, laddy. Just do as he says...and step lively, because Mr. Churchill is a very busy man."

George stood beside me outside Mr. Churchill's office just long enough to see if he was in. When I looked back, George was gone and I wondered why he didn't wait to introduce me...and it wasn't characteristic of George to say so many words about anybody, even in admiration, so I was somewhat ill at ease as I stood alone waiting to meet my new boss.

I didn't have long to wait. A loud Scotch-burred voice boomed from the office, "Come in! Can't you see I'm busy?"

I entered and faced my new boss, a tall, red-headed dynamo of a man with blazing blue eyes and a voice to match. He looked me up and down. "So you're the lad the office sent over? I guess you know who I am. You just stay close and do as I say. I won't tell you the same thing twice, so listen close."

He handed me a rolled-up blueprint. "Here, take this back to the engineering office and tell them to give me the right one this time. And step lively. I need it right away."

Blueprint in hand, I hurried over to the engineering office next to the template shop, told the person at the counter I was Mr. Churchill's new helper, handed him the print, and with all the authority I could muster, said, "Mr. Churchill says he would like the proper one."

The man fixed me like a hawk, opened his mouth to say something, closed it again without saying a word, and disappeared as fast as a frightened rabbit. Almost as abruptly, he reappeared with another print, and handing it to me, said in a hushed, saccarine voice, "Tell Mr. Churchill we're sorry. It won't happen again."

Such was Mr. Churchill's power.

Hurrying back, I thought "Holy mackerel! I suppose its an honour to be chosen as Mr. Churchill's helper, but I wish I was back with George. I don't know if I can measure up, and I bet he has a terrible temper if I do something wrong."

Mr. Churchill grasped the new print, laid it flat on his work table with a sweep of his lean, muscular arms, scanned it, just as effortlessly rolled it up, and blueprint leading the way, strode out the office door, saying, "Take that toolbox and follow me to the blacksmith shop." The toolbox looked the same as George's, a long slender open wooden box with a handle down the middle. Fortunately it wasn't loaded with heavy tools, merely various measuring tapes, calipers, marking line, cakes of blue and white chalk, a hammer and center punch, square, a can of marking paint, and a few other small tools I didn't recognize.

I followed my new boss down the main alley toward the blacksmith shop, a tall metal building with numerous chimneys and ventilators. I couldn't keep up with his long strides, but hurrying as best I could, kept him in sight as he entered a side door.

The sheet metal door banged and rattled behind me and I peered into the shop's vast, dark interior, and hoping to quickly discern Mr. Churchill's whereabouts within, caught sight of him entering an office across the shop floor. Quickly making my way over, I stood outside the door while he conferred with the shop foreman.

All about me, the blacksmith shop was a wonderously different world of clashing noises, glowing furnaces, smells of coke fires and molten metal, the shop's cement floor carpeted in massive blocks of steel punctuated with square holes like an endless waffle. Within its eerie darkness, slowly moving men in leather aprons and gloves slithered red hot beams across the iron floor and methodically arched them into shape to become the ribs for a new ship.

Clashing ingredients and all, there was a magical calmness about this giant workshop that reminded me of the time an elderly lady friend of Mother's took me inside Vancouver's Catholic cathedral, its vast, dark interior swelling to the sound of the organ's thousand pipes as light from windows away up high filtered through a haze of incense-laden sunbeams. So it was small wonder that later on when I worked in this shipyard after school at night, the blacksmith shop became my favourite place to have my cold supper on dark winter nights.

Mr. Churchill emerged from the office, in a hurry as usual, and I followed him as close as I could. He went everywhere; back down the main alley alongside the ways where a new ship was under construction, up the stairs onto the top deck, to the bow, the stern, into manholes cut into the deck, down ladders between decks, and narrow passageways into a labyrinth of compartments.

Between decks the air was heavy with smoke from heating pots and acetylene torches, the noise deafening from jammering rivet guns and staccato burps of calking guns. Moving about without stumbling was an incessant battle with hoses that snaked and criss-crossed underfoot. I followed Mr. Churchill everywhere he went, measuring, checking, marking, then down the stairs he would fly back to his office for a different blueprint, to the template shop, engineering, the shipwrights' loft, back and forth all day long.

I followed his every move and tried to anticipate what he wanted from me or his toolbox because he seemed to hate to ask for anything, as though I ought to know without being told. Sometimes he just grabbed what he wanted out of the toolbox and glanced at me in silent rebuke that I hadn't read his mind quickly enough.

The worst times were when we were between decks in some miserable, hot, smokey hole and something wasn't done right. If the workman responsible was there Mr. Churchill would get red in the face and berate the fellow. "What are ye man, blind as a pit pony? Could ye not SEE the punch holes?" If the party responsible for the faulty work wasn't around, he would start throwing things, a chunk of angle iron, a piece of 2 by 4, anything within reach, then charge off in search of the man's foreman.

It soon became apparent that Mr. Churchill was an impatient, ill-tempered man.

I suppose that was the way he learned the trade on the River Clyde, birthplace of Britain's mightiest ships, the *Queen Mary* and *Queen Elizabeth*, battleships, cruisers, every type of ship large and small. Shipbuilders are a tough breed, and maybe the Scots toughest of all, accustomed as they are to a harsh, barren land.

But my new boss wasn't always a difficult man. Once in awhile when things were going right, like after a trouble-free launch, he would burst into song out on the open deck and paid no more heed to what others thought than to his outbursts of bad temper. His Gaelic soul took wings in his big, melodious voice, and oddly for a Scot, to the tunes of Gilbert and Sullivan.

He knew their light opera tunes backwards and forwards, every part, word, and intonation. With commanding voice he would launch into *The Pirates of Penzance.*

I am the very model of a modern Major General,
I've information vegetable, animal, and mineral,

I know the kings of England, and quote the fights historical,
From Marathon to Waterloo, in order categorical;
I'm very well acquainted too with matters mathematical,
I understand equations, both simple and quadratical..

Satisfied that he had sung enough verses from *Penzance,* he would shift into a verse or two from *The Mikado.*

A wandering minstrel I—
A thing of shreds and patches, Of ballads, songs, and snatches,
A dreamy lullaby!
My catalogue is long,
Through every passion ranging,
And to your humours changing

I tune my supple song!

Mr. Churchill seemed to crave attention, good or bad, and to watch him stand prominently on the top deck of a new ship as it was about to be launched and let loose in song was a comic but touching scene.

Once a ship was launched and tied up at the finishing wharf, working conditions aboard were more agreeable, but Mr. Churchill's temper got even worse. The finishing work: installation of engines, communication and control equipment, armaments, all the working parts; demanded the greatest degree of precision and attention to detail. The ship swarmed with inspectors, important people constantly overlooking Mr. Churchill's work, and with these high muckamucks Mr. Churchill had to hold his tongue. If anyone of these inspectors didn't like something he had the power to withhold government acceptance of the ship, hence had immediate access to the yard superintendent. Mr. Churchill didn't like this at all, and became even more impatient and ill-tempered with me.

I couldn't seem to do anything right or fast enough for him. "Did ye leave your brains at home this morning, lad?" he'd say. It was unthinkable to talk back, so as the summer wore on I built up resentment toward the man. My consolation was that the end of summer was in sight, only a couple of more weeks, and Dad had told me that logging camps were short of men and that next summer I could get a job in the woods at even better pay than putting up with Mr. Churchill's abuse.

But toward the end of my last week in the yards, Fate intervened and Mr. Churchill and I parted company rather abruptly.

It was Thursday in mid-afternoon. Mr. Churchill and I were on the upper deck of a new ship under construction on the ways. Mr. Churchill had to descend 'tween decks via a ladder and a very tight manhole to check on something, so he told me to remain on the upper deck and have his blueprints handy in case he called. I stationed myself a few feet from the manhole, squatted on the toolbox, and waited. He called from down below for one of the prints, but I didn't hear him, what with the racket of the rivet guns.

The next thing I knew, his head surfaced through the man-hole, his right arm rotated, and a chunk of angle iron slithered across the deck and whacked me on the right ankle, the ankle of my polio leg where I had an operation scar. A horrendous pain shot up my spine to the top of my head. I hopped around on my good leg trying to shake off the pain. He shouted above the din, "Did ye not hear me! I said to hand me the # 3 print!"

I glanced around for the prints, the trouble being that when the angle iron struck, my arms automatically flew outwards spill-ing them onto the deck. Hopping around in excruciating pain, I spied them, all rolled up, resting against an open can of red lead paint, brush sticking out, all ready for the rivet counter to slap-count the newly driven rivets.

Mr. Churchill glowered at me, face flushed with impatience as I hobbled toward the prints. Then someone must have called him from below and he lowered his arm to grasp the ladder. Now only his head appeared above deck.

I reached down to pick up the prints, but instead, as if guided by some unseen force, my hand grasped the handle of paint brush. I don't know what possessed me, but without a second's thought, brush dripping with paint, I hobbled toward the manhole, and, with one back and forth stroke, slapped Mr. Churhill's face from ear to ear with red lead paint.

Needless to say, I didn't stick around to hand Mr. Churchill any prints. Recovering sufficiently to put one foot before the other, I scampered sideways toward the stairs, descended as quickly as I could and rushed down the wharf and through the yard toward the exit gate. If old man Churchill ever caught up with me he would be in such a rage he would not only give me a good cuff-ing but think nothing of chucking me off the wharf—and not a man in the yard would have lifted a hand in my defense, for after all, my boss was the indispensable Mr. Churchill and I a mere summer helper.

It was a warm afternoon and I was running out of breath by the time I reached the labourers' shack just opposite the exit gate. Pausing to catch my wind, I stepped into the shadows of the shack's open end and pulled my pocket watch. It was only 2:30, too early to check out of the yard without an excuse slip, and if I rushed out the gate the timekeeper would know something was fishy and call a security guard to stop me before I reached the safety of the street.

On the other hand, the greater danger was Mr. Churchill catching up with me. So I hastily decided the best thing to do was to lay low in some dark corner or the labourers' shack, hope no one would detect me, and keep an eye on the entry gate through a crack in the shack wall. Then, as soon as men started pouring into the yard for the afternoon shift, I could slip in among them, and out the gate. Of course, if I did this, I would miss checking my number out of the yard and be docked time for it, but on the other hand, it just wasn't worth taking the chance for a dollar or two.

I waited in the darkness of the labourers' shack for over an hour, my feelings alternating between fear of being caught and foolishness for pulling a stunt like that. It was understandable because of my accumulated resentment, but nonetheless inexcusable. Irresistible impulse I suppose. I certainly didn't plan on getting even with Mr. Churchill in some way before parting for the summer. But malice of forethought or not, it was my hand that wielded the paintbrush, and like everything we do, would just have to make the best of the consequences.

I thought of a few. What would I say to Mom, then Dad, for coming home early on Thursday and not working on Friday at all? And to Murray Williams' dad who got me on at the shipyard in the first place? For damn sure this caper would put an end to any more work at North Van Ship Repairs. Mr. Williams was bound to hear about it. He kept in touch with everything going on in the yard. Well, there was no use crying about it. I'd just have to make the best of it and get out of the yard alive. That's all that mattered now.

Soon a couple of men came by the side of the shack. I could see them through a crack between the wall boards. They looked like foremen from the way they dressed, neat and clean with pencils stuck in their coveralls. One was laughing while he said to the other, "Did'ya hear the latest about old man Churchill? Seems his helper, you know, the crippled new kid, got fed up with the old bastard and slapped his chops with a dobber brush loaded with red lead! Jeez, has that kid got some nerve! Churchill will skin him alive if he ever catches up with the cheeky little runt." The other man replied, "Well if you ask me, he got what he deserved. Thinks he's King of the yard." They both roared with laughter and disappeared.

Needless to say, what I overheard made me feel a lot better while biding my time until the men started pouring in for the afternoon shift. As soon as that happened, I opened a door at the rear of the shack, looked around, and seeing no sign of Mr. Churchill, walked briskly toward the oncoming stream of men, and sidling sideways, slipped by the timekeeper's window and out the gate.

Wasting no time, I hurried toward the streetcar stop on Lonsdale and hopped aboard just as she was about to leave, and thanking my stars, rode, feeling rather furtive, to the end of the line. I tried to focus on the positive side. So what if I'd lost a day's pay? I already had enough for the next school year, for clothes and books and a little spending money. That's all the mattered. And besides, I was looking forward to working in the woods next year, something all my older brothers had done, and maybe even going on to university after that.

I decided to take a chance on not telling Mom and Dad about what had happened at the yard because my working life was my responsibility with no direct consequences for them. They were both busy with their own working lives outside the home, and it would just complicate things that were already complicated enough. Chances were that they wouldn't notice a thing if I just fooled around the house reading the next day, so that's what I did, and my guess was right.

The following week when I went to get my paycheck, there it was waiting as usual like nothing had happened, except no pay for the day I was absent. But the timekeeper didn't dock me for lost time on Thursday. He must have heard of what had happened. It was all over the yard. But I suspect that he too had no lost love for Mr. Churchill, maybe even remembered that once upon a time he also had worked under such a boss. At any rate, within a few days I put the whole episode behind me, too busy thinking about the year ahead in high school.

North Van High and The Remarkable "Mickey" McDougall

When I attended North Vancouver High School from 1939 to 1943 the student body was only a little more than 300, about the same number as when it first opened its doors in 1924. So it was a small school compared with the Vancouver city schools like King Edward, Kitsilano, Britannia, or John Oliver. But it was North Vancouver's only high school, drawing its students from both City and District grade schools, hence it was an unique, unifying institution for a sparsely populated area extending from Capilano to Deep Cove and the waterfront to the slopes of Grouse Mountain.

Most students at North Van High came from homes which had a great deal in common, tending to give the school a cohesive spirit. There were no great gaps of rich and poor. They all depended upon the same ferries and streetcars to get around with the use of automobiles the exception rather than the rule. The overwhelming majority were British in background, middle class in identity, and placed a high value on formal education. Most liked to garden, the outdoors, and had a keen interest in athletics. And most were home-owners, or had been before the Depression of the 1930s.

Another factor which contributed to a high level of motivation among the students of North Van High was the fact that it was a privilege to attend at all. School attendance was required for B. C.'s youth only through age 14. Families were large, it not being uncommon for families to consist of four to nine children. Attendance at high school was expensive, what with appropriate clothes, books, carfare, et cetera. Many families could not get by without the earnings of minor children, especially large ones or those with an unemployed or absent father. Thus most of North Vancouver's grade school children never went on to high school, and many who started out had to drop out before completing grade 12, a situation made particularly acute during the 30s.

Such community conditions shaped the high school curriculum in the direction of preparing students for careers as white collar workers in business or the professions to the neglect of skilled trades. It was loaded with courses in English grammar, composition, and literature, algebra, geometry, and trigonometry, British and Canadian history, chemistry, botany, and physiology, Latin and French, with merely one course in Manual Arts. For boys interested in becoming an automotive or diesel mechanic, carpenter, electrician, draftsman, steam engineer, or any of the innumerable skilled trades, high school classes were thus rather boring and they attended largely to participate in athletic and social activities.

All of this and more was understood by an exceptional man, Wilfrid R. "Mickey" McDougall, first teacher, then Principal of North Vancouver High School from 1921 until well after World War II. For thirty-five years that little high school was the focus of this remarkable man's attention. He made it his business to know and follow every student's progress. He kept his hand in as a teacher. He was careful in choosing his teaching staff and seeing that he got the most out of them to enrich the school's program. He involved the parents in the school and the school in the community. He could be charming. He could be gruff. He could be gentle. He could be tough. But whatever he did was always pointed in the same direction; to get every student to rise to his best, that North Van High gave its best, and that all pulled together to make North Vancouver a quality community.

The tone of high expectations set by principal McDougall

was a natural outgrowth of his own background and personality. Born on an Ontario farm in 1896 of Scotch-Canadian parents, as a boy he helped out at his father's store in the small nearby town of Milton. By age 16 his family had moved to British Columbia, he graduated from Vancouver's King Edward High School and enrolled at the fledgling U. B. C.

He had completed his first two years at the university by 1914 when World War I broke out. At 18 he joined the Canadian forces and went overseas, serving, of all things, as a muleskinner. One may assume he was given this assignment because of his early farm background, but one can hardly imagine a better preparation for a future career as a high school principal, a line of work calling for a firm grip on the importance of discipline and order. Graduating from U.B.C. in 1921, he took his first job as a teacher of mathematics and Latin at North Van High at age 25.

McDougall drew upon his own life experience and the perceptions of a keen mind to the job of Principal. Exceptionally bright and ambitious as a boy, he aspired to become a doctor. But he was too young to be admitted to the university when he graduated from King Edward, so he apprenticed for awhile with a pharmacist. Mid-way in university along came the war. During his war service overseas doing his best to get notoriously stubborn mules to haul artillary guns around, he was struck on the head by a piece of shrapnel damaging his eyesight. His wounds caused periodic headaches for the rest of his life. From the mucky business of getting mules to do what he wanted he learned that psychology works better than force.

When he returned from overseas and graduated from U.B.C., he still hoped to become a doctor. But by then he was a mature man; he also wanted marriage and a family. So, not having the funds for both medical school and marriage, he opted for a teaching career, marriage, and raising a family. From this he learned much too, especially as his only daughter was afflicted from birth with a digestive disorder requiring years of care and sacrifice.

Thus, as a man, "Mickey" McDougall brought a lot of learning from the school of hard knocks to being the principal of North

Van High, and it showed everywhere. He told any new teacher, "By the time boys get to high school, they're too old for physical punishment to do any good. We have to use psychology." And he practiced what he preached. To give but one example, a sixteen year old student was always late for school, so McDougall called him to the office and asked him, "Why are you late to school every morning?" The boy replied, "My mother doesn't get up to get my breakfast." McDougall responded, "Why can't you cook your own oatmeal? I often do." Still the boy was late. So McDougall paid a home visit. Finding the house unkempt and the mother still in hair curlers, he said to her, "I want your son in school on time, but he can't learn without breakfast." A few days later, one of the boy's teachers asked McDougall, "What did you do? The boy has completely changed."

Principal McDougall expected his staff of a dozen or so to not only be good classroom teachers but to engage students in a wide variety of extra-curricular activities. Even vice-principal J. D. Siddons helped out with girls' grass hockey, and the same with Mssrs. Chamberlain and McIntyre. Art Creelman spent as much time coaching Canadian football and organizing the boys' cadet corps as teaching physics. Ivan Miller and Art Freedman took the lead in soccer and rugby. William Stewart's forte was French but was just as keen on putting together singing groups, especially to perform Gilbert and Sullivan.

Misses Walker and Dunmore provided leadership for girls' clubs, and Katie Reynolds, a power in Latin and History, took on the girls' cadet corps. And McDougall involved them in innumerable other school activities; paper drives, an annual Penny Carnival conducted by the Parent-Teacher Association to raise money for a school gym and community centre "Mickey" had in mind to be built after the war.

He had a broad conception of what a high school education should provide, and it wasn't just high quality classroom instruction. He believed that the development of character and good citizenship were of equal importance, and that school, home, and community must all work in harmony for the maximum effect on the student and benefit to society. That was why he placed such value on extra-curricular activities, teacher involvement in them, and the school being so involved with the community. His viewpoint wasn't just something he had picked up in a textbook. It came from his own life experience and observation, and he saw it as his calling to carry it out with as much dedication as if he were the medical doctor he once hoped to be.

For all McDougall's seriousness of purpose, he was no sour-puss and the schoolday was not an unhappy one. He knew that youth is a creature of curiosity, pleasure, and play, rather than of work. So there were times when he thought it wise to let youth have its way. He was always prowling around to see how things were going, and one day he paused outside the Study Hall door. From just inside, his ears picked up what sounded like a small musical combo thrumming away, the rhythmic dum-dum-dum of a bass viola, the low howl of a muted trumpet, and the tick-tick-tick of drum sticks.

It was pretty good music, New Orleans style jazz, and he wondered how on earth this could be going on during study period when all else seemed in perfect order. Peeking inside, he could see that the three of them were at it again, three of the brightest students in school, so bright they probably got bored at times; Paul Gilmore, and two of his buddies, all huddled together making music with their improvised band of lead pencils, throbbing lips, and cupped hands. He grinned, gave them a hush sign, and passed on.

It was the same with tobacco. Sooner or later kids were going to try cigarettes. The important thing was to not let it interfere with education. Noticing some of the older boys sneak around to out-of-the-way corners of the schoolgrounds to have a puff, he suggested to one of them that it might be better if they just moved across 23rd to a vacant lot where he wouldn't have to take notice of their unofficial smoking hangout. It worked just fine. From then on there was no smoking on school premises and the smokers kept their end of the bargain by being on time for class just like everybody else.

Many of the teachers were rather awesome, amusing characters. Mr. Shaw in General Science was a tall, quiet, gentle man with a dry sense of humour. "Don't put anything smaller than your elbow in your ear", he would say, cautioning us as to the vulnerability of the human ear drum. To us, he was "Snuffy" Shaw, because he had the peculiar mannerism of punctuating his sentences with a gentle snort.

At the opposite end of gentleness was Kathleen M. Reynolds, the large, bosomy major-general of Latin and the girls' cadet corps. In class she was an awesome drillmaster, pacing back and forth pointing out errors in our blackboard Latin verb drills. Now and again her right hand would plunge 'tween her ample bosoms, extract a dainty handkerchief, just as daintily dab her nose, redeposit the accessory, and resume her martial pace.

Ivan Miller, the large, round-headed teacher of Mathematics and Science thought nothing at all of giving countless hours after school to test wits with a knot of zealous male students. Jacking one leg up on a chair, he would roll a cigarette, and the discussion would begin, much like a seminar for advanced students at the university. Miller was slow-talking, almost ponderous in manner.

Just the opposite was Art Creelman, sharp-witted teacher of Physics and Trigonometry. On the way to school in the morning, Creelman would cut across the soccer field like a steam locomotive, chest thrust out, arms and legs like pistons churning with relentless precision, a disciplined tornado of a man. That's the way he walked, talked, taught, did everything including driving the football players to give their all for the old green and white. And so it was with the other teachers; Siddons, McIntyre, Stewart, Chamberlain, Freedman, Sprague, Walker, and Dunmore, all bright, competent in their subject area, interested in their students, and each an amusing, distinctive character in our eyes.

Even McDougall himself was a rather comic, lovable figure with his bow-legged rambling walk, whether it was coming down the long hallway on the lookout for one of us late for class, or after school when he, puffing his pipe, headed homeward down 23rd. No doubt he was cogitating his next deft scheme to put North Van High on the map.

McDougall's skeletel frame was punctuated at the top by a round, bony face, a wide mouth, and eyes that either sparkled or blazed behind spectacles. Normally, his eyes sparkled, the keen mind behind in a state of amused contemplation. When pleased, his mouth stretched in a broad smile from ear to ear. When angry, his eyes sizzled with indignation, and his broad mouth loomed as grim and forbidding as a fortress gate.

There was one sure way to tell if McDougall was upset. Out of the office and down the hall he would stride rapping his knuckles on walls or lockers. Somebody was going to get it, usually back in his office, doors shut. One such day in late April 1943 it was the turn of Bob Handel and Jack Grant, both seniors and players on the Canadian football team looking forward to a championship season.

The day previous had been a gorgeous spring day, and, feeling their oats, had cajoled Lorna Lang, normally a very well behaved top student, to play hookey and come along with them on some sort of expedition. But somebody spied them on their way and got word to McDougall. Next day by 10 o'clock Bob and Jack were in McDougall's office, doors closed.

That morning McDougall was sizzling. Fixing one, then the other, McDougall said in icy tone, "Bob Handel, you ought to be ashamed of yourself! Playing hookey! You, vice-president of the student council! What kind of example is that to set?"

Sweating, Bob tried to evade McDougall's demanding stare.

Then he turned on Jack, "And you, Jack Grant! Do you think that just because you're a good football player, that's going to keep you out of the army? Well, we'll see about that!"

Letting the two truants sweat for awhile, McDougall walked around them and stood looking out the window. He had a problem. The provincial football championship of the Lower Mainland was coming up. North Van High was in the running despite being a small school with barely enough players to field a team.

Handel was the brains of the team, and Grant, although not too smart in school, was a tremendous ballplayer, the fastest runner on the team. So what would he do? Reaching a decision, he returned to his desk. Staring the two down, he paused to let what he was about to say sink in, then said, "Now let this be a lesson you never forget. Both of you are suspended from playing football games until further notice. Now get back to class."

The afternoon before the big game he lifted the suspension and North Van High went on to win the championship.

As a postscript, both Bob Handel and Jack Grant graduated, did their stint in the service, and went on to successful careers after the war. Apparently they had learned a lesson. As for Lorna, McDougall knew she needed no punishment from him to learn from the experience. The scolding she got as president of the girls' Hi-Y and the example she should set was enough. From then on, she was an even better student than before.

McDougall employed an endless repertoire of leadership savvy to get the best out of staff and students. If a threat was needed, he could apply one with exquisite precision, as with Handel and Grant. But a negative approach was always his last resort. His face usually bore an impish grin, eyes sparkling with pleasure when he discovered something of interest in the individual, rather like an amiable parish priest. But behind the eyes, his brain was always at work sizing up the person in terms of his education mission, and like an ethical priest, he was equally mindful of the individual's well-being as well as that of the school.

A tragic exception was the treatment accorded to students of Japanese origin following Japan's attack on Pearl Harbour on December 7, 1941. On February 19, 1942 U.S. President Roosevelt signed executive order #9066 authorizing the U.S. War Department to carry out the wholesale evacuation of all persons of Japanese origin from the Pacific coast and their internment for the duration of the war. All of Canada's Pacific coast was included under the joint military Western Defense Command headed by U.S. General John L. De Witt.

In concert with the U.S., the Canadian parliament authorized Public Proclamation #5 resulting in the evacuation of 22,000 persons of Japanese ancestry then living in B.C., meaning children as well as their parents, most of whom were Canadian citizens.

North Vancouver had numerous families of Japanese origin, usually occupied in fishing, boat-building, or forestry, and many children in public school. Among those at North Van High were Harold Ishii, highly prized hook on the rugby team, Hoshiro Takahashi, and Pauline Hiramatsu, all of whom would have graduated along with the rest of us by 1943.

But by the summer of 1942 they, and all North Shore's Japanese-Canadians were in internment camps in the interior.

I don't remember anything being said about their absence. Certainly neither McDougall nor the public schools had anything to do with this decision by the American and Canadian governments in this time of great wartime anxiety, fear, and hysteria. Government officials were under great pressure from anti-oriental prejudice among many citizens. In hindsight, the apparent lack of protest of the abuse of one segment of the population, hitherto widely respected for their law-abiding and industrious conduct, is a striking example of how different Canadian society was in the early part of the century.

As appealing as life was in North Van during those years, the truth is that it was a Victorian society with its share of prejudice and discrimination, all of which tend to be more openly expressed in times of stress such as severe unemployment or war.

The prolonged unemployment of the 1930s made it impossible for women to gain more equal status with men legally or in educational and occupational opportunity, and reinforced the Victorian notion that the only fit role for a woman was as wife, mother, homemaker, or quasi-maternal occupations such as primary school teacher or nurse. The code was that if a man could do the job, he should have first choice regardless of a woman's often superior qualifications.

A certain high school student's mother challenged that code by clerking at the most popular market on lower Lonsdale. One of the male teachers suggested in class, not mentioning names, that she should stay home and let a man have the job. The student, knowing it was his mother the teacher was referring to, of course resented the remark and told his mother.

The mother had seen a lot of tough times raising her family during the Depression, needed the job, and wasn't about to be pushed around, so the next day she was up to the high school knocking at McDougall's door. He called the teacher in, she gave him quite a tongue-lashing, and that's the last time any teacher at North Van High preached that a woman's only place was in the home.

The wartime need for womanpower in industry and the armed forces did more than anything to break down this gender prejudice, but the war had the opposite effect with prejudice related to race and nationality. Betty McLeod remembers a teacher at Queen Mary requiring pupils of German or Italian extraction to stand up and be recognized in class. Jimmy Gallozo remembers a lot of taunting in grade school because of his name, saying fifty years later, "I feel more at ease today being Canadian than growing up then." The same is true of Ralph and Hugh Kuntz, whose father changed their name to "Koonts" in an attempt to lessen the anti-German prejudice directed against his children. So although those of Japanese origin suffered the most, they were not alone in being victimized by prejudice heightened by wartime hysteria.

On the positive side, the war offered an escape and opportunities hitherto unimaginable to hundreds of North Van's youth. Life could hardly have been worse than for Patricia Lindblom struggling to grow up in North Van before the war came along and she was accepted and sent off for training in the R.C.A.F.

In the first place, she and her twin brother Bill were half Indian, their mother being a Haida from the Queen Charlotte Islands. That alone caused feelings of inferiority because her mother was raised to feel ashamed to be Indian and wouldn't talk about it with her children. Then there was no father in the home. Mr. Lindblom had been a fisherman of Scandinavian descent who disappeared when they were only infants.

And to top it all off, her mother made the mistake of becoming pregnant without benefit of remarriage when Pat and Bill were still in grade school, had her child allowance taken away, and the family forced to leave their settled home in Lynn Valley to live in poverty near the Indian reservation in lower Lonsdale. Bill quit school and got a job in a local sawmill until old enough to join the Royal Canadian Navy.

Pat did everything to make money and stay in school; baby sat, mother's helper, Woodward's part time, all she could until she got a chance to get into the service like her brother Bill. Accepted by the Air Force, she quit school in grade 11, and never looked back. Two years later, with an excellent service rating, she went on to U.B.C. and teacher training, and wound up thirty years later on the U.B.C. faculty. And that's to say nothing of getting married and raising a family.

McDougall had a hard time keeping boys in school during the war years. With both shipyards operating in high gear, jobs were easy to come by, and with overtime, a high school student could earn as much per month as a teacher's salary. Despite doing everything he could to make staying in school attractive and exciting, many boys dropped out, among them Gerry Green who got a chance to learn drafting in the shipyards, Harvey Marshall to learn steam engineering in the merchant marine, and many others who seized the opportunities opened up by the wartime shortage of manpower.

Sports were probably the biggest drawing card for boys, particularly rugby and Canadian football, with soccer and baseball seeming to drop in interest after grade school. Rugby was the preeminent sport for exuberant boys to rough it up. Every high school in the greater Vancouver area fielded Junior and Senior league teams which went at each other every Saturday morning during the Fall. King Ed. vs. Kitsilano, South Burnaby vs. Lord Byng, North Van vs. Britannia, every Saturday morning from September until mid-November high school teams huffed, puffed, grunted, shoved, tackled, and yelled up and down Vancouver's soggy playfields.

It wasn't easy for North Van High to compete against the big Vancouver schools. Aside from being a small school, the others didn't want to come over to the North Shore to play. So every Saturday morning the North Van team had to get up an hour or so early and travel by ferry to fields all over the city, particularly tricky during heavy fogs when the ferries were often late and city blanketed in fog.

Playing against North or South Burnaby was the worst. One morning the fog was so thick, the ferry was a half hour late, by the time the team reached Renfrew Park it was an hour late, and the field so shrouded in fog no one could locate the goalposts or Burnaby team. Ivan Miller blew a few blasts on his referee whistle, waited a couple of minutes, blew a couple more, and North Burnaby emerged from the mist.

The two teams milled around while Miller and the Burnaby coach conferrred, sent out scouts to find the goal posts, and decided to begin the game. The fog began to break up and drift in pockets just as they completed the toss. North Van won the kickoff. Miller coached Roy Siddons to keep the kick low so North Van could follow the ball.

Roy made a good kick, downfield a good fifty yards, and North Van swarmed forward in pursuit of the receiver. Burnaby made a good retrieval, formed up, and advancing to their right with several lateral passes, returned the ball almost to centre field. In hot pursuit, North Van was closing in fast.

Suddenly the Burnaby ballcarrier and line vanished in the fog. From somewhere within that drifting void the Burnaby team yelped like a pack of dogs, their exact whereabouts growing more distant by the minute. Following the play as best they could, the two coach-referees likewise disappeared.

Having no idea of Burnaby's location, the North Van team circled about in confusion, hearts chilled with the absurdity of pursuing a vanished foe. Then, from within the cold morning air came the distant shriek of whistles and muffled shouts. The fog thinned, and from it straggled a dozen mud-drenched figures.

From the largest among them came a command, "Scrum down, North Van!"

Gathering the North Van team around, Coach Miller said, "Boys, we're calling it a draw and we'll play another day. Burnaby got lost in a swamp. It wouldn't be fair to play them in the condition they're in. Let's go home."

Once a month the president of the Student Council called the student body together for a noon-hour Assembly in the study hall. It was a way of building school spirit by sharing information and revving up enthusiasm for the school's teams and projects.

The stars of the event were the cheer leaders, N, V, H, and S, four of the most popular and smart girls in school, organized and trained by the girls' Pep Club. Dressed in green and white colours from shoes to chin, they mounted the stage, and bursting with enthusiasm, led the jammed auditorium in rousing cheers for North Van High. "We don't quarrel! We don't fight! We're the gang that's alright! North Van High! North Van High!"

The four chosen to be N, V, H, and S; Sylvia Dyson, Dot Smiles, Lorna Lang, and Jeanne McKay, were just the lucky ones. North Van High had a   surplus of smart, pretty girls. To the boys, it didn't particularly matter who it was up there in their jazzy uniforms.

For students who didn't have the inclination or time for team sports, other activities were going on all over the school; ping-pong on tables set up in the hall, putting out the school paper and *Annual,* a boys' chorus led by Mr. Stewart, experiments going on in the chemistry lab, and the woodshop where Mr. Gee gave some latitude for boys to work on projects of their own.

One who favoured the woodshop was Wally Firth. Wally had gotten himself a good-paying job working at Horne's cedar shingle mill for after school and Saturdays. He was used to working around big, dangerous saws, so Mr. Gee's little shop saws were toys in comparison. Nonetheless, Wally liked to make things out of wood, so the woodshop was his favourite haunt at noon-time, and there he made all sorts of tables and chairs for use at home.

Another was Paul Gilmore, who had become so fascinated

with the woodshop lathe, he wanted one of his own, so he made a small one with his mechano set, but needed a motor to power it. So one day he asked Mr. Gee if he could make a water turbine that would use the water power of the kitchen tap. Mr. Gee was skeptical of the idea but nevertheless encouraged his initiative. Paul's tap-power driven turbine did work alright, turning its little spindle at a furious rate. So what if it was merely peeling a carrot instead of a stick of wood?

For students like Wally and Paul the woodshop enabled them to take a small step in the direction of their life-time careers. In Wally's case, after the war he went on to university, then teaching manual arts in public school. With Paul, who found his niche in mathematics, he wound up in the main research lab of I.B.M. in New York, and later headed the department of Computer Science at U.B.C.

For the most part, boy-girl relationships were dealt with by the code of safety in numbers. Even in grade twelve, the standard procedure was for students to go to and from dances in two or more couples. Murray Sumpton had the only automobile in school. There was no such thing as drive-in movies. Nobody smoked cigarettes on a regular basis, the use of alcohol was absolutely out of the question, and as for illegal drugs, that's something the Chinese did in Chinatown's opium dens. Sex? Nothing to it; covered in one sentence by teacher Charles McIntyre, "Boys, just remember when you're out with your girlfriend to keep your pecker in your pants and you won't get into any trouble."

It was the era of big dance bands, swing, and jitter-bug contests. Glenn Miller, Artie Shaw, Benny Goodman, Kay Kayser, Guy Lombardo, we knew all of them from Lucky Strike cigarette's *Saturday Night Hit Parade* on the radio. Friday nights we danced our hearts away at St. Agnes' Hall to tunes like *Moonlight Serenade, I'll Walk Alone, In The Mood,* or *Somebody Loves You.* At 10 o'clock the dance would end, then some would stop in at Johnny's Inn for a hamburger and shake for 20¢, play the juke box for a nickel a tune, then go home, and always by midnight, unless you wanted to face a lecture for being out too late.

I suppose it's safe to say that every teen-ager craves attention and approval from his peers. At North Van High, brains and a winning personality were most valued, but among boys, prowess at sports was probably number one. Try as I did, with my bum leg, I wasn't first-string at any sport. So I went into politics, first as campaign manager for Monica Handling to become president of the Student Council in 1942, then to become president myself in 1943, with Anna Laubach as my campaign manager.

I suspect that I won against Bob Handel, a brain, football player, and great personality, because of the girls' vote and the long-time rivalry between the City's two biggest grade schools, Ridgeway and Queen Mary. Bob was from Ridgeway, and very popular there. I was popular at my grade school too, but North Star wasn't a quarter the size of Ridgeway, so I had to get a lot of votes from elsewhere. That's where Monica and Anna came in. Both were very popular, and, Monica came from Queen Mary and Anna from Ridgeway, so with them rounding up the vote from both big schools, I won in spite of being neither a brain nor a jock.

That's the outcome that McDougall preferred too. Not that he and I always agreed, but Bob Handel was a handful for any principal. He was so smart he often got bored in high school and had a way of getting into mischief periodically. If it wasn't playing hookey, it was rounding up some of his pals to carry Mr. Sprague's baby Austin up the school steps and depositing it on the second floor hallway. Or after winning the Canadian football championship in Victoria, partying it up on beer on the way back on the C.P.R. ferry.

Not until years later did McDougall shape Bob Handel up into one of North Van's most solid citizens by getting him involved in the Kiwanis club. There he more than made up for his various high school capers with community-building deeds, all the while conducting an outstanding career as an electrical engineer designing hydro-electric power plants in various parts of Canada and the world.

My senior year at North Van High was a busy one but I still managed to hold down an after-school job at the shipyards. As soon as school was out, I jumped on my motorbike and put in the afternoon shift at Burrard Drydock tallying the rivets pounded in by the day shift's piece-work crews.

It was the perfect job for attending high school, good pay, and not physically exhausting. As soon as I completed my quota I could get my homework done, then get home shortly after midnight and get enough sleep for the next day at school. I did my homework on the deck of a ship under construction using white marking chalk and while having supper in the blacksmith shop. The warmth of the furnaces in the vast shop provided a cozy corner and sufficient solitude to do my quadratic equations and Latin verbs in an atmosphere as agreeable as a university library were it not for an occasional intrusion of a large wharf rat skittering across my outstretched legs as I sat, leaning my back against a charcoal sack.

The fact that I was crippled caused my only confrontation with McDougall. Every boy in grade 12 received a notice from the government to report for physical examination and possible induction into the armed services. The examination was done at the armoury on Burrard Street in Vancouver. When the day came, a bunch of us from North Van went over together and went through the procedure; undressing completely and standing in line stark naked for what seemed hours in this huge drill hall, all waiting our turn to stand in front of a medical examiner sitting at his desk.

For me, it all seemed slightly ridiculous, as it was a foregone conclusion that I, with one leg as skinny as a stick and two inches shorter than the other, was obviously unfit. What I did not anticipate was how acutely personal my brief examination was to be.

When I finally presented my naked self at the head of the line, the examiner, looking only directly ahead at my face, carried on with his usual sing-song interrogation. "Your name?" "Your birth-date?" "Open your mouth and say 'Ah'". "Any infectious diseases?" "Tuberculosis?" "Diptheria?" "Whooping cough?" He even had me look at an eye chart. Finally, he came to his part of the script saying "Now turn around and bend over", happened to glance at my legs, and, totally surprised, said, "Oh goodness, you'll never do." Quickly jotting a number on a card, he waved his backhand as though shooing away a bug, then looking beyond, said "Next!"

I don't want to sounding self-pitying, but to a teen-age boy who grew up in an athletic family and a society in the midst of a war in which all wanted to march off and become heroes, my little examination became the ultimate humiliation. Roiling inside, I put on my clothes and returned home alone. In silence, I raged within with feelings of irreversible inferiority, shame, and anger at the examiner's stupidity.

In hindsight, my reaction was of course immature, unadaptive, neurotic. But from that dreadful day on a sour suspiciousness, hitherto foreign to my nature, entered, and remained to plague my soul. But that's another story which we shall get to later.

McDougall was very keen on North Van High doing all it could for the war effort. We had contests between home room classes as to which could sell the most savings stamps toward purchase of a war bond, Vancouver's high schools competed against each other for the same purpose, and now and again North Van would win first place and publicity in the *Province* or *Sun*. The girls knit hundreds of socks, scarfs, and sweaters for distribution by the Red Cross and marched around in Katie Reynold's girls' cadet corps. And of course all the boys were expected to take part in either an army or airforce cadet corps.

McDougall knew of course that as much as I wanted, I would never get accepted by the armed services. Nonetheless, he thought it important that I, as president of the student body, should set an example by marching around on the upper playfield along with everybody else. He probably also assumed that trying to perform close order drill was good for my morale and character.

So I went along with it all through my senior year, tromping back and forth, forever out of step, and feeling like a fool. It may have been good for the appearance of North Van High's war effort, but for me, every drill day was a day of dread and senseless humiliation.

Along came Senior Matric, first year university courses taken at the local high school, I was no longer a Big Shot on campus with the responsibility of setting an example, but McDougall thought I should continue to set a good example by turning out for drill once a week. As far as I was concerned, my stumbling around on the parade ground contributed absolutely nothing to the war effort, and I had better things to do with time, such as prepare myself for university and hence be of greater value to the country some other way than military service.

So we had it out behind the closed doors of his office. He stated his position, catering to my supposed importance still as a leader around the school, and that I shouldn't expect special treatment just because I was crippled. I admired the man immensely, agreed completely with the war and North Van High's war effort, but I had made up my mind that McDougall or not, I was not going to continue to make a fool of myself on the parade ground.

Neither of us would budge, so finally I said, "Alright, I will quit school, go to work full time in the shipyards, and next year I'll enroll at U.B.C."

That did it. McDougall was stunned. Glaring at me he said, "What? Quit school and waste your time in the shipyards? You can't do that! You've got a pretty good brain and you've got to stay in school straight through to university."

We sat for awhile looking at each other in silence. Perhaps then he finally realized the depth of my feelings and decided that I was right.

His smile and twinkle returned, and he said, "All right, Robin, show up for Mr. Stewart's boys' chorus during drill period. Maybe you will learn some Gilbert and Sullivan. We parted friends. Within a year he recommended me for university.

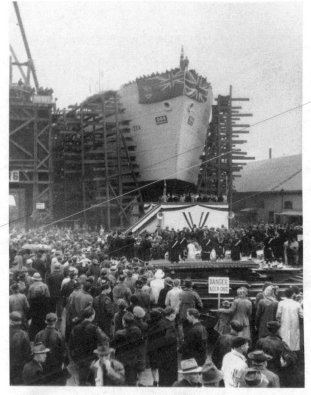

Ship launching at North Vancouver shipyard during W.W. II

North Vancouver High School, sketch by Sydney Baker

North Vancouver High School staff, 1938

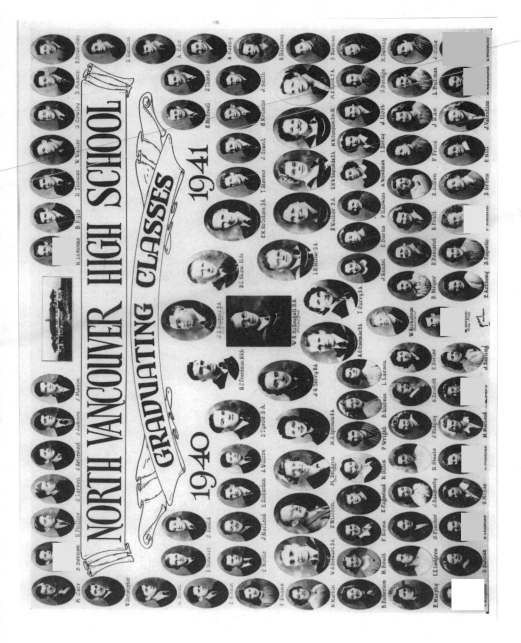

North Vancouver High School, graduation class, 1940–41

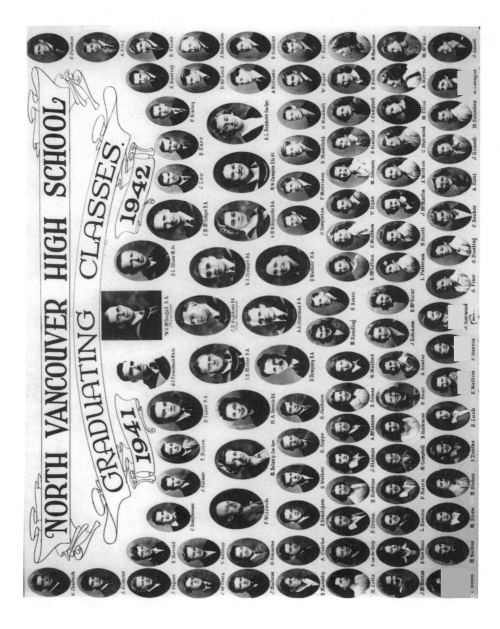

North Vancouver High School, graduation class, 1941–42

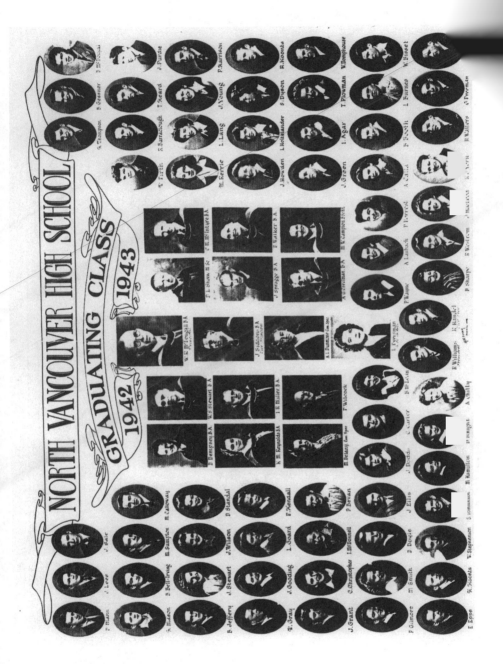

North Vancouver High School, graduation class, 1942–43

North Vancouver High School, graduation class, 1943–44 (Photo damaged by fire)

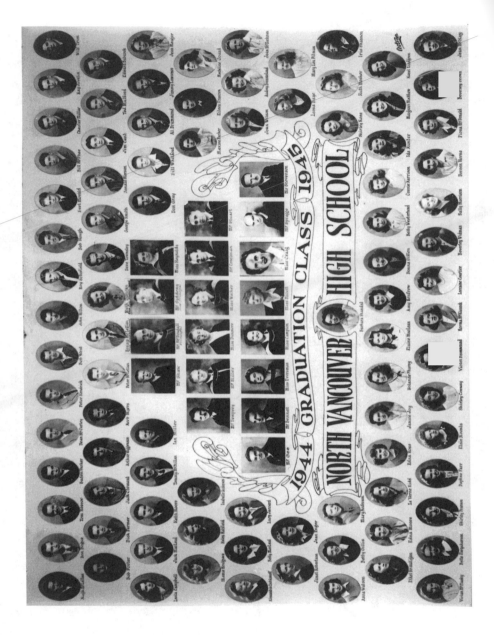

North Vancouver High School, graduation class, 1944–45

North Vancouver High School, graduation class, 1946

North Vancouver High School, graduation class, 1947

PHOTOS BY WAND STUDIO

NORTH VANCOUVER HIGH SCHOOL
GRADUATING CLASS, 1948

North Vancouver High School, graduation class, 1948

North Vancouver High School, graduation class, 1948–49

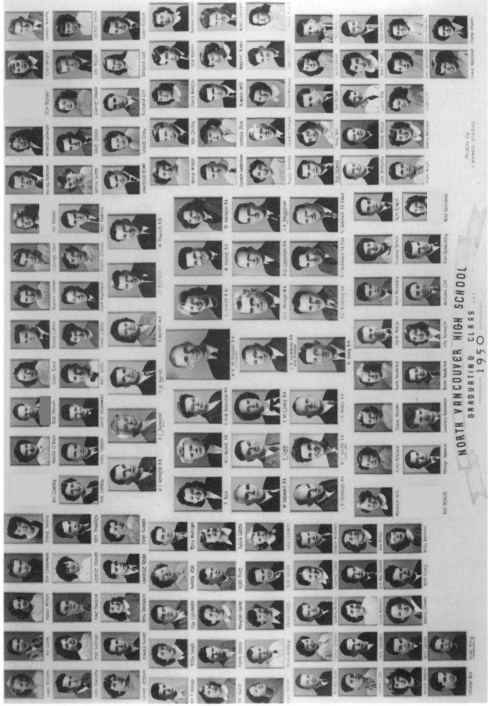

North Vancouver High School, graduation class, 1950

8

QUEEN CHARLOTTE SUMMER

This is the story of leaving the sheltered life of home to work for the summer in a logging camp in the Queen Charlotte Islands. After three days travel by boat I entered a different world, a world of iron men at work in a dangerous trade. At times I wasn't sure I would return home alive.

It was the summer of '43, I was seventeen, just graduated from North Vancouver High School and needed the money for Senior Matriculation. Then I hoped to transfer to U. B. C. the following year. I could have made almost as much remaining in North Van and working in the shipyards, but that didn't include room and board, and besides, it was part of growing up in most B. C. families for sons to leave home to work once through high school. Every summer B. C.'s logging camps, lumber mills, mines, smelters, and fish canneries swelled with young men like me.

Young bucks usually followed in their father's footsteps. My dad was a forester, so all but my brother Asa went into the woods during the summer to support themselves during the next school year. Ace liked to climb mountains, so he got a job at the Trail smelter to be near the Rockies. But logging was in my family, so I wanted to work in a logging camp like my brothers Larkin and Don.

The giant Sitka spruce of the Queen Charlotte Islands were a vital part of Canada's war effort because the wood of this tree is unusually light and strong, ideal for the construction of warplanes. So while most logging in B.C. was shut down for the duration of the war, a high priority was given to recruiting manpower for the Queen Charlottes. Most of the Canadian-born loggers like my brother Larkin were in the armed services, hence logging crews were to a large extent first generation immigrants with only a sprinkling of key personnel being Canadian-born.

Despite this manpower shortage, there was no government employment agency in those days. If you wanted to work in the woods you had to buy a job at a private employment agency on Vancouver's skidroad, Cordova Street between Carrall and Cambie, today's Gastown.

Even a stranger would know he was on Vancouver's skidroad from the injured loggers missing an arm or leg lounging in front of stale-smelling beer parlours, frowsy whores drifting up and down the street, signs like ROOMS, SWEDISH BATH, OUT-DOOR FITTERS, and pawn shops like PACIFIC COLLAT-ERAL with windows loaded with guns and tools.

I found what I was looking for on Abbott Street. "BLACKWELL'S EMPLOYMENT AGENCY" the sign said. That's where Dad said to go and ask for Mr. Sharky.

Inside, a half dozen men stood looking up a huge blackboard on the wall. Listed in neat columns were the jobs. "Kelsey Bay...choker setters (3)...$5.50 a day", "Port Hardy...cook...$6.00 a day", "Powell River...Master Mechanic...$250 plus house". The list of jobs went on and on covering the whole board.

I moved up to the counter beneath the board and asked for Mr. Sharky. A sharp-nosed man with glasses looked down at me. "I'm Sharky. Whatcha lookin' for, son?." I replied, "My first job in the woods."

It would have been foolish not to be forthright and get sent out to a job I couldn't handle. "How old are you, about eighteen?" he inquired, suggesting slyly to me the minimum age to work in this dangerous occupation. "Just about", I said, hoping that would be good enough. "Anything wrong with you?" he fired back. Again I thought it wise to stick close to the truth. "I have one bad leg, but I've worked clearing land and the shipyards and can get around pretty good", I said, hoping that would slide by too if he was hard up for men. To my relief he said, "You better start with a cookhouse job then." I knew I couldn't handle the kind of work Larkin did.

Mr Sharky looked up at the board. "How would you like to go up to the Queen Charlottes? They need a flunky. Three twenty a day and room and board." His sharp eyes fixed me as though I'd better not say "No."

"How much is the fare?" I asked. He shot back, "Thirty-five first class, eighteen steerage. Union Steamship. Leaves tomorrow. Three days to Charlotte City. You got the fare?" Mr. Sharky wasted no words so I had to think quick, "I don't have thirty-five, so I guess I'll go steerage", I replied. "Alright, come over here", he directed.

He led me to the end of the counter and within a minute I was signed up; a contract to pay a third of my first month's wages to Blackwell's, a slip of paper referring me to the timekeeper of Kelly Logging Co., and final verbal instructions from Mr. Sharky. "The camp boat will pick you up at Charlotte City. Give this to the timekeeper. And don't miss the boat, the *Camosun II* leaves tomorrow morning, eight o'clock sharp, Union pier."

I wove my way through a clump of loggers and out the door to Abbott Street. There was nothing to it. I had a job in a logging camp. Now all I had to do was go home and pack and make sure to catch the boat in the morning. To make darn sure, I went to the Union pier on Water Street and got my ticket. There tied up at the pier was the *Camosun II,* an old tub sitting high in the water next to the *Princess Patricia,* both taking on cargo for the camps up North.

It still being late morning, I walked up to Dad's office in the Shelly Building, told him about getting the job, and we went to lunch at the Trocadero cafe to celebrate. The rest of the day I spent at two of my favourite places in the city, Chinatown, and the Vancouver Public Library just down the street on the corner of Main and Hastings.

I took my time in Chinatown, the nearest thing to being in the Orient. The open air market between Pender and Main bustled with vitality; live ducks, geese, pigeons, and rabbits in woven branch cages, rows of vividly coloured fruits and vegetables, smells of spices and barbecued meats, and everywhere a sea of commotion, Chinese men in black skull caps haggling with merchants and excited Chinese children laughing and skipping about as though life was one great barrel of fun.

I bought a small bag of candied ginger, some leechee nuts, spent the remainder of the afternoon at the library with a Richard Haliburton adventure story, then caught the North Van ferry home.

After supper Mother helped get my clothes together and I went to bed filled with excitement. Come morning I was going off like my brothers for adventure away from home.

At eight o'clock sharp I mounted the *Camosun II's* gangplank, small suitcase in hand. The Purser looked at my ticket and pointed to a door just aft of midship lettered "Steerage." I descended the narrow stairs. At the bottom was a storage room jammed with crates of vegetables and fruits. To the left a doorless opening and sign above indicated "galley." Smells of cooking food and decaying fruits and vegetables blended in the dark, warm air.

To the right of the vegetable locker a dark passageway led to the sleeping quarters; a double layer of bunks with barely room to squeeze between the rows. The air was sickly sweet with odors of diesel fuel, oranges, fried food, and stale mattresses. I looked for a porthole. There was none.

I placed my suitcase on a lower bunk and thought "Oh well, it won't be so bad when the ship gets under way and the fresh sea air comes whistling through", and went back topside to look the *Camosun II* over.

A white enamelled sign First Class above a door aroused my curiosity. I opened the heavy door and stepped into a spacious lounge. The handsome room was bathed in light, the fixtures shiny rich in polished brass. Photographs of ships looked out from panelled wood walls. Round tables surfaced in green felt rested casually upon a carpeted floor, each encircled with captain's chairs. Upon the far wall a large brass plate announced the ship's registry. Undisturbed, I approached and read "*S.S. Camosun II*. Built 1907. Ailsa Shipbuilding Co. Ayr, Scotland. Length 241.7' Beam 33.1' Depth 11.1' Tonnage gross 1344 net 767. Passenger lic. 150 berths 87 Speed 13 knots."

The deck crew cast off the hawser lines, the propeller throbbed, and the *Camosun II* backed away from the pier, turned, and headed for the First Narrows. Back on deck, I leaned over the rail to take in the scene, Burrard Inlet, Stanley Park, the mountains of the North Shore, when a man approached, a skinny little man in white starched jacket and white cap too large for his head. He addressed me in a high-pitched, petulant voice. "Your ticket says you're Steerage. You can't stay up here. You have to stay below."

A weak smile crossed his face. Shocked by what he'd said, I rejoined, "You mean to say I can't come up here for a breath of fresh air, even if I get seasick?" He replied, "It doesn't matter. There's a W.C. below. The only time you're allowed up is lifeboat drill or for games in the lounge." "What games?" I asked, and he replied, "Poker, blackjack, whatever you want." He kept his eye on me as I descended the narrow stairs to that dark hole called Steerage.

I didn't know what to make of it. I could understand First Class having a private stateroom with its own porthole and wash basin, and better meals served in that attractive lounge. They paid for it. But to go without sunlight and fresh air just because I could afford only Steerage, that was a different matter. Being kept down in that dark, smelly hole night and day for a three day voyage was akin to transport on a slave ship. I was outraged.

Book in hand, I sat on the edge of my bunk and thought about it, the first time in my life I had come up against raw class distinction. It wasn't just a matter of money buying a little luxury. It was more the Purser's condescending attitude, his abuse of power over another human being, depriving that person of fresh air and sunlight merely because of being less affluent. The injustice of it stung like a cat 'o nine tails. It began to dawn upon me that up until now I had lived a sheltered life, and was not at all sure leaving it behind was a smart idea.

Then I recalled what he said about getting to come up to the lounge if I wanted to gamble. Money again. That was probably it. The Purser probably got a cut to run the games. So from his point of view, it made sense to make life so miserable down in Steerage joining the games would be the only way out. But I didn't have any money to spare, just $7 that I might need when I got to camp.

I resolved that one way or another I was not going to let that little bastard of a Purser keep me from getting a breath of fresh air at least twice a day.

In the meantime, I went into the galley with one of the books I had brought along, Edward Bellamy's *Looking Backward*. The galley was the only place with enough light to read by, one porthole, the only attractive feature to this cramped, grimy cell. In the centre a single oblong table was bordered with stools. A shaft of light cast a glint upon a whitish oilcloth punctuated with cigarette burns.

Seated beneath the porthole, I took in the sounds of a ship underway, the throbbing beat of its propeller, the creak of its ancient joints, and the gentle rattle of dishes upon the galley's shelves. A surly Chinese cook in slippers patted in with the noon meal; two steamed weiners, two slices of white bread, and a couple of tablespoons of canned peas upon a thin, white porcelain plate.

I asked "Any dessert?" and he replied, "Tonight lice pudding. Tomollow bled pudding. Coffee here", with which he placed a thick mug in the middle of the table and filled it from a black porcelain pot. Wiping his hands on his apron, he retreated to the galley as though cleansing himself following a disagreeable chore.

I stared at the unappealing handout. Apparently I was the only passenger in Steerage. A pair of glass salt and pepper shakers sparkled in the morning light, my sole companions at this wretched meal. Downing it, I returned to my book.

Henceforth the galley Mess would be my lounge. Lousy food

or not, it was the only place I could read a book. Dinner consisted of fatty cornbeef, watery tasteless cabbage, the usual two slices of white bread, and pudding. Breakfast was a bowl of oatmeal and coffee. To console myself, I conjured up images of logging camp meals at the end of the voyage, meals legendary for quality and variety.

The second day out of Vancouver the *Camosun II* passed out of the protected waters of the Inside Passage into Queen Charlotte Sound and the open Pacific. A Japanese submarine was reported off Estevan Point, so that evening the ship ran without lights.

The little steamer pitched and rolled in the half light of the moon. Unable to read, I lay in my bunk queezy with seasickness until, overcome

with nausea, I groped my way in darkness to the W.C. and threw up dinner. I sat on the stairs until, feeling better, went topside for a few minutes of fresh air.

In the lounge a half dozen loggers were playing cards, seemingly unbothered by the tossing boat. Drawn by both curiosity and the possibility of some brief comfort, I pulled on the heavy door and entered. A cloud of cigarette smoke hovered above two tables of gamblers. The room smelled of beer. One of the players glanced in my direction. "Want in?" he said in casual, friendly tone, motioning with a handful of cards for me to come forward.

Coming from a family that didn't play cards, I hadn't the slightest idea of what they were playing, so sat back on a chair near him and asked, "Do you mind if I just watch for awhile? I'm not feeling too hot." Turning to the others around the table, he said "Okay with you fellows?" They answered by making a space for me at the table.

Now hatless, the skinny Purser moved between the tables too busy to notice me. Balancing opened beer bottles on a round tray, he reached down and placed a bottle into a cradling devise attached to each chair. So this was another of his little rackets, bootleg beer. Neither the *Camosun II* nor any coastal steamer was licensed for liquor in those days.

After awhile the Purser eyed me with disapproving glances. By then I had begun to get the drift of the game, so thought I'd better get in for maybe a dollar's worth of chips or I would have to clear out. The next time the dealer glanced my way, I pulled out a dollar, placed it on the table in front of me, and said as nonchalantly as possible, "A dollar in chips, please." The loggers were gentlemen enough not to laugh at this punk kid asking to get in the game with such a pittance.

The game was stud poker, and after divvying up to the pot for a couple of rounds, I thought I had a pretty good hand, an Ace and two Kings, and bet a quarter of my chips. All but one other player dropped out. He raised and I matched with the remainder of my chips. Grinning, he said, "Show your hand, son." I laid my hand on the table. His grin widened as he laid his hand out; two pair, sixes and fours, and swept in the chips.

I didn't mind so much losing a dollar, but it meant I'd have to go below again. I would be a total fool to cut into my savings any more. I lingered awhile on deck as the *Camosun II* rolled and pitched in the half moonlight, wretched what little was left in my stomach over the side, returned to my bunk, and lay in darkness for what seemed an eternity.

Eventually the ship settled down. From the galley came the clatter of dishes. Slivers of daylight came down the stairwell. I went into the galley mess and through the porthole I saw a strand of beach and dark forest beyond. We were passing the southern tip of Moresby Island, most southerly of the Queen Charlotte chain.

At two o'clock in the afternoon we came around the R.C.A.F. seaplane base at Sandspit, entered the harbour, and docked at Queen Charlotte City. Suitcase in hand, I made my way up the stairs and stood next to the gangplank scanning the pier. A short stout man with logger's boots stood alone on the dock. I followed the first class passengers down the gangplank. The robust man approached, stretched out his hand, and with an affable smile said, "Hanson, Superintendent, Kelly Logging." Glancing at my papers, he continued "Williams, give a hand with the freight."

Orange crate in one hand and suitcase in the other, I followed Mr. Hanson to the company speedboat. He cast off, gunned the motor, left the harbour, and heading south, slithered past miles of uninhabited beach. Within an hour we entered a small bay full of logs. Superintendent Hanson throttled the boat down, maneuvered behind a log boom, and came alongside the camp dock.

A lean, curly-haired fellow grabbed the bowline, tied the boat up, and without saying a word, placed whatever Hanson handed him on the float. Climbing out, I waited on the float while the two exchanged words and passed mail back and forth. The man freed the bowline, Mr. Hanson spun the little boat around, looked back at me and said, "Just do what you're told and you'll get along fine." With a roar, Superintendent Hanson was gone.

The lean, curly-haired man sized me up and said, "Williams eh?. I'm James MacArthur Jenkins, otherwise known as Sparks. Grab a box. You're just in time for supper."

I followed Sparks up the plank walkway to a collection of shacks on log floats. He stopped at the first little shack, lifted the latch, pushed the door open with his foot and said, "Put your suitcase in here. This is the flunkys' bunkhouse." Proceeding to the next building, much larger, he beckoned me in. "This is the cookhouse. Matt will be glad to see you. He's been short a flunky a couple of weeks."

I followed Sparks down the aisle between rows of tables laden with white porcelain pitchers, bowls, and platters. Benches of men hunched over heaping plates. We entered a kitchen and Sparks went directly to a huge fat man in white.

The man's smooth face glistened with perspiration. Atop his head perched a starched cook's cap ridiculously small for his girth. His arms from the elbow down were huge, pale, and hairless.

Sparks said, "Matt, here's your new flunky, Williams." The huge pale man fixed me with gray-green eyes, grasped my shoulders with a firm grip, and repeated my name several times, "Villyums. Villyums. Villyums", all the while shaking with laughter. He made me feel uncomfortable, as though I was a new pet he owned. I hoped I was wrong, for this man was to be my boss for the next several weeks.

Our introduction was interrupted by a short, fat woman in white. "Matt, let the boy go", she said, and taking me my the hand, led me toward a closet. She reached in, wrapped an apron around me, tied it in back, and standing in front of me, inspected her handiwork. Then she too burst out laughing, only in a warm, maternal way, and said, "I'm Saimi, Matt's wife and second cook. What's your name?" "Robin", I replied, feeling rather foolish from her maternal attention. Nonetheless, I liked her genuine warmth, as though I could trust her.

She too had a way of repeating herself. "Robin. Robin. Robin. Nice name. I call you Robin. Come. I show you what you do." Grateful that she didn't take me by the hand again, I followed behind as she showed me where things belonged, what my duties were, and introduced me to the other two flunkys, Alex and George, both grown men. Then, realizing I hadn't had supper, she sat me down at one of the tables where there was an empty space and I pitched in for the only decent meal since leaving home, steak and fried potatoes, salad, fresh baked muffins and apple pie, and all the milk I could drink.

As curious as I was to see the rest of the camp, after supper I went directly to the washroom, flunkyshack, and to bed, an army cot next to a small wood stove. I was tired, and my first day of work would begin very early in the morning, four o'clock to be exact. Alex said he'd wake me up, something I could count on because my arrival would make less work for him.

The camp had 120 men to feed, twelve tables at ten men per table, so that meant that each flunky had four tables to take care of. The dishwasher stayed in a different bunkhouse, evidently feeling he was a notch higher in the camp pecking order, and that's true. He was paid a little more. No one in camp is lower on the ladder than a cookhouse flunky, and no one works longer hours, from four in the morning until seven at night, with four hours off in the afternoon. Sunday was a day of rest for everybody except the flunkys, just somewhat shorter hours.

By Sunday I had learned enough about camp to write home.

Kelly Logging Co. Cumshewa Inlet
Queen Charlotte Islands, B.C.

June 11, 1943

Dear Mom and Dad:

I like it here. I stay in a small bunkhouse next to the kitchen with two other flunkys, Alex and George. Its Sunday afternoon so I have time to write.

Every morning we get up at four and go to the vegetable shed, sit around metal washtubs and peel two sacks of potatoes and a half sack each of carrots and onions. Then we serve breakfast to 120 loggers, eat, and clean up the tables and floor. The loggers are out in the woods except Sunday, so there's no noon meal to serve and we have four hours off. Before serving dinner we make sack lunches for the next day. We usually don't finish until 7 or 8, so its a long day. But I'm making $3.20 a day plus room and board, so its worth it. By the end of the summer I should have over $200 saved.

The people here are interesting. Matt the cook is a great big Finn who seems mad all the time. But I like his wife Saimi. She is second cook, a short, fat, jolly woman who swears worse than any man I've ever heard, but she is good-hearted and seems to like me.

Hardly anybody here speaks English, only Superintendent Hanson, Sparks, the timekeeper, the logging foreman, or Push, the master mechanic, and a couple of the top loggers. Saimi and the master mechanic's wife are the only women. About a third of the men are Finns, another third Swedes, and the rest what the timekeeper calls "Bohunks", meaning every other nationality. Alex is Polish and George Rumanian, so when we peel vegetables in the morning we can hardly talk to each other. George is a funny little man who walks like our Chinese vegetable man in Shaughnessy and seems to have it in for women. Every day he repeats two or three times, "Women. Long hair. Short brains. No good."

The camp is built on log floats in a little bay. The bunkhouses, washroom, cookhouse, and different sheds for the office, saw shop, and bullcook's headquarters are all interconnected by a boardwalk of thick planks. The logging roads are wooden too, ten or twelve feet up in the air, made of hewn spruce logs. They go for miles into the forest. I've never seen trees like these spruce, some twelve feet thick and they grow straight up like asparagus. They bring the logs down these aerial roads with old solid rubber tired Reo trucks, then the logs are dumped in the saltchuck and formed into booms for towing to the mill.

Don't worry. My work isn't dangerous. I'm glad I brought an exercise book. I think I'll try my hand writing a story or two, the people here are so different and interesting.

Your loving son, Robin.

It took me awhile to learn the Who's Who in camp. At the top were managers, salaried men like the Superintendent who may run several camps, and the foreman or "Push" of logging operations in a particular camp, men who stayed with a company year after year. Then came the timekeeper who was also the radio operator and first aid man, the master mechanic in charge of maintaining all the machinery, and the foremen of specialized crews, all salaried men.

Among the crews the tops in pay and status were the fallers, followed by the buckers who saw the fallen trees into certain lengths, riggers and yarders who brought the logs to a central place called a "landing", the loading and trucking crews, and the boom ground crew who assembled the logs into rafts for towing to the mill.

Two other specialists stayed in camp, the saw filer and bull cook. The saw filer's job was particularly vital to the fallers and buckers, requiring much skill to keep their saws in top condition. One must remember those were the days before chain saws, an invention making falling and bucking much faster, easier, and requiring less skill, strength and endurance. Camp Cumshewa fallers and buckers did it all without machine power, using a variety of saws as long as ten feet, a man at each end and often standing on a springboard several feet off the ground. They had to be iron men, usually paid by their production, so the saw filer had better keep their saws and axes razor sharp or he would be run out of camp.

I thought a handsaw was a simple tool until I stepped into the filer's shop and saw the variety of shapes, sizes, and tooth designs necessary to handle trees as large as the Sitka spruce. Unlike a carpenter's simple rip or cross-cut saw with teeth all the same, the teeth of an eight or ten foot long falling saw are intricately shaped to alternately bite into the tree, then drag the wood chips out of the cut as the fallers at each end pull the blade through. So the slicing teeth and alternating raking teeth must be perfectly even and sharp on both edges or the saw blade will bind in the cut, particularly dangerous when making the final strokes before a giant tree is about to topple over.

The faller's was just one of many types used, all requiring a machine shop full of special vices, jigs, measuring tools, and files to maintain them with precision. Buckers' saws were of varying lengths, often shorter and thicker for sawing through trees toward the smaller, tapered top. The high climber requires a light, one handled saw to lop off the top of a spar tree. Then there is the odd-looking contraption called a "Swedesaw" the bullcook uses to cut firewood for the cookhouse and bunkhouses.

The bullcook was a kind of male housekeeper responsible for keeping the camp up, meaning firewood, linen and bedding, and generally keeping things neat and orderly around camp. But he was also a special kind of character in camp, usually an older logger, often injured so he couldn't work as hard as he used to, but with the experience to know the ropes among loggers. He knew everybody and everything that was going on in camp, and if there was liquor in camp he was usually the bootlegger. But I'll come to that later.

Another afternoon I hiked up the log-hewn road to watch logging operations. I must have gone three miles on this road as it snaked its way through the forest when it came to a clearing. From ahead came a choog-a-choog sound of a steam engine, a sound I was familiar with from watching a pile driver at work on the North Van waterfront. I proceeded into the clearing toward the sound, walked around a large pile of logs, and ahead, not 200 feet away, was the machine, a large black puffing steam engine at work.

Standing in front of the towering black boiler the operator was manipulating levers. He faced a huge spool from which ran a steel cable to the top of a spar tree at least 150 feet tall. Atop the spar tree, large pulleys directed the cable to another spar tree, rather like the clothesline on the back porch at home. Away down below men scrambled about afixing logs to dangling cables, logs then transported through the air to a central unloading point.

What I was watching was a method of logging called "high lead", the transport of logs through the air by means of an intricate system of cables and pulleys activated and controlled by an operator of a powerful steam engine. The steam engine, nicknamed the "donkey", is mounted on large hewn logs making it a sled. By anchoring a spooled-out cable to a distant large stump, the operator can skid the machine forward, hence the name "skidder" for this logging locomotive.

My father did much to develop and introduce this method of logging to British Columbia when he came from the East representing the Empire Locomotive Co. and other machinery manufacturers in 1912. As a result he acquired the nickname "Skidder" Williams up and down the coast. This method of moving logs through the air rather than on land or water surface was particularly suitable for the steep slopes of B.C.'s mountains and canyons.

High lead logging with a skidder took a crew of five working together like the fingers on a hand, all coordinated to grasp and transport a huge log several hundred feet through the air and deposit it at a precise location appropriately called a "landing". The boss of the crew in this complex, dangerous, operation is the donkey operator, so he picked his men carefully. He knew every one of their jobs because that was the way he worked his way up to become the machine operator.

Next was the fireman whose job it was to make and feed the wood fuel to the skidder's steam boiler, maintain the machine, and learn how to be an operator. Then came the ground crew, first the rigging slinger to see that the mainline, blocks, and subsidiary cables were set properly, the choker setter to wrap a smaller cable around the log, and the whistle punk who stood on a nearby stump and signals the donkey operator when everything is ready to pull the log skyward toward the landing.

Each depended on the other to do his job properly for safety and production. The whistle punk was usually a young buck just starting out in the woods. Although he didn't have to be as strong to handle the heavy rigging, he had to be agile, alert, and trustworthy, so even he was looked over carefully before being allowed to become a member of this tightly knit crew.

When a high lead crew moved into an area cut by the falling crew, it was a tangled snarl of logs and stumps called a "show" or "side". Getting them out and into an orderly pile required tremendous strength, stamina, quick thinking, and teamwork, an incessant contest between production and safety.

The most dangerous jobs were those of the rigging slinger and choker setter. These two had to run and crawl like monkeys along, over, and under logs pulling heavy cable all day long. The quickest way to get from one log to another was to run along the top surface of a downed log, and to do that without slipping off, the soles of their knee-length boots were studded with sharp steel spikes called "calks", pronounced "cork".

Scrambling around with their calk boots, these two had to unsnarl the mass of logs fast enough to suit the donkey operator, their boss. Often the logging company paid him a bonus for high production, so he was tempted to "high-ball", pushing his crew too fast and hard, one reason so many riggers and chokers setters were injured or killed.

The skidder was a huge, noisy machine, and because of the noise and great distances involved, crew members communicated with hand signals and steam whistle. One false signal could mean broken bones or death to a ground crew member. Danger could come in a split second from any direction; one log sliding over another, rolling down a hillside, or shattering on a stump flinging fragments everywhere, a cable whipping off a stump with the speed to cut a man's leg off, any number of things could happen in this dangerous game.

I watched for an hour and returned to camp reconciled to my menial cookhouse job. With my bum leg there was no way I could qualify as even a whistle punk on a high lead crew. But in a logging camp not one man was there unless needed for some essential task. By the third week I had become a reasonably adept cookhouse flunky. My job was to feed the fuel to these iron men.

Each morning began at four with the vegetable peeling marathon, Alex, George, and I gathered around washtubs like dumb puppets flaying away at sacks of potatoes, carrots, and onions in the cold vegetable shed. Then came our reward, hot coffee and a cinnamon roll, before setting out food on the tables. By five the tables were laden with pitchers of milk and orange juice, plates of fresh rolls and doughnuts, and plenty of butter and syrup.

The first men to come in were the firemen on the donkeys. They had to eat and get out before the others to fire up and grease their machines. Then came the hungry horde, a hundred loggers tramping up the boardwalk from their bunkhouses. In a minute they would fill the dining hall and the coffee had better be hot and the grub good or they would raise Hell, pitcher after pitcher of coffee, milk, juice, platters and plates loaded with hotcakes, fried and scrambled eggs, bacon, sausage, fried potatoes, and cornbread fresh out of the oven. Some insisted on hot oat meal, "mush" they called it. For thirty minutes it was a mad rush back and forth to the kitchen.

The only way I could keep up was learning how to carry four platters at a time, two in the right hand, a third balanced on the right arm, and the fourth in the left hand. The most difficult were the oval bowls of hot oatmeal. It had to be steaming hot or the men would send it back. The problem was the bowl that rested on my right arm was so damn hot it would burn the skin off my arm if I couldn't put it down in a hurry.

It was with that steaming hot mush that one of the loggers played a dirty trick on poor George one morning. There was no excuse for it. They all knew that the funny little flunky in bedroom slippers had a nervous disease that made him sensitive to touch. If anyone bumped him, or even touched him lightly on the shoulder, he jumped like a frightened rabbit.

It happened one Saturday morning during the busiest time at breakfast. George was hurrying along carrying the morning mush, four bowls of it, steaming hot. A young smart-aleck choker setter came in late for breakfast and slapped George on the butt. George couldn't control himself. He jumped straight up flinging the bowls of mush everywhere. The one in his left hand arched in the air and came down on the top of his head. Gobs of hot mush slithered down and around his ears. I was right behind him and saw it all.

It was terribly funny to see, like a Charlie Chaplin movie, but awful too. He ran into the kitchen, stuck his head under the cold water tap, and the dishwasher wiped him off with a cold towel. Matt grabbed a long wooden soup paddle and chased the choker setter out the door yelling "Sonofabeech, next time I keel you!"

Sad to say, the tables of loggers roared with laughter, a brief moment of comic relief in their dreary, dangerous routine. And after all, George was just a flunky. Fortunately, George got to the cold water tap in time and wasn't badly burned. But he had his pride, and from then on he refused to serve the choker setter's table, taking one of mine instead.

Naturally, the best part of the day was the time off in the afternoon. If I didn't feel like reading, writing in my diary, or taking a nap, I went exploring up the road or fishing in one of the creeks the road passed over.

If I heard gunfire coming from the beach, it was Matt shooting crows or seagulls that hung around the camp. He had several guns and was an expert shot. For crows he usually used a .22 and shot with one arm only. Bracing the rifle against his right arm, he followed the bird's flight and BLAM, with one shot the bird twirled earthward. Then he let out a wild, barbaric laugh. He would pick off two or three a day and never seemed to tire of blasting them out of the sky.

George and I both liked to hike up the log road into the forest on warm afternoons. He always preferred to go alone, shuffling along in his slippers with short, nervous steps.

The road crossed over two fair-sized streams, clear enough so the gravel gleamed beneath the cool water, fine trout streams. The first was George's favorite place to stop and rest. There he would sit on the hewn log buffer gazing down at the gently flowing stream. Often I would pass by him on the way to the stream further up the road. We never spoke. He plainly wished to be alone. But as I would pass I could overhear him muttering in some tongue unknown to me, muttering in fury, as though in combat with some secret foe. Poor George, nowhere did he find peace, from himself or others.

But I couldn't let George's apparent misery spoil these beautiful afternoon hours, particularly if I had fishing in mind. Having no fancy pole, I whittled one from a willow branch. From Sparks I bought some line and hooks, and with scraps from the kitchen, managed to catch some fine rainbow trout.

This particular day I caught two trout, beautiful ten inch rainbows, and was almost back in camp when I heard a girl's voice from the direction of the master mechanic's house. "Do you call them fish?" the voice said. I hadn't heard a girl's voice for weeks. It was like music. I looked, and there were two girls, one blond haired and the other brunette, both about fifteen and beginning to fill out. One was as pretty as the other.

I wondered which one had spoken. But they both just stood there looking up at me, like young deer in the forest. Then they turned toward each other, giggled, twisted their slender bodies as girls do when they flirt, and the brunette said teasingly, "Where'd you get them, up second creek I bet."

Looking directly at the brunette, I said, "Want one?". Instead of answering me, she turned to her blonde companion, they laughed, then the brunette sallied forth again, "I don't want your old fish. But you can bring me something else some time." Again they giggled and wiggled, then disappeared down a path toward the master mechanic's house.

It was a totally unexpected, delightful encounter, but maddeningly inconclusive. I didn't even learn their names.

Before dinner I presented the trout to Saimi and asked about the girls. She laughed, and said teasingly, "Irene and Patricia, master mechanic's girls. Which one you like?" I didn't know how to respond. It was like a choice between light or dark chocolate. So I said, "Which one has dark hair?" Saimi tossed her head back, laughed, and replied, "Irene."

Then Saimi moved close to me, and chuckling with sensuous delight, pinched my cheek and said, "Robin betta be careful. Pretty soon you fall in love with Irene." We both laughed as though sharing a delicious secret and went back to work.

There was nothing big, but Matt did some things that made me think he had a real mean streak and could be dangerous. It wasn't just the uncomfortable feeling he gave me the first day, or his wild kind of laugh when he killed birds. Several times I was aware of him watching me as though trying to catch me at something he could pounce on.

It bothered me, so one afternoon I hung around the time shack and contrived to ask Sparks about Matt in a round about way. Sparks was the closest thing I had to a friend in camp, but I couldn't ask about my boss directly. So I said, "Matt sure is a good shot isn't he? Do you think he enjoys just the skill of it, or does he like to kill birds too?"

Sparks discerned what I was getting at. "Oh, don't worry about Matt. He has to keep proving he's a man. Before he came to Canada he was in the Finnish army. That's why he's such a good shot. They even train them to shoot while skiing. What gripes him is he used to be a faller until he got hurt. So he had to take up cooking. He's good at that too, but he still wants to be a faller. Another thing is he and Saimi don't have any kids and that bothers him too. So sometimes he gets mean but he won't hurt you." I wasn't sure, but at least I understood Matt better.

After Saimi told me the girls' names, I wondered how I could get to see them again. I didn't have a preference for one or the other. What was important was that they were girls, those deliciously different, intriguing, maddening creatures who seemed empowered to make males do whatever they wanted. I could have fallen in love with either one as easy as falling off a log. So I decided to take something nice to each of them the next afternoon.

It was an unwritten code that a member of the cookhouse crew can take anything he wants to eat, anytime, just as long as it doesn't interfere with work. I always took apples and cookies to the bunkhouse for afternoon snacks when reading or for walks up the road and Matt never said anything.

The next day was warm and beautiful, a good day for a hike regardless of whether I ran into Irene and Patricia. But I decided to be prepared just in case. After cleanup I went into the cold storage locker and picked out two plump peaches, put one in each front pocket, tucked an apple for myself in my shirt, and walked out into the warm summer air.

I was about to turn the boardwalk corner by the dining hall when suddenly before me there appeared a pair of large shoes and white pants blocking my way. It was Matt, hitherto never seen hereabouts at this time of day. More surprising, dangling from his right arm was a meat cleaver, an impressive, thick bladed knife about a foot and a half long.

Taking a wide stance, he stared coldly first at my face, then lowered his eyes to my bulging pants. "What you got there?" he said in an accusatory tone. I was about to reply "A couple of peaches" and reach into my pockets to show him. He didn't give me time. With two adroit strokes of his cleaver, WHAP—WHAP, the flat of the blade slapped against the uppers of my legs reducing the peaches to juicy pulp.

In astonishment and fear I stood looking into Matt's gray-green eyes. Cold peach juice ran down my legs. His huge frame stood motionless before me, his face of stone. As abruptly as he had appeared, he pivoted and walked away leaving a fiendish laugh in his wake.

Emptying my pockets of the peach mush, I walked quickly up the road to Second Creek. There, like poor George, I sat eating my apple staring down at the flowing creek thinking about Matt, that mysterious, strange man, now clearly a danger to me. I worried about what crazy thing he might do next.

When it came time to go I kept a steady pace down the road, not pausing to look as I passed the master mechanic's house. Feeling defeated in good intentions, I hoped they would not appear this day. As the days passed my yearning to see Irene and Patricia grew. Many more afternoons I walked up the road hoping to catch a glimpse of those lovely creatures. I never did. They had vanished, as though they had existed only in my imagination.

But Saimi kept teasing me about them until I had to admit that for some reason they were now avoiding me. I'm not sure whether Saimi was making something up to console me or not, but she said, "Patricia tell mother on Irene. Mother tell girls to stay away from men from camp. Dangerous for young girls. For you I am sorry, Robin. I like to see you in love with Irene."

A week later Matt gave me another scare. I was taking an afternoon nap in the flunky's shack after finishing my diary entries in the exercise book. I had laid my notebook down on the little table by the window and was drifting off in dreamland. Suddenly, my slumber was interrupted by some giant force pulling me up by the hair. Still drowsy, I found myself propped up on the edge of the cot like a rag doll. Before me again stood the huge frame of Matt and the cold stare of his eyes.

I searched my foggy brain for some explanation of what was happening. Matt thrust something in front of me. It was my notebook. His eyes now blazed, his face flushed with anger. "What you write my name in book!" he shouted. "You spy for police, eh?" Waving my notebook in my face, he continued to glower at me in fury. Then, taking hold of my notebook with both hands, he yelled, "I teach you!", and tore the notebook into shreds with his powerful hands.

The torn fragments of my notebook fluttered to the bunkhouse floor. Matt turned his back and stomped out the door. Speechless, I sat on the edge of the cot trying to comprehend this man's intense dislike for me.

I bent over and picked up the pieces thinking what a fool I was to have left my notebook on the table. I should have put it away in my suitcase as I usually did. It would take hours to patch it all together again, maybe impossible. What a crazy man. What harm could I possibly do him? He obviously lived in a different world. What the dickens will he do next? Thoughts like that went through my head as I struggled to cope with the shock of Matt's latest assault.

But then I tried thinking about it from Matt's point of view. I remembered reading somewhere how the Nazis in Germany had schoolchildren make reports on their parents. Matt had grown up in Finland, a Fascist sort of state with secret police. And then they had been invaded by Russia. So maybe it was no wonder he had a suspicious sort of mind toward strangers. On the other hand, there was the peaches episode. That seemed like just plain meanness, maybe jealousy of youth and not having a son of his own like Sparks said. Anyway, whatever the reason for what went on his head, he plainly had it in for me and I would just have to be careful. Increasingly, I looked forward to the end of summer and going back home.

Then Matt really went off the deep end, and before it was over I wasn't sure I would leave the Queen Charlottes alive.

🚲

The first signs of trouble came on Saturday morning at the end of a long hot week. Matt must have had some liquor smuggled in with the supplies on Friday, because getting ready for breakfast he pranced around the kitchen laughing and singing like he was half drunk. I thought, "Oh, oh, what's going to happen when the men come pouring into the dining hall?"

They came through the doors and sat down as usual. There was little conversation. They were tired and looking forward to a day off. Matt couldn't have picked a worse time for foolishness. He came out of the kitchen swinging the infamous meat cleaver through the air like a Turk warrior with a scimitar. Pacing slowly and deliberately up and down the dining hall aisles, he whirled this thing over his head, stopped briefly beside each table and asked tauntingly, "Anybody got any complaints about my hotcakes?" He moved from one table to another taunting the men with the same sing-song question.

Naturally, not a man expressed a complaint. They had to go to work. Here and there one paused to look up, but mostly they just grumbled among themselves and continued eating. Soon they all sullenly filed out the door and the dining hall was empty. Matt returned to the kitchen and that seemed to be the end of it.

Come afternoon, Matt was down at the beach firing at birds as usual. Only I noticed a slight difference. The shots were louder. Instead of his .22 he was firing his .30-.30's, one braced against each arm. Rifles were like toys to this man. He was one helluva shot, just as accurate with two as one. I hoped he would blow off steam this way and settle down.

But at supper he started the same thing as breakfast all over again. He seemed determined to pick a fight with somebody. What was really worrisome was that in the kitchen all his guns were stacked against a wall with boxes of ammunition beside them.

Every trip I made out of the kitchen there was Matt at differ-ent table swinging his cleaver, just begging for somebody to stand up and complain. None did, and I figured out why. It wasn't out of fear of taking on Matt and knocking him to the floor. Any number of these men could have done that. No, it was some-thing bigger than that.

Every man in camp knew that if any of them did, all Hell would break loose. You see the problem was that Matt was a Finn in a camp where a third of the best loggers were of the same tough breed, known up and down the coast as men you didn't mess with, or before you could bat an eye a knife would open your guts. And they were clannish. They stuck together. No one in camp, including the Finns, wanted warfare, so they just put up with the crazy cook. Sooner or later he'd be run out of camp and that would be the end of him.

Like an officer reviewing his troops, Matt moved up and down the aisles enjoying his command. The men ate in sullen silence. The clock on the kitchen wall ticked back and forth interminably. One by one the men ate and left, until only half remained.

Suddenly, Matt moved quickly to the dining hall entrance and concealed himself next to the open door. Only then did I notice that he wasn't wearing his usual leather slippers. Instead, visible beneath his apron, he had on his faller's boots, complete with rows of spikes. Nobody more than Matt knew these were forbidden in the dining hall, for soon the floor would be in shreds. So I thought, what the devil was he up to?

The answer was not long in coming. Down the boardwalk came the sound of a single pair of boots. It was Scotty, a fireman, late as usual from work. Scotty was a top fireman, first out in the morning and last in at night. He was one of the few Canadian-born loggers in camp, and well-liked by everyone. Except Matt. For some reason, he had it in for Scotty.

Scotty was not three feet from the open door when Matt, quick as a cat, stepped out from his hiding place, and raising his right boot skyward, lashed Scotty up the side with his razor-sharp calk boot. You could hear Scotty's canvas pants rip as Matt's spikes dug in. The kick was so hard it knocked Scotty over the siderail and into the saltchuck six feet below.

The dining hall froze. You could hear a pin drop. Outside, Matt cut loose with his maniacal laugh as Scotty splashed about in the water. Like ghosts, the men at the tables put down their forks and drifted out, tramping down the boardwalk toward their bunkhouses, Swedes in one direction, Finns in the other.

In the kitchen Saimi burst into tears, blew her nose on her apron, ran out the back door, and hid in the vegetable shed.

I was considering which way to go when Matt waved a .30-30

in my direction and commanded, "Veelyums, put bar on door and watch window. Anyone come, you tell me." He repeated the same command to Alex, George, and Pete, the dishwasher. He thus closed off all four doors in the H-shaped dining hall. Remaining in the kitchen, Matt had a commanding view of the whole dining hall.

There was no doubt Matt meant business. His voice was confident, as though he had rehearsed the whole episode. George shivered and twitched as he stood by his door periodically peering out the window. I couldn't see Alex or Pete, but imagined they were trying to figure out how to escape from this mess just as I was. I wasn't worried so much about the disgruntled men outside. The question was what this crazy man with the loaded rifles was going to do next.

The minutes went by. The only sounds came from the ticking of the kitchen clock and the squeak of Matt's boots as he paced back and forth checking on his conscript platoon of flunkies.

Then I heard a slight noise, a scratching sound, like something moving up on the roof. I listened carefully. Maybe it was only a crow wrestling a garbage scrap or clamshell around. The noise grew more pronounced, too much for a crow I thought. Maybe one of the men had gotten up on the roof to stuff the chimney hoping to smoke Matt out. I sure hoped so. That might distract Matt enough that I could unbar the door and run for it.

My hunch was right. At first I could smell the smoke. Then it began to drift out into the dining hall. I could hear him rattling around, then the hiss of steam. He must have doused the stove's firebox with cold water to stop the smoke.

I inched close to the door and, keeping an eye on the kitchen, quietly eased up on the door bar. I had one end almost to the top of the cradle and was working on the other when Matt checked me from the kitchen, and BLAM off went his 30-30. The bullet clipped the heel of my boot, hit a nail in the floor and zinged through the cookhouse wall. "You stay" Matt said calmly.

Soon I thought I heard the sound of feet coming up the boardwalk, not many, but I was pretty sure I wasn't mistaken because the cookhouse waved and creaked a little from the weight of men on the boardwalk.

My mind tumbled with questions. Are they going to rush the cookhouse? If so, which doors? Would Matt actually shoot to kill? Did they too have guns? Could I make it to the pastry pantry ten feet away if shooting broke out? Would the Finns try to rescue him? If so, would a pitched battle break out between them and everybody else? And what had become of Saimi? Surely they wouldn't use her as a shield to advance on Matt. And what will she do once this thing is over? Even silly questions came into my head, like who would take over the cooking once they'd collared Matt.

My speculation was interrupted by the tinkle of breaking glass. At first it came from the windows near Alex's door. Then George's. Then a stone went CRACK and glass splattered all over me. BLAM BLAM BLAM BLAM. Matt fired four rounds about 20 seconds apart, one through each door just above our heads. The shots echoed through the dining hall.

Outside, all went still for awhile.

In the stillness my ears picked up another familiar sound. It sounded like the distant hum of a motor boat. It grew more pronounced. It was heading our way. By the sound I could tell it was coming around the point. There was no doubt about it now. From the VROOMing sound of its powerful motor it had to be the company speedboat. Ordinarily the Superintendent didn't come on Saturdays. Sparks must have radioed him to come from Charlotte City.

Thank God. If there was any one person who could put a stop to Matt's rampage, it was Superintendent Hanson, the only man Matt seemed to respect.

The rest wasn't long in coming. I could hear the thump, thump, thump of Hanson's boots tramping up the boardwalk from the dock. By the sound, someone else was with him. Their footsteps halted at the first cookhouse door. Hanson's voice boomed through the shattered window, "Matt, its Hanson. Hand your guns out and unbolt the door. Sgt. McCurdy is with me, so let's not have any trouble."

What I was about to see was astounding. As soon as Matt heard the Super's words, he picked up his guns, ejected the shells, walked straight to the window, handed them out stocks first, unbarred the door, and welcomed Hanson and Sgt. McCurdy like they were his bosom friends.

Sgt. McCurdy, R.C.M.P. looked every bit the guardian of law and order. He was tall, erect, a splendid sight in his blue and gold uniform and polished boots. He addressed Matt quite matter-of-factly, "You had better gather up your things. I'll have to take you to the mainland." He meant Prince Rupert, the R.C.M.P. headquarters, where Matt would undoubtedly be charged with assault with a deadly weapon.

Matt stood there with superintendent Hanson and the officer like a pleased little boy having his picture taken. It was an extraordinary sight. It was so contradictory; this huge man in a cook's uniform and logging boots who only minutes before was terrorizing a camp now stood looking pleased as punch in the clutches of law and order.

It took some figuring. After all his meanness, why was he suddenly so submissive, even jubilant, in surrender? It must have something to do with authority. It was perfectly clear Matt felt comfortable only when under the thumb of persons more powerful than he. Perhaps in his demented mind only the control of Hanson and McCurdy could resolve a conflict he could not manage on his own. He felt safe, reassured somehow, only under stern authority. Perhaps he was raised that way in Finland, an armed camp under authoritarian rule, and could feel safe only under similar circumstances.

Matt and Saimi were a pitiful sight being escorted down to the speedboat. They looked like war refugees, their fat bodies crammed into ill-fitting city clothes. Bent over with the weight of their suitcases they trudged down the boardwalk to the wharf. Hanson and McCurdy kept their distance, ten paces behind the disconsolate pair.

Loggers lined a nearby boardwalk and pelted Matt with produce from the vegetable shed. Occasionally a missile would miss its mark and strike Saimi. I cringed with pity for this good little woman. She had become rough and course in some of her ways. But who could blame her? At one time long ago she must have been joyous and beautiful, in the springtime of marriage to a handsome young logger named Matt.

Hanson and McCurdy let the men take their retribution. The superintendent had a more practical problem. Where would he find a replacement for one of the best cooks on the Coast? He didn't have a quick solution. Matt's successor would have to be whoever he could dredge up in Prince Rupert.

He showed up with Hanson the following Monday and was no match for Matt. His eggs were greasy, doughnuts tasteless, steaks overcooked, the grub just plain lousy. Before long the men wished Matt and Saimi were back. It didn't much matter to me. In a few days I was going home.

Right after breakfast Sparks said, "Lets go", and we headed for the speedboat. The *Camosun II* was due to leave Charlotte City for Rupert at ten. Sparks eased the powerful little boat around the logboom, gunned the motor, and the camp faded into the forest. A light chop ruffled Cumshewa Inlet as we skittered past endless stretches of uspoiled beach. Now and again a family of deer foraged on the beach. With almost total indifference, they merely lifted their heads to scan us with large innocent eyes.

In my pocket I had two hundred dollars for the summer's work. My mind raced ahead. This time I would travel first class on the *Camosun II*. No more steerage for me. And when I got home I was going to buy my first motorcycle. I'd noticed some at Fred Deely's, black little 125 c.c. Excelsiors from Britain. I could get one for close to $100. It would be an investment really. With it, I could zip down to the shipyards after school and work the night shift. That way I could sock money away for U.B.C. the following year. The university, wow! Thats what I wanted more than anything. Then I could learn what really made things tick.

Sparks wished me good luck and I boarded the *Camosun II*. I felt mighty good when I told the Purser, the same little bastard,

"First class to Vancouver, please." "Yes, sir" he replied respect-fully, handing me the ticket as though he had never seen me before. I was tempted to tell him off with some sarcastic remark when distracted by something of far more interest.

Nearby, a girl's voice said, "Daddy, will we see any more whales on the trip to Prince Rupert?" She was fifteen, maybe sixteen, her slender figure just beginning to blossom, a pink bow tucked in the back of her hair. She was looking up at her father, a tweedy gentleman about fifty. Both were leaning on the rail watching the crew on the dock readying the ship to depart.

I was tempted to introduce myself, instead, went to see my new sleeping quarters and tidy up. For obvious reasons I wanted to look my best if we had a chance to meet.

What a pleasure it was to have my own little stateroom with decently made up bedcovers, wash basin, and mirror! Only when one has done without does one relish the luxury of such simple comforts. I washed my face, combed my now quite long hair, put on a shirt Saimi had freshly ironed for me, my best clothes, and went back on deck.

The girl and her father were still there. Thinking it best not to appear too hasty, I leaned on the rail about ten feet away, on the father's side. Evidently I did the right thing. In a few min-utes they moved up where I was and the father asked in a good-humoured tone, "I suppose you have been working all summer in the woods? I've often wondered what that would be like."

He had probably observed me coming on board and decided I was fit company. The daughter smiled at me and waited shyly for my response. "Yes sir, I have been working all summer for Kelly Logging at Cumshewa Inlet. It was quite an experience, my first job away from home." He smiled warmly and said, "Won't you join us for lunch and tell us all about it?" Trying not to show excessive delight, I replied, "Yes, I would very much, sir."

The girl smiled with pleasure and the father continued, "May I introduce ourselves? My name is Asseltine, provincial Minister of Mines, and this is my daughter Nancy." Shaking hands, I in-troduced myself. We strolled for a few minutes on deck, separated to wash up, and sat down in the lounge for lunch.

Mr. Asseltine was a genial, diplomatic, and discerning man, not at all stuffy as I imagined a man of his importance would be. He wanted to know the logging operation, life in camp, and what I planned to do when I got home. He wasn't the slightest bit condescending, as though genuinely interested. Nancy followed our conversation with evident interest, smiling and laughing at appropriate times.

After two months of rough camp life among people who could barely speak English, I enjoyed their company immensely, to say nothing of the comforts of first class instead of that stinky hole called Steerage. Somehow, I didn't want to tell them about that.

Evidently Mr. Asseltine found me fit company, inviting me not only to have supper with them but to join them on a short motor tour of Prince Rupert the next morning.

After a most agreeable sleep in my little cabin, then breakfast, I followed the Asseltines down the gangplank at Prince Rupert and his waiting chauffeured car. Mr. Asseltine sat up front while I sat with Nancy in the back.

The chauffeur took us over much of Prince Rupert and surroundings, all mildly interesting, but I must admit that Nancy was of more interest to me. Unfortunately, the Asseltines were taking the railroad from Prince Rupert, so dropped me off at the Union dock, I re-boarded the *Camosun II*, and that's the last I ever saw of Nancy or the genial Mr. Asseltine.

The Minister of Mines friendliness to me did not go unnoticed by the crew of the *Camosun II*. For the next two days down the Inside Passage to Vancouver they outdid themselves accommodating to my every need. I thought how smooth and easy life could be with a little money and a government Minister for a friend.

But that was not to be my fate, as we shall learn in the next chapter.

9

ALASKA GRUBSTAKE

On the morning of June 6, 1944 Allied forces under General Dwight Eisenhower crossed the English Channel and established beachheads on the coast of France. That day, D-Day, marked the beginning of the end of World War II. Despite fierce resistance, British, Canadian, American, and Free French divisions forced their way into Hitler's fortress Europe while Russian forces continued to press forward on the Eastern front.

None of this would have been possible without first winning the Battle of the Atlantic by keeping the sea-lanes open between North America and the British Isles. The corvettes, minesweepers, and cargo ships produced by North Vancouver's shipyards had played a small but vital part in winning the battle against German U-boats, so there was pride and rejoicing among North Van's shipyard workers, many of whom had sons and daughters in Canada's forces overseas. But they were also aware this meant less need for their ships and there would be layoffs at the yards.

By then I had worked myself up to being an oxy-acetylene burner at North Van Ship Repair earning journeyman wages of 92+ an hour. By the end of the summer I would have saved enough to see me through the first year at U.B.C. All that came to an end by the middle of July.

The night of the layoff I talked to myself in the dresser mirror. "Okay, you can't make it in North Van, so why not take a year off and work up north, go to Alaska where the big money is? The newspaper says they're working ten-hour days, seven days a week in construction up there. In one year I could save enough for two or three years of university."

But I had a problem or two. I didn't know anybody up north, knew nothing about construction, it would take all my savings to get there, and besides it was getting late in the summer to head north expecting to find a job. But what chance would I have to go to university if I stayed in North Van? The yards were laying off all sorts of men with more seniority than I, and pretty soon servicemen would be coming home, then I'd have no chance at all. So I decided I had to take the risk of going north. But I had to go now, today, or it might be a day too late to get on for the rest of the season, let alone find a job that would last a whole year.

Once I had made the decision, I was relieved and grew excited as I gathered my things together. Boots, socks, underwear, work shirts, pants, and shaving kit went into a canvas paratroop bag Don had left behind when he went into the U.S. Army Airforce. Then I put on my best casual clothes; gray flannel trousers, red tartan shirt, gray herringbone sports coat, tucked address book, family photos and birth certificate inside, and dividing my savings, put half in my wallet and half inside a buttoned back pocket of my work pants. Stiffening myself, I took one last look at myself in the mirror and went out on the back porch to tell Dad.

It was Saturday afternoon and Dad was in his beloved vegetable garden. He was a comic figure bent over his hoe among the potato plants, a skinny scarecrow of a figure in floppy hat and paint-splattered pants that sagged between the cheeks of his rump.

I dropped my bag, leaned over the rail and announced, "Dad, I'm going to Alaska. I got laid off at the yards and don't have enough money for U.B.C., so I'm going north for a year."

He stopped hoeing momentarily, then resumed slowly, taking his time to think before responding, if at all. I wasn't surprised. He didn't have much to say during the last few years, getting old and beaten down by the Depression I supposed. It seemed to go on interminably until the war. Then, one by one, his sons left for the war. Don was the first to go, now a bomber pilot somewhere in Europe. Then Larkin, in the paratroop corps at Camp Shiloh, Manitoba. Then Asa, in officer training at Maple Creek, Saskatchewan. Now me. I suppose he thought that because I was crippled I would always be around.

Waiting for his response, I took one last look at the garden and orchard beyond. I knew I was leaving home for good. The big old house was now a mere shell emptied of all its young, and the same was true of North Van. All my friends had gone off to war.

Being left behind hurt more than I cared to admit. Working in the yards building ships for the war helped some. I felt proud doing what I could for the war. With the money I could look forward to a future. Good old "Mickey" McDougall, my high school principal had put it right. "Robin, your body isn't good enough for the army, but you've got a pretty good brain. You've got to go to university. That's the best way you can serve your country." For me, that meant U.B.C. and I had even checked out housing, ready to start in the fall. Now that was out of reach.

Going to university was the only thing that mattered to me. But now I wasn't sure it would be U.B.C. As of last night, that place had become a part of the general pain of my little world that was all falling apart. Nothing was working out for me here. I had to get away from Vancouver

and take my chances somewhere else.

Dad straightened up, leaned on his hoe, slowly turned his scarecrow head toward the porch, and said, "Son, you're a damned fool", bent over his hoe, and resumed his work.

It was so much like him. One no-nonsense sentence. He wasn't any good at business, but was plenty smart. He knew my mind was made up, so what was the use of arguing? Besides, he'd left New York and never looked back over thirty years before, so what could he say? Now it was my time to go.

But it wasn't easy. For a short while I looked down at the old man who was my father. It was all I could do to muster "Goodbye, Dad. I'll write", then picked up my bag, and headed down the Windsor hill to the carline.

I decided to call Mother at her real estate office on lower Lonsdale from the train station. It would be easier for both of us that way. The streetcar swayed and creaked its way down Lonsdale. It was hard going past my old high school. I felt guilty, as though Mr. McDougall was sitting across from me on the streetcar and wondering where I was going with my paratroop bag, like a deserter slipping away in the night.

"Mickey" McDougall was quietly but devoutly Canadian. It took character to stay Canadian, to put up with the climate, poor wages, high prices for everything manufactured, a country little populated and unsure of itself. All kinds of things made it enticing to cross the line to the easy life in the States.

I imagined him saying, "We're different. We're not Americans and we're not English. We're used to hardship and proud of it. Of course, if you have to leave to get an education, then you should go. But don't forget where you came from."

I imagined answering, "How can I be anything but Canadian no matter where I go? I'll remember, and if I'm lucky, you'll see me in a year and be proud of me."

The imaginary talk with Mr. McDougall brought an immense sense of relief. He had understood, and given his blessing to my hasty departure. Now I could leave North Van feeling no shame.

Boarding the ferry and going to Vancouver had always exhilarated me. That day I needed more than ever to savour all the good memories of that place, to carry them away with me, and to recall them again and again, until I had mastered what lay ahead.

I recalled so many events to cherish, most of them small episodes, but deeply satisfying to a boy growing up. Like a breeze turning the pages of a story book, memory upon memory visited awhile, then left. Going to Dad's office and lunch together at the Trocadero Cafe. Saturday morning trips to Chinatown and the Vancouver Public Library, that old musty place with so many exciting books to read. Trips in the fall to play rugby at Renfrew Park when it was so foggy I could hardly follow the streetcar tracks with my bike. And the day I went to Fred Deely's up on Broadway to bring home my first motorcycle, riding it for the first time straight down Oak Street, all through downtown Vancouver, and onto the North Van ferry.

Taking a deep breath of salt air, I got off the ferry, boarded the streetcar on Hastings, and headed for the Great Northern station thinking that if I could ride that black little motorcycle clear through downtown Vancouver and not get smashed up, I could darn well make it to Alaska and back. I got to the station in time to wash up and call Mother. It felt cruel and unnatural leaving her like this, but it was more than I could bear saying "Goodbye" to her face to face in North Vancouver, something to do with the special dependency tie to Mother that had to be broken sooner or later, but harder than with Dad.

I needn't have felt bad. I told her all the details and she didn't make me feel guilty at all, in fact, said she understood that I had to prove I could travel on my own now. How different than years ago when last in this huge conduit of a railroad station with her always by my side! In a way, she still was, only giving me love and encouragement by telephone, so no matter where I went on my own, I wasn't all alone after all.

The conductor looked at his gold pocket watch, scanned the platform, and announced, "Seattle...Portland...all aboard." He then swung onto one of the coach cars, the train jerked forward, picked up speed, and settled ito a comforting clickety-clack rhythm. I secured a window seat, placed my paratroop bag in the rack above, and settled in to enjoy the passing scene.

We soon reached Blaine and the familiar Peace Arch astride the border, symbol of amity between the two countries. But it was also a painful reminder of the division within my own family. In my parents' case, it had now become clear to me that my thoroughly Canadian mother was not well matched with my American father. His overbearing attitude was suffocating to her personality and spirit. They lived together, side by side, not in harmony or unity, but by accommodation, her accommodation to his will and power. I hated to think it, but this pretentious monument to Canadian-American unity, from the standpoint of power and equality in a relationship, was as much a sham as my parents' marital relationship.

Born and raised in Canada of a Canadian mother whom I dearly loved and respected, there was no doubt where my national heart lay. But I, like thousands of other young Canadians ambitious for an education, had little choice but to cross the line to the States.

Actually, I was better off under my present circumstances than most young Canadians for having an American father. Treaty between the two countries allowed dual citizenship until age 21 unless swearing allegiance to one or the other to enter its armed forces. Both Larkin and Asa had done so to enter the Canadian forces. Don was in the gold fields of Alaska at the time Canada entered World War II, stayed until Pearl Harbour gave him a chance to become a pilot in the U.S. airforces, so became an American citizen. But I, being neither 21 nor service-eligible, retained dual citizenship enabling me to move freely back and forth across the border.

The U.S. Immigration boarded the train and asked, "Where were you born?", I replied, "Vancouver", and her responded, "You're a Canadian citizen then?" I replied, "No, I'm both. Here's my birth certificate." Scanning it quickly, he returned it saying, "So you are." and went to the next seat.

That little document could become my ticket to university. I looked it over. "Name of mother....Eliza Bell Larkin. Place of birth...Alberton, Prince Edward Island. Father...Asa Starkweather Williams. Place of birth...New York City, U.S.A. Name of child...Robin. Place of birth...Vancouver, Canada. Date of birth...September 30, 1925." I tucked it back inside my sports coat feeling comfortably legitimate. The train rolled on toward Seattle.

I was tired and hungry when the train pulled into the King Street station so I looked for the nearest hotel. Three blocks up on Fourth Avenue the Holland Hotel looked clean and respectable. "Dollar and a half a night" said the desk clerk, a thin wrinkle-faced man with a green eyeshade.

Key in hand, I climbed the carpeted, creaky stairs and opened the door to room 206. The room was rectangular, white, and lifeless, not a picture on any wall. Bedspread, bathroom, everything about me was dull white and soundless, totally without colour, warmth, or vitality. It was like being isolated inside a white box, except for one little object. Resting upon the nightstand was a book, all black but for its name in shiny gold letters on the cover. "The Holy Bible" it said.

I put my bag in the closet, sat on the bed, and lifted the book's cover. "Donated by the Gideon Society", a label on the inside said. What is the Gideon Society? I wondered, so read on to learn that it was a fellowship of travelling salesmen dedicated to spreading the word of the Lord. Closing the book, I looked again at my surroundings, this clean but utterly barren room. I thought surely no setting could be better contrived to bring lonely travellers to the Lord.

As lonely as I felt, the Holy Bible held no interest for me. I was anxious to get on with my urgent mission. First, I'd get a newspaper, something to eat, and find out where there was a travel agency, thinking that if I was lucky, I would be on an airplane heading north on Monday. As for tomorrow, Sunday, nothing would be open, so I would see a little of Seattle, get to bed early, and be all ready to go first thing Monday morning.

The old gentleman at the desk was helpful. He told me where to eat, that the United Travel Agency was down the block on Third Avenue, and most important, that he was pretty sure I cold get work in Alaska. "A lot of fellows stay here when they come 'outside' he said. He even told me where to stay in Fairbanks, saying, "Go to the Hotel Fairbanks, a good, clean place and not too expensive."

My spirits were good as I walked down Yesler to the Owl Cafe. I was beginning to get some place. I bought a *Post Intelligencer,* the local Hearst newspaper, and a glance at the first page left no doubt I was in the U.S.A. Flying from the masthead was an eagle spreading its wings from corner to corner and in big

letters, AMERICA FIRST. AN AMERICAN NEWSPAPER
FOR THE AMERICAN PEOPLE. Below, the headline, three
inches high, announced SUICIDAL JAP DRIVE FORCES
YANKS BACK. It was July 16, 1944 and the U.S. forces in the
South Pacific were on the counter-offensive to retake territory
the Japanese had conquered almost to the doorsteps of India and
Australia.

I had the Owl special, roast beef dinner, and read the P.I.
from front to back. Almost everything in the newspaper was about
the war. "General MacArthur's Headquarters...New Guinea July
15...Japanese 18th army troops, desperately striving to fight their
way out of a jungle trap, succeeded in crossing the Driniumor
River." "Reds Smash Nazi Nieman Line." "Supreme Headquarters, Allied Expeditionary Force, July 15...American troops, hammering units of 11 or 12 German divisions into steady but fighting retreat along the western half of the Normandy front."

The news was all good from the war fronts. We were finally
on the offensive and maybe Larkin and Ace, still in training in
Canada, wouldn't get killed before the war was over.

Out of curiosity, I red some of the Want Ads. One said,
"YOUR WORK AT BOEING HELPS TO BOMB JAPAN.
Men and physically qualified women needed NOW! Minimum
average monthly earnings $185 on 38-hour week. You are paid
while training. APPLY TODAY. Boeing Employment Office.
2nd and Union."

Those wages sounded might good, twice what I was making
in journeyman pay at North Van Ship Repair. But I didn't come
down to Seattle to work in an airplane factory, so turned to the
movie ads. At the Paramount was "Home in Indiana", the Music
Box had "White Cliffs of Dover" with Irene Dunn, and at the
Liberty, "Once Upon a Time" with Cary Grant and Janet Blair.
But I didn't come to see movies either, besides, didn't want to
spend the money, so went back to the Holland Hotel and turned
in, figuring I'd get up early and see the city.

Killing time is ordinarily a stupid thing to do, but that's the
truth about how I spent Sunday, just waiting to get going first

thing Monday. After breakfast at the Owl, I took in the sights in the old parts of Seattle around Pioneer Square and sleazy First Avenue with its pawn shops, taverns, Swedish bath houses, and working mens' clothing stores, the counterpart of Vancouver's Cordova Street.

Alaska Way along the waterfront was more interesting. Soldiers and sailors were everywhere. The streamlined ferry Kalakala pulled into Coleman Dock and emptied a horde of shipyard workers from the Navy Yards at Bremerton. The Old Curiosity Shop was worth a couple of hours; a treasure house of strange creatures, mounted animals and exotic fish, skeletons, Eskimo and Indian carvings, wondrous objects from all over the world.

I bought a couple of postcards, one for Mother and the other for my high school girlfriend, Dorene, picked up a pack of razor blades, returned to the Owl for supper, then to the hotel and early to bed.

The next morning the lady at United Travel did not sound encouraging. "Give me a deposit, twenty dollars will do, leave me your 'phone number, and as soon as one shows up I'll call you. One way to Fairbanks by Pan Am. is $280. You can pay the balance before you go. It might be two or three days."

That transacted, I walked out onto Third Avenue to the cold realization that I had not planned this trip very well. The air fare would take just about everything I had, leaving me with hardly enough to get by in Seattle if I had to wait two or three days, and leaving me nothing for food and lodging once I got to Alaska, so it became obvious that I had to get a short-term job in Seattle darn quick.

I hit it lucky at the employment office on 4th and James. Wile waiting in line, a stubby little man in overalls came up to me and said, "Want a job right now? I pay twelve dollars a day, cash." Without hesitation, I replied, "Yes, sure" and he responded, "Okay, come with me." The money wasn't much, but it was enough to get by, and I wouldn't feel bad quitting in a hurry when my 'plane showed up.

I soon found out what he did; Pacific Metal it said on the side of his old flatbed truck. He was a junk dealer picking up car batteries at service stations all over town, then dismatled them for their lead back at a greasy storage shed. Little did I realize that four days later I would pay dearly for such haste in joining his enterprise.

All day we picked up used batteries, loaded them on his truck and unloaded them at his shed not far from the railroad station. "There's nothing to it" he said, "Just be careful not to spill the acid on your clothes or skin. Its nasty stuff, eat right through you if you don't watch what you're doing. Here, use these gloves and hold 'em out in front like this."

He paid me off each day as promised, and this went on for three days. Each morning and at noon I checked with the hotel clerk, and again at the end of the day. By the end of the third day, Wednesday, I was getting worried about the reliability of the travel agency, but when I came through the hotel lobby headed for the desk, the old room clerk reached behind him to the mail slots, thrust out a small piece of paper, and said, "Message for you, Mr. Williams." I grabbed it and read the short message, "Pan Am. flight 203 to Fairbanks via Whitehorse. One stand-by seat. Departs Vancouver Thursday 1:30 P.M. Pick up ticket 8:00 A.M. United Travel."

Departs Vancouver? There must be some mistake! First thing next morning I was at United Travel with my bag at ten to eight, ready to go just in case I had to move in a hurry. At five minutes to eight the same lady came down the sidewalk, opened the office, and explained, "No, there's no mistake, your 'plane leaves this afternoon from the Vancouver airport. Boeing Field has been closed to all but military aircraft ever since they started building bombers in '42. All Alaska traffic leaves from Vancouver or other area airports."

My God, how could I have been so ignorant not to know this? I guessed she didn't tell me before, assuming that I would know such an important fact. Feeling quite ridiculous and a bit of a panic about how to get back to Vancouver in time to catch the 'plane, I was surprised she seemed so calm, as though there was no problem at all. "You should have just enough time to catch the 9 o'clock train, arrive in Vancouver at noon, and catch a bus to airport." I handed over the $270 balance, got the ticket, thanked her, hurried out the door down to the King Street Station, and got there with time to spare to get on the train. Everything worked out as she had said. Nerves frayed and thoroughly humbled, I arrived at the Vancouver airport at 12:45.

I made my way through a waiting crowd of construction men to the ticket confirmation window and stood in line to board the 'plane. I'd made it just by the skin of my teeth. No doubt about it, Dad was right. I had acted in haste, foolishly. But I sure as heck wasn't going to admit it by confirming it with a telephone call to him or Mother from the Vancouver airport when I was supposed to be in Alaska by now.

God takes care of little children and fools, so I was told. I'd just have to learn to be more careful, smart, in the future, and hope my luck held out.

There was standing room only among the men waiting for the next 'plane north, mostly seasoned construction men judging by their talk and dress. They were confident, exuberant guys with tanned leather faces and dressed in sharp-looking engineer jackets, neatly pressed pants, and expensive looking cowboy boots.

Have you ever been in a crowd where you wanted to belong, obviously didn't, and wished you could become invisible? That's how I felt. These guys had it made, were good at their profession, knew it, and dressed the part. The best I could do was to just slip in among them hoping to go unnoticed in my herring bone jacket and gray flannel pants like some schoolboy. I figured I'd better change into my work clothes at Fairbanks and at least look more like a construction worker when I went into town.

It was small comfort, but I was glad that nobody knew except myself what little I had in my pocket, the grand sum of eight dollars and thirty cents, all that was left of my savings. On the other hand, I had a ticket, it was still mid-summer so I wouldn't freeze to death, and I could always wash dishes in some restaurant until a real job showed up. Anyway, there was no turning back, I'd just have to make the best of it, enjoy the ride, and keep my fingers crossed.

The line moved up and I was lucky to get a window seat, on the right side, just behind the wing. I tucked my bag aloft, settled into my seat, and peered out the window anxious for my first ride in an airplane.

From the back of the 'plane came a loud Bang-click as the stewardess locked the door, then walked up the aisle to check our seat belts. The 'plane jerked forward, taxied down the runway, turned at the end, and came to a halt. The DC3 thundered and shook as the pilot checked the engines, the NO SMOKING sign went on, the 'plane thumped, bumped, and roared down the runway. We were up and away, and I didn't want to miss anything. Down below I could see Vancouver, my city, for the first time from the air. I was surprised how small the city looked down there nestled on a small penninsula of land beside Burrard Inlet with the Fraser River to the south and to the north, the mountains of the North Shore.

Soon the city disappeared and from then on it was endless mountains, occasional rivers and lakes, and tiny settlements below. Gradually darkness came and all I could see were miniscule clusters of lights from remote settlements in the mountain wilderness of British Columbia.

Early next morning the 'plane dropped altitude, turned, and below lay the town of Whitehorse in a bend of the Yukon River. The stewardess announced, "We will have a two hour stop in Whitehorse to refuel. For those going to Fairbanks, please be back on board by one o'clock. Thank-you."

I left the 'plane with the other passengers and thought "What could be better than two hours to see this famous old mining town on a beautiful summer day!" Whitehorse was a frontier town indeed, board sidewalks a foot or so above street level ran the whole length of the main street's wooden buildings, all two storeys with false fronts, signs advertising every type of goods and services, and more Indians than I had ever seen before. Dogs were everywhere, big, easy-going dogs that acted as if they owned the town. And the townspeople seemed in no hurry to go or be anywhere, apparently content to just take in the sunshine and informal conviviality of this famous old frontier mining town.

I was sitting on the edge of the boardwalk enjoying the sun too, not feeling at all like an out-of-town spectator, when I overheard a conversation, a couple of husky young men talking outside the Gold Nucket Cafe. A slight burr and "eh?" at the end of their sentences marked them as Canadians. "So they turned you back, eh?" said the first fellow and his friend replied, "You can't blame the Yanks. It's our own government. They don't want us getting their high wages, eh? It's a bleeding shame. We could make twice what we make here, eh?" The first fellow rejoined, "That's right. They've fixed it with the Americans so they won't let us in, eh?"

What they said was disturbing enough to get me off my rump, resume my walk to see more of the town, and think about it. The boardwalk's wooden planks squeaked underfoot with my every step, as if warning me of danger ahead. What if the U.S. Immigration turns me back too at Fairbanks? I thought, "Well, I've got my birth certificate right here, and it says I was born in Canada and Dad in New York City. But how can I prove that he's still a U.S. citizen? I can't. If those guys are right, they'll peg me for a Canadian and send me back too. Damnit! It would be total disaster to get turned back now. What the devil am I going to do when the 'plane lands at Fairbanks?" I reboarded the 'plane feeling a conflicting mixture of excitement and apprehension, of being a half-baked outsider all over again just when I was beginning to feel at home up north.

It was close to six in the evening when the 'plane landed at Fairbanks. A gentle rain was falling.

All the passengers lined up at the entrance to a small tin-roofed building at the municipal airport. I was in the middle of the line with ten men or so behind me as the U.S. Immigration officer went down the line. He asked me the usual question, "Where were you born?" and I replied simply "Vancouver" hoping he might think I meant the one in Washington state. No such luck. I just looked and talked like a Canadian even if I didn't say "eh?" at the end of every sentence. "So you're a Canadian citizen, then?" he said. "No", I replied, "my father is American. I have dual citizenship. Here's my birth certificate." He took it from my hand, looked at it briefly, then, apparently impatient standing in the rain, handed it back, saying, "This is too complicated. Go inside and wait."

I went inside the shed feeling very apprehensive. I looked around. The place had no seats, just three doors marked MEN, WOMEN, AND EXIT. The agent's reaction to my birth certificate really had me worried. He was so indecisive, as though he was new to the job or a little slow-witted. In either case, he could be a real problem, the kind of man who says "No" unless he feels absolutely safe in saying "Yes".

The stakes were too high to trust a man like that, I reasoned to myself. But on the other hand, I didn't have a problem with U.S. Immigration coming down to Seattle on the train, so why should I worry? And another thing, if I made a run for it, that would be doing something illegal, and the thought of that made me feel extremely uncomfortable.

I looked at the EXIT door again, then behind me, and said to myself, "You wouldn't be doing anything harmful. You either trust yourself or him, and you don't have much time to decide." As soon as the fellow behind me in the line came into the shed and walked straight to the EXIT door, I followed him out. He went directly to a yellow bus and got in. Parked next to it was an olive drab sedan with "U.S. Government" printed on the driver's side door. No one was behind the wheel. I skirted both vehicles and started walking as fast but inconspicuously as possible down the long dirt road. It was full of puddles, so I had to weave and bob, moving as quickly as possible but not running or seeming to be too much in a hurry.

I got about two blocks down the road when I heard the bus start up. Hugging my paratroop bag, I jumped a small ditch bordering the road and ran, half stumbling on the uneven ground, toward a thicket of birch trees, then continued into the thin forest until I could no longer see the road. My heart was poundir and I was out of breath. I flopped down facing the road anc listened. The bus passed by. A minute or two later I heard the agent's car start up. Soon it came adjacent to where I lay concealed as best I could in the thinly treed forest, then passed slowly by, slopping its way down the puddly road until I could no longer hear it.

Just to be sure, for several minutes more I lay watching the road and listening for any sign of the agent's return. It grew darker as the gentle rain continued to fall. No danger seemed to be coming from the road, no lights, no sounds of a motor approaching. My dress clothes were soaked through, so standing up, I changed into my work clothes, thinking also that I might be less recognizable if perchance I should come upon the agent. Retracing my steps toward the road, I periodically stopped and listened before proceeding.

Upon reaching the road, I looked up and down, listened again, and detecting no sign of danger, threw my bag across the ditch and jumped. A sound like the ripping of a gunnysack came from my backside. Cold air travelled up the side of one leg and around my buttocks. Reaching for my bag, one bare lag showed. My pants had split half way up my rump and down one side to the knee.

I then recalled what the Seattle junk dealer had said about battery acid and clothes. I'd be lucky if I made it to the Hotel Fairbanks before my pants fell off.

It was awkward going down the road, paratroop bag slung over my right shoulder, hand holding onto what was left of my pants. But by eight o'clock I reached it, a four storey wooden building that could be taken for a warehouse were it not for a lighted sign above the front steps that said, HOTEL FAIRBANKS.

I was tired, soaked, and hungry, but hesitated beneath the sign, wondering how much they'd want for a room. I decided I would go as high as two dollars for that night just to get out of my particular predicament and get a fresh start in the morning.

olding my bag in front to conceal my disreputable appearance, opened the door to a small lobby, approached the desk, and asked the man behind for a single room. "Sorry," he said, "the only thing left is a cot in the basement."

He had a straightforward, agreeable manner, an older man who didn't act old, the same sort as the clerk at the Holland Hotel in Seattle. He volunteered, "It's a little damp down there, but the cots are clean, and you can have it for a dollar and a half a night."

I was in no condition to haggle, so I said, "I'll take it", handed him two damp dollar bills, and followed him down the wooden stairs. Duckboards squished with every step as we passed alongside a double row of army cots. Two naked light bulbs dangled from the ceiling. "Take any one you want," he said, and noting my lack of enthusiasm, added, "the breakup was late this year. It's usually dry by now." As he turned to leave, I asked about a bathroom. "Upstairs, at the end of the hall," he replied, then pointing upwards, added, "Let me know if there's anything else you need."

The damp cellar reminded me of a book of photographs I'd seen at the Vancouver Public Library showing the trenches of France during the first World War. But I found a dry section, put my bag down at the foot of a cot and rolled back the two army blankets to check what kind of bed I was to get into that night. It was reassuring to find clean white sheets, and the pillow at the head was just as acceptable, no luxury, but when travelling on the cheap as I was, a fellow can't be too fussy. I had a bed for the night, and my next thought was to get back into my other clothes and get something to eat.

Mounting the stairs again with my bag, I found the bathroom, a real one with a bathtub, changed back into my town clothes, damp as they were, and went across the street to the Lucky Strike Cafe. I sat down at the counter and picked up a menu. "Hamburger steak and fries...$4.50, Bacon and eggs...$3.25," on down it went to the bottom, where it listed, "Stack and coffee...$1.50." I mumbled to myself, "Holy mackerel! I can't afford these prices, for sure. I've got to get a job to-morrow or I'll starve."

The waitress came, set a place and a glass of water in front of me, and asked, "Ready?" and rather sheepishly I asked her, "What's a 'stack'?" "Three hotcakes," she said, looking me over with a slight smile. "Okay then, give me a stack and coffee, please", trying my best not to let on my state of finances but cheering myself up with a dose of high-minded self-talk that I had no reason to feel ashamed just because I was darned near penniless.

She brought me a stack of hotcakes almost as big around as the plate, plenty of butter and syrup, and with two cups of coffee, I was full. I paid, left no tip, figuring I'd make it up to her when I came back after I had made some money, and walked out the door with $5.32 in my pocket. But somehow it didn't bother me. Fairbanks felt right, like I was going to make it here. After what I'd been through the last couple of days, here I was in Fairbanks with a full stomach, a bed to sleep in, and with a little more luck, a new lease on life.

I returned to the hotel and got to talking with the old room clerk. "So you're up here to make money for college?" he said. One thing led to another, and as he seemed such a decent fellow, I asked him, "Is there any chance I could do some work around here to get free rent until I get a job?"

My question didn't seem to surprise him, and he came right back, "Oh, I don't see why not. Let's see, you could save me the trouble of cleaning up this lobby every morning, how's that?" and I replied instantly, "Well, you're sure doing me a favour. I'm a little short right now. Just show me what to do."

He showed me where the broom and dustpan were, I thanked him again, and went to bed feeling the best I'd felt for a long while. Thanks to the old room clerk, things were beginning to go my way. Now if I could just be careful and not somehow make a fool out of myself again, I just might have a winning streak. "Tommorow," I thought, "after I clean up the lobby and have a little breakfast, I'll get to know the town and maybe line up a restaurant job to tide me over until I find a good paying job."

The next morning, Saturday, I tidied up the hotel lobby as Frank had shown me and went across the street to the Lucky Strike again for breakfast. This time I had a bowl of hot oatmeal, toast and coffee for $1.50. With plenty of milk and syrup on top, that's all I needed to keep me going to see the town. The rain had stopped, the sun was out, and I headed down Cushman Street toward the Chena River.

From the bridge, the river was so small, not over sixty feet across, that I wondered how Capt. Ebenezer Barnette could have brought a steamboat up such a river. A few days later I got hold of a book on Fairbank's history that told me about the significance of what I was seeing from that bridge. It was here where the town of Fairbanks began in 1902. That's when a Mexican miner named Felix Pedro discovered gold nearby, and Barnette built a trading post to profit from the stampede.

From 1902 until World War II stopped gold mining, over 200 million dollars in gold had been taken from the rivers and creeks around Fairbanks, so they gave Fairbanks the title of the Golden Heart of Alaska. I was after a different kind of gold. Construction of military bases, roads and airfields now dominated the economy of Fairbanks, but the town still had the character of a frontier mining town. The public library was a one-storey log building, much the same as many of the surrounding houses, their thick sod roofs sprouting with northern wildflowers.

The town had a settled and comfortable feeling, a far cry from how Judge Wickersham described it in his diary in 1903, writing, "Sourdoughs, and Cheechakos, miners, gamblers, Indians, Negroes, Japanese, dogs, prostitutes, music, drinking! It's rough and healthy, the beginning I hope of an American Dawson."

By noon I had walked over a good part of the town and was returning to the hotel when a bus saying "Ladd Field" stopped at a corner on Cushman Avenue and began to fill with construction workers and G.I.'s. None of them paid a fare, so I got on, too, a chance to see this huge military base before going out there on Monday to apply for a job.

The M.P. at the gate waved the bus through, and it stopped at

a cluster of Quonset huts, the half-moon shaped metal
that squat by the thousands on U.S. military installation.
where. The civilians got up to leave, so I went along. The,
persed to different huts, and not knowing what to do next, I
tered one that said LATRINE, giving me time to get my bearing.

Coming out of the latrine, I saw that the hut saying PER-
SONNEL OFFICE was closed, but nearby a line of men stood
in front of two huts joined together. They entered the door on
one and came out the other. I moved closer to get a good look.

The sign above the door where the men entered said CIVIL-
IAN MESS, and above the other hut's door another sign said
EXIT. Between the two doors was a long table and a row of
garbage cans. Men coming out of the EXIT door banged their
metal trays inside one of the garbage cans and put their trays on
the table.

Beside the EXIT door stood an M.P. Occasionally he stopped
one of the exiting workers, pointed to his tray with his nightstick,
said something, and the worker dumped his tray and kept going.
But what I noticed of particular interest was that not once did
the M.P. check anyone going through the entrance door. By then
I was hungry, and it occurred to me that before my eyes lay a
potential solution to my problem.

But that raised another problem; with my town clothes on I
didn't look like a construction worker. If the M.P. stopped me
either going in or out, I might wind up in the stockade and God
knows what, certainly no free meal or chance of a job at Ladd
Field. I could go back to the hotel and change clothes, but that
presented another problem; in my only pair of work pants, even
if I could find a way to patch them up, I would look more like a
bum than a bona fide construction worker.

I had no choice but to get back on the bus and see if I could
find a decent pair of work pants. During my walk I hadn't come
upon a Goodwill store or other place I could get a cheap pair of
used pants, so I turned again to Frank. "Frank, you don't happen
to have any old work clothes around, do you? I'm pretty sure I'll
get a job next week, but I'm short of work pants." I couldn't tell

.c planning to sneak into the Ladd Field chow hall, and
want to admit what had happened to my work pants.

started to say I would pay him as soon as I got my first
check, but he just chuckled and said, "Oh, I guess we can find
omething in the storeroom."

He led me down the hall to a small room and switched on the
light. Inside, the room smelled like a pawn shop. There were
shelves of travel gear of every description, scuffed leather suitcases, cardboard boxes tied with rope, duffle bags, steamer trunks,
some covered with dust as if they had been there for years. He
blew off the dust, flipped and moved them around, and examined their tags, seeming to be looking for a particular one.

At last he found the one he was looking for, a sturdy old brown
suitcase with a belt around the middle. He wiped the dust off the
tag and said, "Yup, this is it, Rudy Thompson, P.O. Box 659,
Seattle, Washington. He won't need it any more. Here, take it
out to the lobby and we'll open it up." I took the suitcase out to
the lobby, placed it on a sofa, and waited for Frank. Its owner
seemed somebody special to Frank.

Frank locked the storeroom door, returned to the lobby, and
said, "I've got the key back here in the drawer somewhere." He
kept talking as he hunted. "Old Rudy. He was a real old timer,
one of the best prospectors around in those days. Now he's gone
like the rest. Died last year at the Pioneer Home in Sitka. Got a
letter from his sister in Seattle not long after. Said to give whatever he left to the Salvation Army. I just didn't get around to it.
He wouldn't mind. Come to think of it, that's what he would do.
He was always grubstaking some young fellow. That's the way
he was. Yessir, he was a real sourdough. Struck it rich and gave it
all away."

My stomach was beginning to groan, but Frank seemed to
want to reminisce about his old friend as much as find the key, so
I just sat down and listened. "Stayed here every time he came to
town. Stay a few days, visit the girls up the row, have some good
meals, and off he'd go again, always lookin' for one more strike.
Yep, I miss old Rudy. Not a big man, about your size. Yessir, I

think he'd like the idea of you wearing his clothes."

After two or three minutes of scratching around in the desk drawer, Frank found what he was looking for, a little brass key on a short string of beads, and at the other end, a little horse made of gold. Picking up the key, he dangled the little gold horse so it shone in the morning light, then chuckling to himself, he unbuckled the belt around the suitcase, inserted the key, and the suitcase popped open.

Laying back the lid, he lifted up the corner of contents. It was packed with layers of freshly laundered workshirts, brown canvas pants, red flannel longjohns, a red bandana, suspenders, and a green crusher hat. At the bottom was a large photograph. He lifted the old brown photo out, held it up, and chuckling to himself, kept looking at it, seemingly oblivious to the clothes or me. It was a picture of an old prospector leading a horse laden with mining gear. "This is ol' Rudy," he said, handing me the photograph. At the bottom was printed, "Me and Lazy Nag. Rampart, July 4, 1928."

Frank went through the clothes and handed me a shirt, suspenders, and a pair of pants, saying, "Here, try these on." It didn't take me long and I was back. "Look, Frank, they fit perfectly. The pants are first class, made by Stilson in Seattle, and this shirt is the smoothest I've ever had on, a soft kind of flannel."

I don't think he even heard me. He just stood by the window looking at the picture of Rudy Thompson and his horse, every now and then chuckling and looking out the window as if looking for Rudy and Lazy Nag to come down the street.

Finally aware that I was standing there, he looked me up and down, nodded his approval, and resumed talking about his old friend. Hungry as I was, I could hardly run off in my new clothes until Frank was finished so I again sat down on the sofa and listened.

"This here picture was Rudy's big day, him and his partner Lazy Nag. He owed his strike to that horse, told me the story himself, came to town about this time in the summer of '28. It seemed he and Lazy Nag were heading up a steep grade beside this creek, Icicle or Morelock, one of those creeks that come into the Yukon between Tanana and Rampart. Anyway, old Lazy Nag got thirsty and stubborn and wouldn't go any further. So Rudy went down to the creek with his canvas bag to get some water for Lazy Nag. He was scraping around in the gravel making a hole big enough to dip the water bag into when he got the surprise of his life, the best looking colour he'd ever seen, real black and heavy like there might be some real gold down there. So he takes the bag of water up to Lazy Nag, goes back to the creek with a shovel and pan, and begins workin' the bed."

Frank must have sensed my impatience, and turning toward me said, "Well, to make a long story short, he camped right there and worked that stream all summer 'til he had all the gold Lazy Nag could carry. He took close to sixty thousand in gold from that creek, all because of a horse wanting a drink of water."

Frank paused, took a good look at me this time, and said, "Yessir, you look all right in Rudy's outfit." He then reached into the suitcase again, pulled out the green crusher hat, plopped it on my head and said, "There you are. Now you go out and find YOUR gold."

I just wanted something to eat, caught the next bus that said Ladd Field, and headed for that chow line. It was after one o'clock by then, but three men were still in line, so I joined them.

Rudy's outfit did the trick. In five minutes I was sitting down to the only real meal I'd had since leaving Seattle: pork chops, mashed potatoes, green beans, apple pie, and all the milk I could drink. The only things left on my tray were bones. I carried the tray out the door, passed by the M.P., banged the tray on the garbage can like a veteran construction worker, and caught the bus back to town. Of course I felt a little sneaky, but also triumphant. I would no longer have to worry about going hungry until I found a good-paying construction job, hopefully right there at Ladd Field. Then I could repay the government with good, honest work.

First thing Monday morning I was back in the chow line for breakfast, then pestered the superintendent for a job. By Thurs-

day my persistence paid off. He turned to the heavy e.
foreman and said, "Mike, put this kid to work. I'm tired o
ing at him." I followed Mike out to his red pickup, and he
"Jump in and let's see what you can do."

He tried me out first on a Ford double axle dump truck loaded
with river rock. I had never driven a truck of any kind, let alone
a double axle dump, but I got it started, figured out the gear shift
pattern, got it rolling, and did okay as long as we stayed on the
road. But half a mile down the road Mike said, "Okay, turn right
here and dump her this side of the 'cat." That's when the jig was
up. The ground was soft, I lost momentum fast and got stuck. "I
guess you don't know how to double shift," he said, but I shot
back, "Yeh, but I can learn how fast, just show me once."

He didn't bother to reply, just opened the door on his side and
motioned for me to slide over. He shifted into low gear, worked
the clutch pedal, rocked the truck back and forth until the rear
end bounced and came out of the hole. As smooth as ice-cream,
he pulled alongside the 'cat, dumped the load without even stopping, shifted one gear after another, and headed down the road
without saying a word. All I could do was pray, expecting him to
say, "Sorry kid, we can't use you."

But he didn't say a word, just parked the dump truck, motioned for me to get back in his pickup, and drove down the road
awhile until we came to the river and the biggest piece of machinery I had ever seen. He parked fifty feet away, got out, and
motioned to me to follow. The machine was on steel tracks like a
steam shovel, only three times as big and with a long boom. At
the back it said NORTHWEST, and in smaller letters below
GREEN BAY, WISCONSIN.

I stood by Mike behind the machine while the operator swung
the huge boom around, dumped its load of river rock on a huge
pile and gracefully lowered the boom to the ground. The diesel
engine throttled down, the operator swivelled around in his seat,
stepped down onto the tracks, jumped to the ground, and walked
over to Mike.

He was not a big man, just a little taller than me, but lean,

the oil filter or checking the engine oil level with the dipstick.

The engine was a Caterpillar taller than I, took up the whole rear end of the cab, and put out a lot of heat and noise when even throttled down and idling. After showing me its oil and fuel filters, he went up behind the operator's seat, and taking a red Pyrene fire extinquisher from the wall, squirted some of its contents along the edge of the break bands on the drums that control the cables. "Keeps the break bands free of grease", he explained.

The oiler's job was to keep all these working parts regularly lubricated, plus doing anything else directed by the operator, such as directing trucks at loading. It doesn't sound like much, but with dozens of grease fittings, often in awkward positions, it kept a person busy crawling, climbing and jumping most of the time, hence the term "grease monkey".

Happy covered the essentials of the job, took his thermos bottle from   behind the operator's seat, jumped off the tracks, poured his coffee, and just as patiently explained the work schedule. "We work ten hours, everyday, until the job is done. I come at six, leave at five. At eleven the crummie comes and I go for lunch for an hour. You come at five, eat at ten, and finish at four. Every morning and at lunch you grease and keep everything clean, like my watch", with which he drew forth a large gold pocket watch and held it up, smiling with admiration.

"Tomorrow I will come early and show you how to change the filters. Now you just stand by the pile and when a truck or Uke comes, you signal him to stop here.", saying which, he made a line in the dirt with his boot, the precise distance from the dragline to bring the end of its boom directly above the vehicle to be loaded.

I stood by the line as directed waiting for a truck and watched in admiration as Happy operated the dragline, dipping in and out of the river and dumping the bucket of cascading rock and water on the pile, back and forth, back and forth, as rhythmically as an expert flyfisherman casting into a stream. There was absolutely no waste motion, the machine's body revolving and swinging as precisely as the ticking of Happy's watch. And as a teacher he was just the same, thorough, precise, patient, and always smiling and gentle. I had never met a boss like him and could hardly believe my luck that I showed up just when he needed an oiler.

Before long a large rubber-tired vehicle came bouncing and snorting down the road and stopped where I was standing at the line. It was like a mechanized waddling duck, probably the 'Uke' that Happy talked about, an odd looking contraption with a snorting diesel engine sticking out above two huge rubber tires, a driver's cab mounted above the wheels, and behind this front end, it trailed a long steel box supported at the rear by two more huge rubber tires.

The door of the operator's cab swung open and out sprang a muscular brown body. He could have been a boxer on the cover of *Ring Magazine.* He landed as light as a cat, paused to hitch up his pants, spat, and bounded over to me. He spoke in a quick, staccato sentences like a boxer's jabs, his feet always moving, and just as nervously, he alternately pawed the ground and kicked rocks with thick black boots. "I'm Brownie", he shot out like he spat, "So you're Happy's new oiler, lucky bastard. He's the best operator on the base. Where you from?"

He paused to spit again, giving me time to respond, "Vancouver", I said, and he came right back with "Oh, so you're a Canuck. That's what I'll call you. Gotta go now. See ya later." He left as quickly as he came, back-pedalling and prancing toward his Uke, and sprang back into his cab. Brownie's energy was overwhelming. Trying to carry on a conversation with him was like being a punching bag in the middle of a boxing ring. He and his Uke snorted and bounced down the road and I returned to the peaceful world of Happy and his dragline working the river.

The rest of the day went as planned. At ten I rode the crummie to the chow hall, returned to grease the dragline, Happy let me off early to sign up at the Personnel Office, and I was assigned a bed in quonset hut B2.

Inside were twelve army cots, six on each side, with an oil stove in the middle. Beside the cots were improvised night stands made of apple boxes. One in the corner had no apple box or

clothes hanging on the wall so I assumed it was mine. No
had to do was go back to town to get my gear at the hotel and
Frank the good news.

Frank wasn't surprised I had landed a job. "I knew you would',
he said, and taking two books off his desk, said "Here, take these
back to the library after you read them." Their titles were *Old
Yukon* and *Cheechako Into Sourdough,* the first by James
Wickersham, one of Alaska's first judges and the man who gave
Fairbanks its name, and the other by the 'Klondike Kid'. These
two little books were my introduction to the log cabin Fairbank's
Public Library, to become my favourite town haunt in the months
ahead.

Paratroop bag in hand, I headed back to my new lodgings to
set up housekeeping among my new neighbours.

The first to greet me as I came through the door was the Uke
operator Brownie. "Whadya know, its Canuck", he boomed out
in a taunting tone. Then, turning to the others, anxious to tell
them the latest, announced sarcastically "Heh fellows, look who's
our new cellmate. He's a Canuck." Under ordinary circumstances,
I would have been honoured with the tab, but coming from
Brownie with his sarcastic tone, let alone my misadventures in
getting to Alaska, it was an unwelcome introduction to quonset
hut B2.

The other men, most of whom were lying down on their cots
listening to their radios, merely cast a brief glance in my direction, paying less attention to Brownie than if he had announced
the presence of a stray dog in their midst. It was a relief to notice
that he did not seem to have very high standing among them.

I hung my motley assortment of clothes on the nail-dotted
wall and lay back, book in hand, hoping a more compatible in-
habitant would appear. Soon, one did, a shy appearing young
fellow about my size and age. Reaching out with a friendly hand-
shake, he said in a soft Southern drawl, "Ahm Elby, Elby Hooper
from Arkansah." His smile and eyes were as gentle as his voice,
so I responded in kind, saying "I'm Robin Williams, Happy's
new oiler on the Northwest", hoping that might establish some

...on bond with this agreeable fellow.

...lby seemed pleased with my arrival. "That's swell. Ah'm an ...er too, on the P & H furthah down the rivah. We cin gah ...ahgetha in the mahnin'. Ah'll wake yah up in the mahnin if yah like." "That would be great!", I replied, we shook hands again, he returned to his cot and radio, and I returned to my book wondering if Elby realized how important his introduction was to me. From that moment, Elby and I became regular companions. Each morning we went to work together, often had supper in each others company, and shared what we had in common, each working up north for our separate dreams.

Elby was a shy country boy not used to talking much, especially to strangers, but at dinner one night he shared his dream. "Ah'm savin' everthin' foh when ah git back home in Arkansah. Ah know jes the fahm ah'm gaunta buy. Foughty acahs, good land, buttonut trees, an' a fine house an' bahn. Ah cin live real cheap, an' good too, back in Ahkansah, nevah want foh nuthin'. An' ah knows jes the right li'l gal too."

So of course I told him what I was saving for. Our dreams and other interests were so different we didn't have much in common, so our friendship was based largely on the here and now, but that was good enough for the both of us.

He showed me his pay stubs so I'd know how much to expect to earn. We were paid time and half for everything over 40 hours a week, and we worked every day, ten hours a day, that meant being paid for 85 hours per week at the oiler's hourly rate of $1.37. We got paid twice a month, and Elby's take home pay after deducting room and board, not much, and income tax, was $197.30, just short of $400 a month, more in one month than all my savings for a year at North Van Ship Repairs! If the job held out for a year, I'd have almost $5,000, more than enough for three years of university. My gamble seemed to be paying off, my spirits soaring higher with each pay check.

Every day Happy showed me some new part of the dragline to inspect and maintain, how to grease the cables, adjust the brake bands, numerous points of keeping the machine in perfect running order, and every day my admiration for him as a machine operator and boss grew.

Working for Happy was fun. He was in harmony with everything around him. He was not only master of his machine, he loved it, taking care of it as though it were a living thing. He didn't force it, get mad at it, or abuse it.

He was the same with me and other people; no anger, no shouting, no demanding, no boasting, he just said or did what was necessary with no waste motion or conflict, so naturally I was hoping that I would work with Happy for the next twelve months.

The mornings grew cool as summer turned to fall. Along the river, the birch trees turned to feathery gold, their leaves quivering in the river's updraft as though performing a dance of the seasons for Happy and me. From the airfield's runway warplanes buzzed and hummed like angry bees as they took off for their long flight across the Bering Sea and the expanses of Siberia. Still they would fly on until reaching their destination, Russia's eastern front, to vent their fury on Hitler's barbarian hordes. Almost 15,000 of them, mostly fighter planes, flew to the Russian front from Ladd Field between 1942 and 1944, and they were America's best; P 39s, 40s, 63s, and big bombers like B-25s and C-47s. When one would come close enough to see, I would sometimes imagine the pilot could see me down there by the river, waved my hat, and gave a cheer.

Each morning Happy and I had coffee together on the river bank, and one morning he said something that caught me by surprise. "What are you going to do when the freeze comes?" he said in his usual gentle manner. Seeing that I didn't understand what he meant, he went on, "The river freezes over in October. No more dragline until spring. During the winter I operate a shovel loading the piles I make during the summer. No oiler on the shovel, too small." I was shocked. Happy was letting me know in his typically kind way that within two or three weeks I would have to find a different job.

I thought about it all that afternoon and night, and by the

next day I had a plan. Across the road from where we were working a D8 'cat sat idle for an hour or so every day while the operator went to lunch. I thought that if I watched the 'cat skinner closely and asked a few key questions, I could jump on his 'cat while he was gone, learn how to operate it, and get a job as a 'cat skinner.

The next day I put the plan into effect, at every opportunity going across the road and observing every move the operator made. I watched his hand and foot movements every time he did something different, moving forward, backward, turning, raising and lowering the blade, everything but starting the engine, as he always left that running. Happy didn't know what I was up to, but he didn't mind me being gone for short stretches, and of course I timed it so I wasn't needed then.

The second day, after I got all the greasing and cleaning done and Happy and the 'cat skinner were at lunch, I hurried over, climbed on the 'cat, and started practicing. It was scary at first up there in the operator's seat for the first time, especially as I didn't dare stall it because I didn't know how to start it again. I didn't try operating the dozer blade while it was on the ground, figuring I'd make a mess of it, the operator would notice, and that would be the end of learning how to be a 'cat skinner. I just practiced raising and lowering the blade while the 'cat was stationary, then, with blade raised, moving the 'cat forwards and backwards, then turning left, then right, to get the feel of the steering clutches and levers.

Everything went okay, so I dropped the blade and left it where it was before, hoping the operator wouldn't notice. I worried all that afternoon and the next morning that he would tell Happy and put a stop to it, but didn't, so was emboldened to move ahead with my learning sessions.

The second and third day I put the two together, first back-blading, just dropping the blade and moving backwards making a smooth path where the track marks had been. Then I started to learn the tough part, laying an even grade while moving forward. It's a lot tougher than it looks. The blade wants to dig in, making troughs and dips and pretty soon your 'cat is moving up and down like a bucking bronco, so I had a dickens of a time trying to smooth the ground out so he wouldn't notice. I was damn lucky. He must have noticed the mess, but still didn't say or do anything to stop me, just straightened things out himself and forgot about it I suppose.

But it was necessary not to push my luck too far, so that afternoon I watched him, paid particular attention to how he laid such a smooth grade, and finally caught on. I noticed what he did was always started out on level ground, dropped his blade, and only then, started forward. That made sense, the only way to do it unless you were a magician. There's no way to eliminate the bucking bronco effect and make a smooth, level grade if you're moving forward on uneven ground and drop the blade, at least I couldn't figure it out.

Anyway, once I'd learned the secret, I practised laying grade for the next two weeks, until I figured I was good enough to hit Mike up for a 'cat skinning job. He probably figured out what I had been up to, but gave me a chance anyway, knowing from Happy I'd done a good job on the dragline and would soon be out of a job.

He watched me on the 'cat for a few minutes, putting me through various maneuvers, then said, "Okay, you're not much good yet at laying a grade, but I can use you on a 'pusher'. Stick with Happy the rest of the week, then report to me." By then I knew what he meant by a 'pusher', the same sort of 'cat with a blade, but assigned to just keep other equipment from getting stuck, so the operator doesn't have to have the same degree of skill as one who moves dirt to build roads and runways.

The next week I was on my own D8 'cat pushing Ukes and carry-alls, a contraption that scoops up the dirt from the bottom of its steel box as it moves forward scraping the surface of the ground. My job was to get behind and push the scraper, keeping it moving through soft ground so it didn't get stuck. It demanded a certain degree of skill to catch the back of the carry-all at just the right speed to keep it moving, and not too hard so as to jolt the operator.

It was the first of October, ice was beginning to form along the quiet eddies of the Tanana, but I was saved again; I had a job to see me through the winter. And I loved my new job, simple as it was, because I now had a machine of my own to run. My 'cat was a beat-up, ugly old D8, the kind you hardly see anymore with the blade operated from a lever in back of the operator's shoulder that activates a cable running over the top of the cab to the blade. It was all mechanical, with pulleys and brakebands, not hydraulic like all the tractors today.

Ugly as my 'cat was, all banged up with dents and a rusted cab, it did the job, and more importantly, it meant earning $1.75 an hour from an oiler's $1.37. Now I could save close to $500 a month instead of $400, so I was mighty pleased with myself.

By the end of October I had saved my first $1,000. About my only expenses were cigarettes, 50¢ for a carton of Lucky Strikes at the PX, clothes, stamps, and an occasional meal in town. Almost all by paychecks went into savings at the Post Office. I bought a little radio from one of the men who moved out, and of course I always had my nose in a book, a no-expense pleasure because every couple of weeks I went into town after work to the library and to see Frank.

Sometimes I got homesick, especially on Saturday nights when the "Lucky Strike Hit Parade" came on the radio. It took me back to dances at St. Agnes' Hall with Dorene and high school classmates like Murray Sumpton, Bob Handel, Anna Laubach, and Lorna Lang. Murray and Anna were very good dancers, flinging and whirling themselves like tops as they did the 'jitter bug'. Not being so hot on my feet, I liked to dance the slow ones with Dorene like Glenn Miller's *"Moonlight Becomes You"*, *"In The Mood"*, or Guy Lombardo and his Royal Canadians playing *"I'll Walk Alone"*, or *"Somebody Loves You"*.

When the nostalgia got too much, writing letters helped; to Mom and Dad, Dorene, or one of my brothers. First thing after work each day I went to the base Post Office to see if there was a letter for me, something I looked forward to even more than dinner after a hard day's work.

Aside from Elby and Oscar, the master mechanic from Minneapolis, I didn't have much in common with the rest of the men in the bunkhouse. Elby and I were the youngsters and both of us liked Oscar, a great big jolly Swede who was sort of our big brother. He could tell us anything we wanted to know about machinery, and being a father himself, looked out for us and wouldn't stand for any loud swearing or bullying in the our Quonset hut home.

Brownie never let up teasing me about something. If it wasn't calling me 'Canuck' in a snide voice, it was 'Professor' or 'Hotshot'. He'd yell out, "What are you always doing, reading them books for Professor?", or "Here comes 'Canuck', the red-hot catskinner. Who'd you brown nose to get the promotion, 'Canuck'?" I tried to ignore him, and he backed off whenever Oscar told him, "Brownie, lay off the kid."

But one night Brownie went too far for Oscar. I had just returned from the library with some new books and Brownie pipes up, "Heh 'Canuck', been to town to get a little pussy eh? I know just the right one for you, one-legged Annie, just like you, could be your sistah." He made me so mad, I felt like tearing into him, boxer or not. But Oscar got to him first, just reached out with his big left hand, grabbed Brownie by the front of his shirt, and backed him against the wall, saying "One more peep out of your shitty little mouth and your head's going right through that wall!"

Oscar was one man Brownie didn't fool with, and so he backed off, saying "Okay, okay, I was just havin' a little fun", but he gave me a dirty look, as if to say "I'll get you for this 'Canuck'". He left me alone for the rest of the time at Ladd Field, but a few weeks later, after we got shipped to the Aleutians, he went at me again, only this time he got physical, and Oscar wasn't around to bail me out. But that's getting ahead of my story.

Just like Happy said, the river froze up solid by the end of October. By mid-November the temperature got down to minus thirty, the 'cats hard to start, so the Engineers decided to ship us to the Aleutians where they were building more airfields. Some of the men wanted no part of the Aleutians in winter and went 'outside', but I would go anywhere for the kind of money I was making.

They gave us three days to get ready. By Thanksgiving we were to be in Whittier boarding a troop transport for the Islands. So one night I went into town to say 'Goodbye' to Frank, return some books to the library, and take one last look at the town that had been so good to me.

When I got off the bus and headed for the old hotel, so many people crowded Cushman Avenue I thought there must be some sort of celebration going on, of the Gold Rush, beginning of the dog racing season, or something like that. As I came down Cushman, it was clear something big was going on alright, but it was no celebration. Lines of men and women were passing buckets hand over hand toward the Pioneer Laundry across the street. It was on fire, the only laundry in town. Flames shot up the side of the wooden building. Windows popped. Smoke swirled around the bucket passers. "Everybody's clothes is in there" said one man.

The bucket passers were of every description; young men, old men, bearded old-timers, clean-shaven men in business suits, lots of women dressed in every fashion, about every type you'd see in town. I got to the hotel, but Frank wasn't there, almost surely gone to join the bucket brigade. I'd heard about the lady who owned the laundry, and 'half the town' people said, but so what, the Pioneer Laundry was an indispensable institution in town, something you'd risk your life for, so there wasn't a person in town who didn't turn out to try and save it.

The last bus to Ladd Field was about to leave, so I had to leave without saying 'Goodbye' and 'Thanks a million for your help' to Frank. But he didn't need my thanks to do the same for some other young buck suffering temporary financial embarrassment. That's the way Frank was, and now he was out in a darn cold night helping to save the town's laundry. That's what it means to be a 'Sourdough', the kind of men who built Fairbanks from a muddy trading post into a first class town, the Golden Heart of Alaska. The gold that lasted wasn't the stuff they dug out of the ground. It was men like Rudy and Frank, their spirit, the spirit that tells a man that whenever there's trouble, you pitch in and help. I doesn't matter whether its helping just one fellow whose temporarily down on his luck or the whole town, a real man pitches in whenever he's needed.

I hated to leave Fairbanks, but my pot of gold was waiting somewhere out in the Aleutian Islands. Little did I know what a God foresaken frozen patch of misery I was headed for when I boarded the bus and returned to Ladd Field that night.

At eight o'clock Thursday morning, November 21, 1944, the train pulled out of the Alaska Railroad station in Fairbanks with 200 construction workers bound for the Aleutian chain. We hadn't been told which island. Some guessed Shemya, others Kiska, Amchitka, or Adak, all unfamiliar names of distant, barren islands. Their names passed back and forth inside the darkness of the blackedout train, its windows painted over with olive drab paint. All day and through the night the train travelled toward the docks of Whittier, four hundred miles away.

The only thing we knew was who we worked for, the "U.S. Army Corps of Engineers" it said in yellow letters painted on the sides of the railroad coaches. The train crawled westward like a dark centipede toward the stormy coast.

Late the next morning the train came to a halt, opened its doors, and through the wind-blown sleet there appeared the docks of Whittier, and alongside, a gray Army transport.

By noon, the *General Greely* slipped away from the dock and moved westward into the fog of the North Pacific. For four days and nights the ship rolled, wallowed, and heaved its way through the sleet and fog. Below, in the half darkness of the hold, men sullen with fatigue and apathy, braced themselves against the sides of their bunks. The habitual gamblers gathered in dark corners of the hold. Their dice clicked against steel bulkheads and skittered across the deck. I lay cushioned in my bunk against the incessant pounding of the sea, reading one Armed Services Edition paperback after another.

The third day out was Thanksgiving and the sea the roughest

of the voyage. Over the ship's radio came the voice of the President, Franklin Delano Roosevelt. "My fellow Americans, today we give special thanks to our countrymen in uniform all over the world. They are fighting to defend our freedom...in the Pacific, in Europe, everywhere. And everywhere the enemies of freedom are now on the defensive...so, as we sit down to our traditional Thanksgiving dinner, wherever we are, let us give thanks to our Creator..."

No heads were bowed in prayer aboard the *General Greely* that Thanksgiving Day. The ship's Mess had no seats and tables, just rows of stand-up counters. Our steel trays were heaped with the usual Thanksgiving fare, turkey and cranberry jelly, mashed potatoes, and pumpkin pie, but the problem was to hang onto the tray long enough to get some.

The trick was to spread the feet wide apart, brace the chest against the counter, and hanging onto the tray with one hand, use the other to maneuver the fork in and out of the tray, and in and out of the mouth without stabbing one's self or one's neighbour. We could have managed it as smooth as a tango if it weren't for the fact that the damn ship had no regular movement.

It would be rolling one way, everyone would lift their forks to accommodate, then halfway between tray and mouth, the ship would suddenly lurch the other way, and off flew the fork's contents, mashed potatoes, gravy and all, every whichway. It would have been much tidier, let alone nourishing, if the Captain had ordered all of us to squat in little circles on the deck, legs crossed, and pretended to be having a picnic on an island somewhere in the South Seas.

Relief came on Saturday, the 25th of November. The ship settled down to a comfortable roll, and soon, from the top deck came the sounds of winches, clanging chain, and boots thumping up and down metal stairs. The ship's hull made crunching sounds as though scraping against piling or a dock. From the sounds of it, the *General Greely* had reached her destination.

"It's Adak! It's Adak!" The name crackled back and forth in the hold's stale air, skipping down the rows of bunks. Faces lit up. We laughed. We joked. We tossed pillows in the air. We slapped each on the back. "It's Adak! It's Adak!". Roughneck construction workers from every state in the Union exploded with boyish excitement.

From up on deck, the magic isle of Adak was a treeless wasteland, the only signs of habitation rows of Quonset huts, smoke rising from their little tin chimneys. Still, it was our new home, as much as migrant construction workers can look forward to; hot showers, good food, a warm bunkhouse and cot to sleep in after a hard day's work, and firm ground to walk on instead of a tossing army transport on a ferocious sea.

Elby and I found Oscar and trudged up the hill together, making sure to share the same hut, hopefully without Brownie this time. We each settled our gear on a bunk, showered, and went to chow, basically the same menu as at Ladd Field. U.S. army camps are all the same, and not bad; clean, comfortable, good food, hot showers, everything one needs for creature comforts. Not only that, but Adak had a post office, P.X., Rec. Hall with a small library of paperback books, ping-pong tables, free movies on Friday and Saturday nights, a regulated card room and gambling hall, and a weekly ration of four bottles of beer. For that we got tickets, and being more interested in money than booze, I sold mine for a dollar apiece.

The weather was another matter, something I found out on Sunday morning when I got my assignment; another beat-up old D8 'cat pushing dirt at the end of a runway on the night shift. Two hundred feet below, the North Pacific pounded at the cliff. On a hill behind, a small portable lightplant cast a dim glow upon the snowy ground. The feeble light came and went as gusty winds swept up the cliff's side, curled, and swept salt spray and sleet across the baren, frozen ground. Like gravemarkers, small wooden stakes formed an imaginary danger line beyond which I dared not go. Night after night, I chewed away at the hill, moving fill toward the edge. Inside the cab, heat from the engine kept me warm, but once outside, I quickly became numb with cold in the swirling sleet and snow.

Dressed like a penguin, I wore a hooded rubber parka with wool cap underneath, two pairs of long underwear, woolen pants and shirts, and my feet were encased in mukalucks, rubber boots lined with felt insoles and knee-high leather tops. But still it was impossible to stay dry and warm.

The trouble was that every few minutes I had to climb out on the 'cat's tracks to wipe sleet off the windows to see where I was going and check the stakes, barely visible with encrusted sleet. This was absolutely essential, for to go beyond meant certain death, plunging over the cliff trapped in a twenty ton machine.

⚜

One dark night just before Christmas I thought my time had come. It was particularly dark that night with no fresh snow on the ground to reflect the lightplant's glow. Wind-driven sleet clung to the windows of the cab. As usual, I stepped out on the tracks to clear the windows and check the stakes, then, in low gear, moved ahead in the darkness.

Suddenly the earth slumped downward beneath the 'cat. The new fill was sinking and slipping slowly over the cliff's edge. I broke into a cold sweat, heart pounding. I thought I was going over for sure. I jammed my foot down on the clutch peddle, shifted into neutral, eased the cab door open, jumped to the ground, and ran toward the lightplant.

Halfway up the hill I dropped to my knees and looked back. The 'cat was still there, idling quietly in the swirling sleet. Removing my woolen cap, I wiped the sweat from my forehead. My hands were shaking. I was weak at the knees. I fumbled under my parka for cigarettes and lighter. Taking deep draws, my nerves calmed down, and walking slowly toward the lightplant, I tried to organize my thoughts.

The safe thing to do would be to go get another 'cat to winch me back. But I wasn't too keen on that because the other 'cat skinner might tab me as 'chicken', not tough enough to work for the Engineers no matter where.

Then I thought maybe it wasn't as bad as I thought, even my imagination. After all, I didn't exactly see a crack. And if I got help, the 'cat skinner would tell the foreman, he'd come back, and if there was no crack, would say, "I guess you don't have the guts for the job, Williams", and I'd be on the next boat out, still $2,000 short of my savings goal.

I decided to go back and take a good look.

I worked my way back in a zig-zag pattern, checking the ground for softness or any abrupt drop in elevation. I could see no crack, but coming abreast of the 'cat, the earth showed a definite downward slope indicating slippage beginning to occur in the sodden fill. Now there was no doubt about it, it was not my imagination, the ground had begun to slip away.

Now the question was, how badly, and dare I back the machine up? The initial backward thrust of the gripping tracks could trigger a sudden avalanche.

I didn't know what to do. But whatever it was, I had to act fast. In a few minutes the foreman was due.

Undecided, I approached the 'cat slowly, cautiously, as though it was a slumbering, dangerous beast. Coming alongside it, I reached out and touched the outside of its cold, iron body. It slumbered on, puffing black diesel fumes in the air. Venturing further, I climbed upon its tracks and began wiping the sleet off its great purring body with indecisive strokes, irrationally wishing it would tell me what to do. It merely purred, belching diesel smoke into the cold night air.

My indecision ended I know not why, but the next thing I knew I was back inside the machine's warm cab. As though a sleep walker, I lifted the blade, eased the 'cat slowly backwards, and up the hill toward the lightplant. It was as though for awhile I had left myself and some other self had taken over.

After, when safe again, I was so overcome with fatigue that for several minutes I sat listless in the warm insides of the machine. Too tired to think, I was aware only that I was alive.

In awhile, I recovered, and feeling vaguely heroic, resumed my work.

Soon, the headlights of the foreman's pickup bounced over the hill and came alongside. He leaned out the window and yelled, "Canuck, you better call it quits. We just lost 'Red'. We're shutting the nightshift down 'til the weather clears. Jump in, I'm taking you to the mat plant."

I shut the 'cat down, jumped in Mike's pickup, and on the way over to the mat plant, he told me what happened. "He was pushing fill at the other end of the runway. All of a sudden the earth gave way and down he went. Never had a chance...can't even see the 'cat..just a big hole. I feel real bad. 'Red' was a good operator."

I felt a cold emptiness inside. I found it hard to breath. My brain went numb with shock. I found it hard to take in what Mike was saying. Like an echo from a far off voice, his words formed into a terrible message. So 'Red' got it, not me. I knew him from Ladd Field, in fact he was in the same hut with Elby, Oscar and me. He was a real experieced 'cat skinner from Texas, a big, gravel-throated red-headed guy who must have been a cowboy at one time because he walked bow-legged like he had a hernia and was always hitching up his pants with his elbows. He wasn't a friend, in fact, he was sort of ornery most of the time. But he was one of us, and it could have just easily have been me.

I didn't tell Mike about my close call. What would have been the point? Still sullen with shock, I wanted only to get to work at the mat plant and get my mind off that night.

∞

The mat plant was an eerie place to work. Inside a Quonset building three times the size of a bunkhouse, paint vats twenty feet long bubbled and steamed in the corner of the dark interior, the air in the huge oval building saturated with the smell of paint.

Down the center was a long conveyor, steel rollers set waisthigh upon steel legs, and on both sides, men moved like shadows among machines that howled and screeched.

At the far end of the shed, buckled and rusted metal mats by the thousands lay piled in a jumbled heap. One at a time, men placed these on the assembly line and fed them into machines where they were straightened and cleaned, then dipped in bundles in the paint vats. After a suitable interval of drying, the remanufactured and repainted mats were as good as new, ready for service again.

Landing mats were ingeniously designed to fit together into a temporary landing field for aircraft. Each mat was a sheet of metal an eighth of an inch thick, two feet wide, and eight feet long punctuated with two inch holes and serrated along the edges to interlock with others, much like a zipper. Fitted together over soft, uneven ground, they made a useable landing strip until a more permanent runway could be built with cement. The ones we were reprocessing formed the first temporary landing fields in Adak and throughout Alaska, and now were about to be shipped to the south Pacific for the island-hopping campaign against the Japanese.

The job had to be done, but it was a smelly, noisy, repetitious factory sort of work, distasteful to construction workers used to commanding their own machines and a certain degree of independence. So the men in the shed got surly and bored, and it wasn't long before the gamblers among them had a crap game going. Brownie, of course, was in the thick of the game, an incurable gambler, and he didn't like to lose.

One of the few good things about Adak was that I didn't have to deal with Brownie. He was in a different bunkhouse and I did my best to avoid him in the chowline or anywhere we might meet around the base. There was something about me that seemed like waving a red flag to Brownie.

Maybe it was because I was white and he a light-skinned mulatto. Or that I was always reading and never gambled. Oscar told me that Brownie had done time in an El Paso juvenile institution where he learned how to box. Maybe my bookishness reminded him of the judge who sent him there, or a teacher he disliked, I don't know.

But whatever it was that went on inside Brownie's head, whenever he caught sight of me, it unleashed in him a volcanic fury that turned him into a bully. I was no match for him. He was quick and light on his feet, as strong as a steel strap, and a trained boxer who had doubtless pounded many opponents to the ground. So I kept my distance and a wary eye whenever we had be around each other.

It wasn't just the presence of Brownie but everything about the time and place made the mat plant assignment a precarious situation. It was February, the whole crew had been working for weeks in the worst climate imaginable, and far away from any town where they could blow off steam in the usual ways of whiskey, women, and song.

The only females on Adak were three nurses, and there were at least two thousand men on the island, military and civilian. The gamblers had their official gambling hall, and hard liquor could be had for $35 a fifth smuggled in by flyboys willing to take a chance to get rich. But it was no Fairbanks.

The only legal alcohol was our weekly ration of four bottles of beer per man, not much, but it meant different things to different men. To me, it meant an extra four bucks a week when I sold my tickets to one of the men in the bunkhouse who liked a beer after work at night. A few would do almost anything to get more than their share, including gambling for it. The two were a bad mix. But that's what was going on among the few gamblers and boozers in the mat plant.

For those of us still working, they were a pain in the neck. "Why don't those lazy bastards get back to work? They're getting paid just like us", was heard up and down the assembly line, but there wasn't any firm boss to keep them in line, so they just did as they pleased. The gambling and cussing and guzzling beer went on and on. Little empty brown beer bottles stood like totems around the quarrelsome knot of gamblers.

Prominent among them was Brownie, a poor loser, and on the particular night of the incident, there was no doubt he was losing. Above the noise of banging landing mats he could be heard yelling petulantly, "Lemme see those dice, they must be loaded, you muthafuckah."

Tempers were getting hot. The gamblers stood up and circled, glaring at each other like fighting cocks. They pointed accusatory fingers, some looking furtively around for something they could grab in case a fight broke out. It looked as if the game might be breaking up one way or another. One or two made like they were returning to work, and for a moment things quieted down to a still uncertainty. Even Brownie turned his back on the game and moved toward the assembly line. I watched him from the corner of my eye, his face taught with anger as he left the losing game.

He stepped over a pile of mats, caught sight of me, and in flash, moved toward me. Seeing him come full tilt in my direction, I moved backwards, but lost my footing, stumbled, and fell backwards onto a pile of mats. In seconds, Brownie was on top of me, face flushed in anger, and in his right hand he held a broken, jagged-edged beer bottle. He sat on top of me, beer bottle poised to plunge downward. Flat on my back, feet dangling over the edge of the pile of mats, I was completely at his mercy.

I stared up in cold terror into Brownie's eyes. He finally had me where he wanted me. I visualized the awful consequences if he plunged that ugly weapon downward into the soft tissue of my face. For what seemed an eternity, he hesitated, enjoying his supremacy. The paint gurgled in the vats behind my head. All else was stillness as the men stopped work, watching and waiting for what would happen next.

Enjoying the triumph of his dominant position, Brownie withheld the blow. His face slowly relaxed, his fury subsiding. From behind him, two men quietly grasped his shoulders and drew him back. He released his grip on the bottle. It dropped on the pile of mats, and broke into a thousand harmless shards.

They say that a dog, victorious in battle, releases its hold upon it's adversary's throat once his enemy lies still and helpless upon the ground.

That's all there was to it. Both Brownie and I went back to work. I pondered what seething hate could cause him to use a beer bottle when he could have easily dealt me punishing blows with his fists. That night Elby told Oscar about what had happened, and Oscar came over to say, "Brownie's a bully, always has been. He was losing in the crap game and took it out on you. He won't try it again." Oscar was right, and that was also the end of craps and beer at the mat plant.

🚲

By the first of March things got a lot better. The weather calmed down, and they put us outside again. For me, it meant a new assignment cleaning up around a rock crusher. And on the more personal side, I had saved better than three thousand dollars, and one day I received very good news in the mail.

In one of my previous letters to Dad and Mom, I said that I might go to college in the States instead of picking up where I left, returning to Vancouver, and attending U.B.C. Underneath, in my feelings, I had not resolved the painful associations of Vancouver; of always feeling physically inferior, always being 'left behind' in sports or not going off to war with my brothers and friends. I didn't feel good about leaving my city and country to amount to something, but I had strong, conflicting feelings about returning home to pursue my education.

On the other hand, all during my stay in Alaska, life had been made more agreeable by the U.S. Army's pocket-size books. Called *"The Armed Services Edition of Great Literature"*, they brought some of the world's best writing to thousands of G.I.s and civilian employees like me the world over.

These little paperbacks were good stuff; Tolstoy, Hemingway, Faulkner, Conrad, the greatest writers, American, English, of all nationalities, and these little books increased my understanding and respect for some things American. Another influence was my admiration for Franklin Delano Roosevelt, the President of the United States from the time I was only seven years old. He was a hero for me much more than Canada's Mackenzie King. Roosevelt was a bold champion of the underdog and plain people with his New Deal reforms during the Depression, and a world leader on a par with Winston Churchill in fighting World War II.

But aside from Roosevelt's leadership qualities, I felt a personal sort of connection with him because we were both afflicted with polio, yet he had risen above his severe disability to become President of the United States. He was a man whose judgement I trusted and would follow no matter where it lead.

Anyway, when Dad wrote back about where I might go to university, he replied in his typically succinct way, "Son, go where the teachers write the text books." That made sense. I had saved enough for at least two years of the best university, so I thought why not try for Harvard where Roosevelt had gone? So I wrote to Harvard for an admissions application, and two weeks later received one. Beside the usual transcript of high school grades, they required two references from teachers, and a brief autobiography.

So I wrote Mr. McDougall, my revered Principal at North Van High, requesting that he send my transcripts and references to Harvard, and I completed and mailed the application and autobiography.

Within a month I received a reply. The envelope said, "Admissions Office. Harvard College. Cambridge, Massachussetts". Without waiting to get back to the bunkhouse, I opened the envelope and began to read its contents. The letter said, "Dear Mr. Williams: We are pleased to inform you that you are granted admission to the freshman class of 1949 under the following conditions." I was so astonished, for a moment I couldn't read further; me, not a brilliant student, going to Harvard! I could hardly believe my eyes.

Recovering from shock, I read further, and the letter stated the conditions, "Three additional credits in history or social sciences to be completed by May 15."

On the way back to the bunkhouse, I was in a different world talking to myself, numb with excitement. "Me, an ordinary kid from British Columbia going to Harvard! True, I had been president of the student body in high school and showed a lot of ambition, but I was only a 'B' average student. It must have been glowing references from Mr.McDougall, one of my teachers, and plain luck."

Thinking ahead about the immediate future, I decided at dinner that I had better leave Adak a little sooner than I had planned, by the first boat in April. That would give me enough time to find and complete the three credit course, get it graded, and send the results off to Harvard by May 15.

My Aleutian exile was about to end, but I didn't tell Elby and Oscar about the momentous news causing my early departure until the morning came to board the boat. I had good reason. I wasn't about to let word get out that I had been admitted to a fancy Ivy League college like Harvard, having learned years before from working in shipyards and logging camps that working men are usually uncomfortable around 'college kids'. I had taken enough razzing for always having my nose in some book.

The morning for departure came, the 8th of April, I boarded the army transport for Prince Rupert, had an uneventful voyage, and four days later, was riding in the luxury of a C.N.R. train through Jasper and on back home to Vancouver.

I arrived in Vancouver on Friday, the 12th, picked up the *Vancouver Province,* and the headline shouted in a six-inch headline, ROOSEVELT DEAD. The shock of it made me sit down on a station bench, hands shaking, and read the details; a kind of combined obituary and eulogy of this great man's life and achievements for the common man. And he was a Harvard man, class of 1904.

Numb with shock, I got up from the bench, boarded the streetcar on Main Street, and headed toward the North Van ferry dock. As though in a trance, nothing captured my attention as the tram travelled down Hastings. Boarding the ferry, I went directly to the upper deck, leaned on the guard rail, and staring across the waters of Burrard Inlet, struggled with emptiness and remorse. I had lost the greatest hero of my boyhood.

Gradually, as we approached the North Shore, the ferry's

throbbing beat and the swishing of water against its side, soothed my pain. Slowly, my spirit healed. My mind cleared, and as though emerging from a dense fog, there came an overwhelming realization. Within only a few weeks, I would be sitting in the same Harvard classrooms where Franklyn Delano Roosevelt had sat forty years before.

ᚖ

As I stepped off the North Van ferry and headed for Mother's real estate office on lower Lonsdale. I had every reason to be optimistic about the future. The Alaska adventure had paid off, a grubstake of almost $3,000, enough to see me through at least two or three years of university, and now I was about to attend one of the best.

Despite the death of Roosevelt, admired at least as much in Canada as the United States, a successful conclusion to World War II was in sight. Allied armies were closing in on Germany and Japan. The San Francisco conference to establish the United Nations was to open on the 25th. And the Canadian version of the G.I. Bill promised thousands of Canadian servicemen and women the chance for a university education, something they would never have had before the war. Soon they would be streaming home and welcomed as heroes. Everyone believed that World War II was a necessary and just war, and I had done everything I could to help too.

I also had reason to feel good about my family. While all my brothers were still in the service and had been wounded one way or another, they were at least alive. Don nearly had his lungs frozen when he and his 'plane went down in the Arctic, caught fire, and the crew had to run for their lives. Larkin broke a leg on a parachute drop. And Ace came down with tuberculosis, found out only when he returned to U.B.C.

As for Mom and Dad, I had learned from letters that they were now separated, but they sounded happier than I had ever known them to be. Their marriage had apparently come full circle from the divine madness of first love, through hardship and

…isillusionment, and now, peaceful separation. They had stayed together to do their jobs as parents. Now they had now gone their separate ways to resume lives more in harmony with their very different personalities.

As soon as I walked through the door of Mother's office, she rushed over, we had a good hug, and she led me into her back room for tea and cookies. It was obvious that she now felt good about her life. She had gone into the real estate and insurance business with Mrs. L.B. Howard, another able, independent-minded woman. Their business thrived. Mother again had her own car, money in the bank, was active in civic affairs of North Van, and had loads of friends. She was, in short, living a kind of resurrection of the successful, happy life she had known during her Prairie years. Her eyes again sparkled with laughter. She was full of stories and jokes, and from what she said, enjoyed endless conversations over tea with old friends from the Prairies and many a new one she had made in North Van.

Dad had returned to the simple country life he loved, to his own little house on Lulu Island, with his *Saturday Evening Post*, his garden, his dog, and a few old cronies to go hunting with. When I went out to visit him, it was plain that he was a happy bachelor once again.

And I, by correspondence, had fallen in love with Dorene, the North Van girlfriend to whom I wrote just about every week while in Alaska. Dorene, instead of staying for Senior Matric at North Van High, had gone into nurses' training at Vancouver General Hospital. But we stayed in touch, had a date or two, and by the time of my return, our relationship had developed into a love affair, so I was beside myself with excitement to see her.

But there was a slight complication. She had contracted tuberculosis while in training and would be confined to bed at the hospital for several more weeks. On the telephone she said, "But I can see you for a short visit in my room."

That afternoon, I entered her room at Vancouver General clutching a dozen fresh daffodils in one hand and a small box of chocolates in the other. There she was, propped up in bed, my

Dorene, as beautiful as ever with rosy cheeks, laughing Irish eyes, and gorgeously bright auburn hair. We were both excitedly shy, didn't kiss, just held hands, squeezing now and then, laughing and chattering to each other. I haven't the vaguest recollection of what we said to each other. Of course I wanted to kiss her, and I suppose she would have liked me to, but under the circumstances, it didn't seem the appropriate thing to do. It didn't really matter. For both of us, these few moments to be together again were ones of overwhelming joy. For awhile, we were drifting together on a cloud of love, just as we had been a year before as we danced at St. Agnes' Hall to the strains of Glenn Miller's *"Moonlight Serenade"*.

All too soon, they told me it was time to go, and as I left, Dorene's parting words were, "You'll write, won't you?". "Of course", I replied, blew her a kiss, closed the door, got on the ferry, and returned home. That was the last we saw of each other for another year.

I had much to do in preparation for going east. Foremost was satisfying Harvard's requirement for another three units of history or social sciences. My former Latin teacher, Miss 'Katey' Reynolds, came to my rescue despite my having been no hot shot in Latin, and gave me a cram course in Canadian history. Doing much better than in Latin, I whipped through the texts and examination with flying colours, she sent off an 'A' grade to Harvard, and I was in, enrolled in the class of '49 to start in June rather than September as part of Harvard's accelerated wartime schedule.

My luck had held, but of course I would have never made it without the help of a lot of people who went out of their way to lend a hand when I needed it most. One who stood out was of course the remarkable "Mickey" McDougall. We had a good visit in his office while I was taking the rush course from "Katey" Reynolds. "Mickey"'s parting words were "Now give it your best back there, and don't forget where you came from."

And of course I replied, "You bet I won't. How can I? I'll always be a Vancouver boy and Canadian at heart, no matter where I roam."

I decided that I would take the Greyhound bus instead of the train to go back east. I'd see more of the U.S. that way, and it was cheaper too. As the bus pulled out of Vancouver for Seattle, Portland, then heading east, I should have felt completely happy. I was excited, but not happy. It was a mixture of excitement with the great adventure ahead but I also felt a little scared and lonely.

With the end of the Alaska trip, I was no longer a boy. But I didn't feel like a man yet either. It bothered me for awhile. I wondered when I would ever get that feeling. But then, as the bus rolled along, my feelings of loneliness and self-doubt went away. I began to dwell on what it would be like at Harvard and what New England would be like too. Excitement and feelings of satisfaction at having got this far gradually took over and renewed my confidence. "What the heck", I said to myself, "I'm going to make it back east. I just know I am, even if I don't know what I'm getting into any better than when I went to Alaska."

So as the bus rolled along, its droning sound turned into a kind of rhythmic beat, and in my head it kept repeating McDougall's last words, "Now give it your best. And don't forget where you came from." And then my reply, "Of course I won't. Who do you think I am? I'm a Vancouver boy, and a Canadian at heart no matter where I roam."

That little dialogue between the two of us would fade, then come back, again and again, all the way to Boston. It made me feel good, confident, more like a man. Maybe manhood just creeps up on you if you think you know where you're going, and give it your best. And never forget where you came from.

I guess that's why I've written this book.

Union Steamship Co. dock in Vancouver

World War II, Author in Alaska, 'cat skinning for the Army

World War II, brothers Larkin and Asa on leave, Edmonton

World War II, brother Donald in U.S. Army Airforce

World War II, Author and Asa, North Vancouver, April 1945

10

EPILOGUE

Over fifty years have passed since I left Vancouver on that Greyhound bus bound for Harvard College in 1945. I loved Harvard and New England but didn't like the East anymore than my father. It was too formal, lived in the past too much, had a rotten climate, and was too far from home and my girlfriend Dorene. So at the end of my freshman year I transferred to the University of California at Berkeley, known as the "Harvard of the West".

It was one of the smartest things I ever did. Berkeley was a quiet, beautiful college town then, a great place to learn, and abounded with outdoor recreation. In the middle of winter, I played tennis, and with a friend, popped on my motorcycle and roared down to Santa Cruz for a weekend of fun on the beach. It was Paradise, and I remained there seven years to earn two degrees.

Another reason Berkeley suited me was that it was close enough to run up to Vancouver to see Dorene, family, and friends on a brand new motorcycle I bought for myself as soon as I got back West. But after it became clear to Dorene that I was more in love with Berkeley than her, she wisely called off our long distance romance, and married Art Pearson, a classmate from North Van High ready to settle down.

It was at Berkeley too that I later met, wooed, and married Billie Marie Wallace, a very attractive and bright student earning her Master's degree in French. Soon after we were married, she won a Fullbright scholarship for a year's study in Paris, so that's where we spent our second honeymoon. We travelled over much of western Europe; France, England, Germany, Italy, the Netherlands, on a motorcycle naturally, another brand new British machine bought on the Isle of Jersey where Billie's aunt Margaret lived.

After I received my Master's degree in Social Welfare in 1953, I took a job with the State of Wisconsin doing child welfare work, and after three years, moved to the State of Washington and continued in the same kind of work until retiring at age fifty-five. I was "burned out". I needed to get away from other people's problems for awhile and just commune with mother nature. Consequently I have spent the past sixteen years converting eighty acres of cut-over forestland into a combination tree farm and wild life preserve. "Robinswood Tree Farm" I call it. There, with my dog Sandy, I find great satisfaction in planting thousands of trees amidst beaver ponds and in being in the company of every type of bird and animal that dwells in this part of the world.

Billie and I have now been together for almost fifty years, raised three sons, and are now grandparents to a dozen. We have done our jobs as parents and workers, she as a teacher, and I in social service. Now is our period in life to look back on it all, figure out what we may have learned, and transmit whatever we can to our children, grandchildren, and whoever else might be interested.

In the course of writing, I have made many trips to Vancouver and the North Shore to visit libraries and archives, to have many talks with former teachers and classmates in grade and high school, and to revisit the familiar places of my boyhood. I still get great pleasure visiting this city even though much of it isn't the same as it was fifty years ago. It's no longer the little western seaport town it was until after World War II.

Vancouver is now a world-class city, with at least five times the population it had fifty years ago, and different in every respect except in its superb natural setting. My North Shore mountains are still there, that rugged rim of rock, forest, and snow t frames this picture beautiful city. Stanley Park, is still there, th 1,000 acre gem of nature and loving care. My Burrard Inlet is still there, but oh my, how it has shrunk in size! The ferries and boats that float upon it all seem like toys to me now, where before they were huge and mysterious.

I must say though, small as the city now seems to me, this new Vancouver strikes me with awe. Downtown is a forest of new skyscrapers. They loom and stretch skyward in one continuous cluster from the Inlet to English Bay and False Creek. The whole downtown is now so shiny and new, so impressively tall, and much more dressed up and clean than the dull assortment of mostly smoke-browned and stodgy buildings that I knew as a boy.

I had to remind myself that was fifty years ago. Within just ten minutes of leaving Granville street and heading down Hastings street, I had drifted in place and time from the newly sprouted city of Vancouver along Granville and Burrard streets and reentered the old, familiar city of my boyhood. It was both a confrontation with the truth of how old I now was and a return to the world of my youth. On one of my walks down Hastings street, I came upon the Dominion Bank Building, right across from Victory Square and the Cenotaph. There it stood, much the same as when I was a boy and pushed through its revolving door, went up the elevator, and walked into my Dad's office on the 13th floor. I felt the excitement of youth again.

In a way, it has been the same in writing this book. Visiting and talking with my old classmates reminded us all of how old we were. But as we talked about the things we did, about the old school buildings, the teachers, the games we played, the trouble we got into, the ferries, the streetcars, sledding down Lonsdale in the winter, the old swimming hole in the summer, about the war, and working in the shipyards, it was as though we were reliving those days. And then we talked some more, about what we had done since, and where. Our voices were excited as we talked.

Then we had coffee and a sandwich together, or went out to a ›cal pub and talked some more. All the time we talked, we were excited. The time passed so quickly. And still we kept thinking of something else we each wanted to tell the other. For a time, we both felt like the kids we used to be. We felt so good, so young again, no longer alone in old age. In fact, we felt a sense of pride that we had lived so long and done so many things. We both knew that neither of us had made much of a splash in this world. But that too didn't matter anymore. We were rich in memories and sharing them. We were young in spirit again.

We parted feeling closer to each other than we had ever felt as kids in school, and agreed to meet again. When we did, we picked up right where we had left off, and made plans to meet again and share whatever interested us.

Thus, in the process of writing this book, I discovered a totally unexpected and rich dividend. It had taken me back to my boyhood friends, and it took all of us back to the days of youth. We were together and young again, if only for a few hours.

And it all came about because of what good old "Mickey" McDougall had told me fifty or so years ago. He said, "Do your best, and never forget where you came from."

So whenever my old schoolchums and I get together, we all say "Thanks again, Mickey". And we pray that our children, and children's children, will enjoy lives as rich as ours have been, and that they too will share them in their old age.

Author when completed writing this book, April 1997

References

A HISTORY OF THE CITY AND DISTRICT OF NORTH VANCOUVER.
> Kathleen M. Reynolds. Unpublished Master's thesis. University of British Columbia. 1943.

A HISTORY OF SHIPBUILDING IN B.C.
> Boilermakers Union newsletter. 1977.

CANADA: A STORY OF CHALLENGE.
> J. M. S. Careless. MacMillan of Canada. 1986.

MAYOR JERRY.
> David Ricardo Williams. Douglas & McIntyre. Vancouver, Canada. 1986.

THE LARKINS OF ALBERTON, PRINCE EDWARD ISLAND, CANADA.
> H. H. Kerr. Unpublished family history. Toronto. February, 1974.

WEST VANCOUVER, A PLACE OF EXCELLENCE.
> Bruce Ramsey. 1987.

ORDER FOR

A Vancouver Boyhood:
Recollections of Growing up in Vancouver 1925–1945

_____   Copies @ $19.95 (Can) ea. _____
_____   Copies @ $14.95 (US) ea.   _____
_____   Copies @ £9.95 (UK) ea.   _____

$5.00 for 1 book, add $2.00 for each additional book
for shipping & handling   _____

                              Total enclosed _____

Make cheque or money order payable to:
ROBINSWOOD BOOKS

Ship to:
Name _____
Address _____
City, Province/State _____
Postal/Zip Code _____
Phone _____ (work) _____ (home) _____

————————— **ROBINSWOOD BOOKS** —————————
1427 Bellevue Ave. Box 91352
West Vancouver, B.C. V7V 3N9